Extraordinary journeys of individuals, who stepped out of their comfort zone, disrupted existing business models and changed the rules of the game — forever.

The Authors

Gagan Jain is a pioneer in the start-up and e-commerce space and a management professional with over two decades of international experience.

He is the founder of RangRage.in, a unique brand of stylish hand painted lifestyle products. He is also co-founder of Puzzle Desh, a Singapore based startup.

Prior to his own entrepreneurial ventures, Gagan played a key role in setting up operations for several of startups like including Moneysaver (now Snapdeal) and Mad(e) In India.

Gagan holds a P.G. Diploma in Marketing. His interests include teaching and writing; he is also on visiting faculty of reputed B-schools in India and abroad.

In 2014, he was honoured as one of the '50 Most Talented Retail Professionals of India' by the Asian Retail Congress. He can be contacted at gagan@rangrage.in.

Neeti Jain is co-founder and Creative director of RangRage.in which trains artists in new and innovative painting techniques to create designer apparels and home decor products.

Eminently qualified, she holds a Masters degree in Economics, and Post Graduate Diplomas in Brand-Management and Marketing. Prior to that she worked in Advertising, Media and Consultancy, both in India and abroad.

Neeti has been visiting faculty to various business schools in India and Oman. Her interest includes painting and social work. She can be contacted at neeti@rangrage.in

The Startup Diaries

Ordinary Entrepreneurs, **Extraordinary Journeys**

Neeti Jain | Gagan Jain

Orient Publishing

DELHI | MUMBAI | HYDERABAD

To

Indu,

Fighter, Idol, Mother

The trademarks/logos/names mentioned on the cover and in the book are the property of the respective organisations.

ISBN : 978-81-222-0588-6

The Start-up Diaries: Ordinary Entrepreneurs, Extraordinary Journeys

Subject: Business & Economics / Entrepreneurship / Motivational

1st Published 2016
2nd Printing 2018

Published by
Orient Publishing
(A division of Vision Books Pvt. Ltd.)
5A/8 Ansari Road, Darya Ganj, New Delhi-110 002
www.orientpublishing.com

Printed at
Yash Printographics, Noida

Printed on Chlorine-free eco-friendly paper

CONTENTS

Acknowledgements

We would like to express our profound gratitude to all those people who helped make this book what it is:

To all the entrepreneurs covered in the book, for all the time they have given and for tolerating our constant email follow ups. To Divya Dugar, for assisting us and treating the book like it was hers as much as ours. To Rohit and Kunal from Snapdeal, for having introduced me to the world of possibilities, the world of entrepreneurship. To Professor Sundararajan, Mr. Mahendra Ranka, Mr. Sumeet Maru, Mr Rahul Singh for their continuous guidance and motivation. To Gaurav Jain and Devyani Patra for adding a varied perspective. To Nextbigwhat.com, Yourstory.in, Iamwire.com, Venturebeat.com, Trak.in, VCcircle.com, Nurture Talent Academy and many others who are doing excellent job in developing and nurturing the startup ecosystem in India. To our Publisher for showing faith in debut authors. To my elder brothers Shyam and Prashant who have stood by us all along. Lastly, and most importantly, you, the reader, who has taken a leap of faith by picking up this book.

FOREWORD

THERE HAVE BEEN BOOKS ON ENTREPRENEURS, capturing their journeys, their struggles, and the lessons they have learned, with an academic interest and insights. Often the author, through his prose and erudition, has narrated their lives. It is through him that we get to know them. The author stands witness to their life, recording their emotions and conversations, as they unfold. It has all that would make a powerful screenplay for a movie, with twists and turns, punctuated with powerful dialogue. You see them as characters playing out before you, too easy to get involved, feel their pain and happiness when they feel. I myself being the subject of few such books, find this very impactful and of much help as it serves to motivate youth to take this off-beaten path.

Neeti and Gagan Jain's book, *The Start-up Diaries* does that and goes beyond. By telling the stories of six successful Next-Gen entrepreneurs, who had bright ideas and the strong will to succeed, through the story format rather than the essay/interview approach commonly adopted, the authors score a clear plus. For this technique is built on the great Indian tradition of story telling, one that is devoid of myths, where the reader's imagination is ignited by the narrative before them.

The other highlight of the book is the diversity — the entrepreneurs profiled range from a boy hailing from a small UP village, an MBA from an Ivy League school to a professional leaving his cushy job.

Their success along a path that was what others thought as impractical is quite interesting and motivating. Their life could easily have been ours, those arguments, helplessness, loneliness, is common place in our homes. I found while reading the chapters that there is a common theme that laces through the stories in the book.

The authors have taken pains to bring out a fundamental truth that will encourage many to turn entrepreneurs namely, the fact that the people in this book were not extraordinary people or highly talented, and the fact that it was not according to a well written script. The people profiled in this book made mistakes, learnt from them, capitalized on opportunities, hung on and probably got a bit lucky along the way. This I think is another facet which excites me about this book.

Gagan actually spent many days with each of the entrepreneurs and consciously avoided what was already written about them to the extent possible. That he himself is an entrepreneur also helps.

I recommend *The Start-up Diaries* as it will be and can be inspirational for those who want to travel the entrepreneurial road. It could easily be about another person, told in a different time and with the name of another successful entrepreneur.

I appreciate the authors, for the efforts taken and the important insights they have peppered through the stories.

I wish Neeti and Gagan well with the book and their entrepreneurial journey.

K Pandia Rajan
Founder and Managing Director
Ma Foi Strategic Consultants Pvt. Ltd.

PREFACE

If you can't fly then run, if you can't run then walk, if you can't walk then crawl, but whatever you do you have to keep moving forward.

Martin Luther King Jr.

'LET'S START AN E-COMMERCE COMPANY,' I said to my elder brother. He replied, derisively, 'We are traders, so let's stick to trading. These new age businesses, like e-commerce, are for a different league of people who have professional education, exposure, strong financial backing — you know, they are visionaries.'

His instant refusal triggered a series of questions in my mind. 'Why do most people not even consider entrepreneurship as an option?' There is no dearth of entrepreneurs in this country who, like my brother, have started on their own, gradually scaled their businesses, convinced their clients, clinched deals at various stages and generated employment for others. Yet we see the word 'entrepreneur' attached to a selected few.

His reply led me to recall my own start-up experience with Jasper Infotech, which today owns the 'Snapdeal' brand. What worked there was not a big strategy aimed at future growth, rather the handling of day-to-day problems, which later took a strategic form. There I realized that entrepreneurship is not as much about dynamism as it is about patience and perseverance.

Entrepreneurs don't often start with flamboyant board rooms, but begin with humble tea table discussions. The grand picture that we see around big companies is the result of a series of small decisions and actions.

When I delved deeper to understand why the attitude of most people towards entrepreneurship is that of an unachievable aspiration, I realized that it's either due to lack of information or excessive information or both.

There is little information about the ecosystem that is available to support start-ups. Today entrepreneurs can validate their ideas through various business plan competitions; have expert mentors guide them through organizations like TiE (The Indus Entrepreneurs) that foster entrepreneurship, and can raise funds through private equity and venture capitalists. A lack of information of such avenues may prevent people from venturing into this field.

On the other hand, there is excessive glorification of entrepreneurs by the media. Their stature is exaggerated to the level of a superhero as a result of which people look up to them awe-struck and think that they cannot achieve the same level of success.

So, to validate this belief — that inadequate information has led to fewer entrepreneurs — and to obtain more insights into the life of entrepreneurs, I, along with my wife, decided to meet entrepreneurs and ask them about those small anecdotes, their mistakes, funny moments, which can happen to anyone of us.

We were clear that we will not treat this book as a literary work, rather as an entrepreneurship venture in itself. We had read somewhere that 'if an idea excites you for around seven weeks then it is worth pursuing'. This thought enthused us further as we researched about the companies. Our criteria was simple, we wanted to cover companies that had been started after 2000. Why? We wanted to study companies that were young and in their growth phase, for whose founders the taste of success was new and memories of the struggle fresh. We wanted to hear the stories of the founders in depth, capture the moment when they decided to choose the path less travelled, the emotions they went through, the way their families reacted, their experiences while recruiting their first employee, the activities that went on behind the scenes, the way they tackled an unprecedented situation.

After short-listing the companies, and before contacting the entrepreneurs, we approached some experienced people to get their opinion on our initiative. Since we had not written any books before, this decision to document the lives of entrepreneurs seemed too ambitious to us and we had second thoughts on our ability to pull it through. When we met people, we were told 'Before venturing into it, you should work on your language skills, start with reading good authors, and test your calibre through a blog.' Some of our well-wishers went so far as to suggest that we should first practice writing for a year because they were of the opinion that we should either write a good book or not write at all.

The concern that critics would be scathing of a mediocre book was a valid one. While reality does come with a pinch of salt, their feedback gave us enough food for thought. We chose to handle this situation like entrepreneurs for whom the impatience to execute is a virtue. We thought that if we did not execute a good idea out of fear of critics or what people would say, we would not achieve anything in life. In the midst of all the speed breakers, the one line of Mr. Kishore Aher, the founder of www.mygreatstay.in, worked as an accelerator for us. He said 'You want to write, then just write.' It was as powerful a statement as it was simple and we realized that to be an entrepreneur you just need to do it, you can't wait to hone your skills. The mantra is 'Keep working and gradually you will learn and improve.'

Our second step was to contact the companies we had chosen. We had many questions in our minds. 'Why would anyone give us an interview? Did we need strong credentials like a degree from an IIM? Would we be able to land interviews with the people we had chosen?' When we were granted our first interview with www.redBus.in, it was an encouraging experience. Gradually, with each interview, our confidence grew.

When we decided to write this book, we started with the premise that entrepreneurs are not heroes, they are ordinary people like you and me, who just persist more. We did not intend to glorify the entrepreneurs but present a realistic picture about their journey towards success. And after listening to their stories our premise was validated.

We have tried to present each story in an interesting and insightful way. The gist of the book is that there is no particular formula for success, or a set of do's and don't that guarantee success in entrepreneurship. Every story presents a different perspective.

To start with, some entrepreneurs, like Ajit Andhare of Colosceum Media, who made a business plan and raised funds before plunging into the business, were crystal-clear about what they wanted to achieve. Others, like Ashish Dev Kapur of Yo!China, who quitted his job with a dream to open a chain of restaurants, had only vague thoughts about the path ahead. Ashish did not decide on the cuisine he wished to serve, neither did he have the funds to support his venture or a relevant background or qualification. Some entrepreneurs were blessed by serendipity like Phanindra Sama of redBus.in, who accidently got into the business. They had all started with a different set of circumstances and with different approaches, struggled and committed terrible mistakes, accepted their failures and kept walking. They did not yield to the option of 'giving up'.

We hope the thought processes, anecdotes and incidents presented in the book will bring you closer to the reality of entrepreneurs. No, they are not superhumans — each one of us is as capable as any one of them. Eventually there is only one way to move ahead in life, even in entrepreneurship.

Neeti Jain
Gagan Jain

'Let us make a dent in the Universe...!'

One97 Communications Ltd., better known for its flagship product — Paytm — is India's largest digital goods and mobile commerce platform. It is also a leading payment solutions provider to ecommerce merchants using its RBI approved semi-closed wallet.

It delivers mobile content and commerce service to millions of mobile consumers through India's most widely deployed telecom application cloud platform.

Headquartered in New Delhi, One97 is more than 2900 people strong with regional offices across the country and global presence in Africa, Europe, Middle East and Southeast Asia.

It is backed by marquee investors like Ant Financial (AliPay), SAIF Partners, Sapphire Venture and Silicon Valley Bank.

One97 also invests in early stage mobile companies through the One97 Mobility Fund (OMF).

1

ONE 97

VIJAY SHEKHAR SHARMA

'Main garibi hun, aur main tumse pyaar karti hun,
Par sach to yeh hai ke tum mujhse aur bhi jyada pyaar karte ho
Kyunki tum mujhe jyada pyaar karte ho,
Isiliye main tumhe chhod ke nahi jaati.
Main garibi hun!'

(I am poverty, And I am in love with you, But the truth is that you love me more, Because you love me more, That is why I don't leave you. I am poverty!)

IN A SMALL VILLAGE NEAR ALIGARH, Uttar Pradesh, a Hindi teacher in a *paathshala* (school) was discovering a reincarnation of Premchand of the 21st century when he read a short poem scribbled on a sheet of paper by one of his students. He read the poem aloud; it was completely beyond the comprehension and wisdom of the other students, mostly 11 to 12 years old. When Masterji enquired about the writer, Vijay, sitting on a mat in the corner, reluctantly raised his hand.

Masterji marvelled at the maturity of the young boy's thought and asked, 'What inspired you to write this poem? What do you understand about poverty?'

'Masterji, I have observed that the students as well as the teaching staff come in slippers as they cannot afford to buy shoes. Yet they don't seem to do anything about it. Masterji, they are poor not only financially but also mentally,' said Vijay.

'Hmm...But, Vijay, why is the poem incomplete?'

'The poem is complete as this is all I want to say.'

~

Vijay was born and brought up in Harduaganj village of Aligarh district in Uttar Pradesh. His father taught biology at a local school.

Little did his father know that Vijay was a child prodigy; in an era of the Ambassador, he was a Ferrari. Vijay crossed various milestones at lightning speed. He was allowed to skip the pre-primary class and admitted directly to Class I; he was always the youngest in his class. He even finished his exams in mere two hours against the allotted three.

When Class X board results were declared, he was the lone individual in his school who passed with distinction — 72 percent, to be precise. He was among the top ten in the entire village, and yet he had tears in his eyes. Despite his good performance, he had lost the chance of owning a Hero Ranger cycle, promised by his mother on the condition that his rank was among the first three.

Sadly, the cycle was not the only thing that was lost — his father lost his temper as well. 'Why did you leave the examination hall in two hours? Why didn't you utilize the complete three hours?' he shouted. His father was a strict disciplinarian and unhappy with Vijay's always-in-a-hurry attitude.

After 15 minutes of thrashing, the 'verdict' was passed. Vijay's father warned, 'Listen carefully, from here on, you shall not come out of the examination hall before the allotted time. You will opt for biology as your subject.' After all, Vijay had scored 60 percent in math and 84 percent in biology. It was natural for his father to advise him to opt for biology. But Vijay had different plans.

His father's volcanic temper turned Vijay of Harduaganj into Vijay of *Agneepath*. The enraged youngster exhibited his first sign of teenage rebellion when he said, 'No matter what you say I will opt for math, and my decision is final. When I finished the paper, I knew I had done well. It's the examiner's mistake in validating and they should recheck the paper.' However, Vijay had no luck as Uttar Pradesh Board at that time re-checked only the total marks allotted, and did not revaluate individual answers.

This was first time that anybody in his family has raised their voice. Vijay's father was taken back by his rude response. However, his adamant stance helped; his father did not persist further and allowed him to opt for math.

Vijay scored 90 percent in both the Class X and Class XII exams, and that too after answering in just two hours.

The passion to challenge the status quo was clearly reflected in his personality.

~

Vijay was only 14 years old when he cleared his higher secondary exams. He wished to pursue engineering, but he was declared underage for admission. So he decided to take a break from studies to prepare for the entrance exams. Back then in Uttar Pradesh, entrance exams preparation was more for the herd of good-for-nothing lads.

When Vijay started preparing for the entrance exams, he confronted his first roadblock — an inability to comprehend English. He had completed his schooling in Hindi medium, while engineering entrance exams were conducted in English.

To overcome this handicap he started studying the same subject simultaneously in English and in Hindi. Unfortunately even after one year, he was still not eligible for an engineering college admission. Luckily, he came across a news item that Delhi University Vice-Chancellor had the power to approve a seat for outstanding students. He thought he could get selected and be admitted, despite being underage. Thus, he decided to try his luck at the Delhi College of Engineering.

On the day of the entrance exam, he woke up at 3 AM, and at 4 AM, boarded a train to Delhi. It was his first visit to a metro and his first chance to explore the outside world. From Delhi railway station, he took a bus. While travelling, he feared that being sleep deprived he would not be able stay awake, but the sights of Delhi kept his eyes open with excitement. It was a dreamlike experience for him.

He reached the examination center at 8.30 AM; there was still an hour for the examination to start.

Instead of last-minute revisions, he stood at the examination center and examined the surroundings.

He got a glimpse of the level of competition that he had to face ahead, but his major concern was his limited knowledge of English.

To Vijay's relief, it was a multiple-choice test. He still had to answer 200 questions in two hours, and there was negative marking — marks were deducted for each wrong answer. The paper was aimed to test both speed and accuracy. In the first hour, he answered the questions that he could understand. For the next half hour, he tried to solve a few more questions, but couldn't due to his poor English. During the final half hour, he knew that he hadn't answered enough questions to clear the exam.

'I need to answer additional questions,' he thought. Vijay's dilemma was that the questions he had reserved to answer later were questions he could not solve. He had to do something quickly; he started to contemplate his options. Looking at the answers for a clue he suddenly sensed a pattern. 'Most of the answers are either "B" or "C". Should I tick answers as per the pattern? What if some of them prove wrong? There is negative marking, but then if I don't do this, I am fighting a losing battle. That's the chance I need to take,' he thought, even as he doubted his decision, he marked the answers to all the 200 questions.

Coming out of the examination hall, he wondered if his decision was right, and then his philosophical side took over. 'There is no wrong or right in life, there are only decisions that we make and live with. If I clear this exam, the decision of random ticking will be the right decision, or else it will be wrong.' He was ready to live with his decision.

When the results were declared, Vijay passed with flying colours, securing the ninth rank. With the special recommendation of the Vice-Chancellor, he was admitted into the Delhi College of Engineering.

~

'Which branch should I choose?' Vijay asked the fellow students during the counselling session. He wasn't sure of which stream to elect.

'What is your area of interest?' asked Piyush, the topper from MP PET. They had met during the counselling session in the campus.

'Interest chhod. Bhai yeh bata job kisme milne ke chance jyaada hai?' (Forget about interest, brother. Tell me which choice will give me a higher probability of landing a job?) Vijay asked.

'Look, if you select computer science, you can only work in computer-and IT-related industries, but if you choose electronics, you can get a job in computer-related as well as electronics-related industries. All the toppers—' Piyush began, but Vijay cut him short.

'OK, *bhai,* done. I will go for electronics.' The decision was made.

'Hey, wait... all the toppers go for computer branch,' Piyush retorted.

'Koi farak nahi padta (Doesn't matter). If I choose electronics, I have a high probability of getting a job, and that's all I want.' Vijay had already made up his mind.

~

'Oye pajame? Kidhar ja raha hai? (Hey, dudhead, where are you going?)' Somebody shouted.

Vijay looked around and saw a small group of boys looking at him. He recognized one of them as his senior in college.

'Abey o haddi ki dukan, tere se hi bol rahe hain (Listen, you skeleton, we are talking to you),' shouted another guy.

Vijay was taken aback. *'Aap mujhse aisi asabhya bhasha mai kyu baat kar rahe hain?* (Why are you talking to me in such an uncivilized language?)' he asked.

For a minute, everyone kept quiet. Then, they looked at each other and burst into laughter. Vijay could not handle this humiliation and ran to the hostel. In the past, he had seen and enjoyed many ragging scenes in movies, but now he was close to tears.

On his way to the hostel, he brushed past Akhilesh, a senior from a village near his native place of Harduaganj. In the difficult environs of Delhi, he turned to him for solace.

'From now on, you face them or else I will rag you,' Akhilesh said with a smile and gave him some tips to be street-smart.

Soon, Vijay became friends with his seniors and started enjoying their ragging and teasing. Away from the protective environment of his home, he discovered a new family and a new means of survival.

Though he had made a few friends and developed a close rapport with seniors in college, keeping pace with his class was no easy task because the books as well as the medium of instruction was English. A sense of humiliation pervaded Vijay's mind when he could not understand a word in the class. He started looking for ways to avoid attend classes. Soon, he began bunking classes.

Being vexed, he asked himself: 'Why am I here, to study or to get a job?' And answered the vital question himself — his main aim was to get a job. A few of his seniors told him that recruiters looked for engineers with a flair for computers, and with that thought in his mind, his romance with computers started.

One of Vijay's seniors, who ran a computer center inside the campus, allowed him to access computers at will.

Once again, Vijay struggled to cope due to his abysmal English skills. He even used the *Bhargava's English-Hindi Dictionary* to assist him in finding the Hindi synonym of English terms, but there were many technical terms which were beyond the scope of the dictionary. The word 'UNIX' was one of them. He strived to hunt for the meaning, but even dictionary could not help him. Once when he saw the word 'notebook' in an advertisement of a magazine, he went to the library to search for the meaning but was unsuccessful. He searched for 15 days before he quit. Hesitantly, he asked one of his friends the meaning. Phew! The 'notebook' was just a type of computer.

To pursue his interest in computers, he started visiting Nai Sarak regularly, the second-hand book market in Delhi. Once, while browsing through the titles on the footpath, he came across Bill Gates' face with a computer on the cover of the *Forbes* magazine. He picked up the edition and thought, 'Bill Gates, who is this guy?' He bought the copy and read it from cover to cover; stories of Silicon Valley inspired him. Soon, reading *Forbes* and *Fortune* became a habit. Stories of Internet start-ups such as Yahoo!, Netscape, Hotmail, and others inspired him, and he started dreaming of having a start-up of his own.

By 1997, the Internet had started making inroads into India. Luckily for him, his college by that time was connected to the Internet. Soon, Vijay learnt how to build HTML pages and developed his personal page on http://vss.tripod.com/old-index.htm. This marked the beginning of his affair with the Internet.

~

When Vijay went home during the semester break, he had a painful realization that his family was drowning in a sea of debt. Also, it was his first visit after his elder sister's marriage. Later, he came to know that his father had taken a personal loan for the wedding. Vijay was not even aware of the situation his family was in as his father had sent him money regularly for his tuition fees. It was unbearable for him to watch his family cutting back on their basic expenses.

'I just cannot wait to become an engineer to get a job. I need money to support my family and my education right now,' he thought and resolved to start working as soon as he reached Delhi.

Harinder, his computer teacher and batchmate, warned him, 'You have to appear for a supplementary exam, Vijay. For now, focus on your studies. Forget about computers for a while.' Harinder had chosen computer engineering as his stream and knew about Vijay's passion for computers, so in his spare time, he had been teaching Vijay a bit about computers.

'Even Bill Gates was a dropout!' Vijay retorted. The entrepreneurial stories he read in *Forbes* had left an indelible mark on his youthful mind. He dreamed about becoming a billionaire like Gates.

'The truth is that it's easy to get a job, but who needs a job. I will start my own company. What do you say? We can start a web hosting company.'

‘Maybe we can do that? But what’s the basic requirement for starting a company?’ Harinder queried as he was not very sure about the idea of starting a company. A company to him meant a huge office buzzing with a lot of people.

‘Just a business card,’ said Vijay, oozing with confidence. After all, most Silicon Valley start-ups had started in garages!

‘Are you sure?’ Harinder had his doubts.

‘Why can’t we? We have full access to the college computers, and what all we need is an Internet connection. In fact, we should make the card right away,’ Vijay said, springing into action to make a visiting card. He was excited as if he had already created a Fortune 500 company.

‘E-37, DCE, K-Gate, Delhi-6, Phone No. 2453789. That’s our address.’ Vijay winked. He felt excited by this new idea.

‘Whose address is this?’ Harinder failed to comprehend Vijay’s train of thought.

‘See, E-37 denotes my block and room number, DCE signifies Delhi College of Engineering, K-Gate stands for Kashmiri Gate. Nobody should know that we are college students, or they won’t take us seriously,’ Vijay explained.

‘What shall be the name of the company?’ Now Harinder got into his groove and was charged up.

‘XS Corp.,’ Vijay announced smugly.

‘Why XS Corp.?’ Harinder wondered that Vijay had ready-made answers for all his queries.

‘The letter ‘S’ implies Supriya. She never showed interest in me, so I am crossing her name from my life. That makes it XS. And every big company in America has the word “Corp.” attached to its name. So our company will be XS Corp.,’ Vijay clarified.

‘What a noble thought and who will be our customers?’ Harinder was looking at Vijay in awe.

‘There are several companies that post recruitment ads for HTML programmers in newspapers. If they are giving ads, that means they have a job in hand. We will search for the prospective clients, appear for the interviews, and finally we will tell them that we will work as a freelancer and complete the project.'

Thus, they began their venture and started applying to various companies. They started earning a small sum, but this took a heavy toll on their studies. They burnt the midnight oil writing programming code instead of preparing for their semester exams. They followed the mantra of 'beg, borrow, and steal' in the examination hall.

'Arey, Miglani, *answers dikha yaar. Sirf last wala bacha hai. Baaki ke maine dekh liye* (Hey, just show me the last answer, rest I have seen),' Vijay said, requesting his batchmate Miglani to help him. For the last three days he had been working on a project and could not find time to prepare for exams.

'Tune baaki ke answers bhi mere paper se dekh liye! (What! You have copied the answers from me!)' Miglani turned in surprise.

'Haan. Ab to dikha de,' asked Vijay again.

'Why don't you attend classes? I won't show you. Don't disturb me now, or I will call the invigilator.' Miglani was irritated.

Vijay knew that this time he would not be able to clear the exams but he was not worried. Earning Rs. 10,000 per month made him confident and aware that skill was more valuable than a degree.

~

Vijay went home during his semester holidays to share the breaking news of his start-up company. 'I want to start a business,' he declared. The announcement almost broke his mother's heart.

'Business? Why? We are Brahmins, we don't get into business,' said his mother, already worried about her son's future and of criticisms from relatives and friends.

'Arre Ma, mai ghoda nahi banana chahata jiski lagaam kisi aur ke haath mai ho. Mai ghodo ko rakh kar unse kaam karwana chahta hu (I don't want to be a horse whose reins are in someone else's hand, I want to make people work for me).' Vijay quoted Vijay Mallya with great élan.

'Humne tumhe engineering *kya ghodo ka astabal khulwane ke liye karwayi hai?* (Are you studying engineering to open a stable?)' asked his mother. She took his words literally, so he explained about the business he wanted to get into and showed her the copy of *Business Today* that had an article on the Internet boom in India.

For his conservative parents, all this made no sense.

'Arre bhai, humme tum yeh ghode gadhe ki baate na samjhao, duniya dekhi hai humne, tum bas ek achi si naukri kar lo (Don't try to teach us. We are more experienced, so listen to us and get a job for yourself),' the coaxing continued. 'We have to get your younger sister married. If you don't get a job, we will be in deep trouble.'

In the end, Vijay became a victim of his parents' emotional *atyachar* (blackmail). His parents' arguments proved to be mightier than the combined influence of all of the *Forbes's* garage start-up stories, at least for the time being.

'Fine, I will take the job till her marriage, but after that, don't stop me.'

Vijay kept his promise. He started preparing for campus interviews. While studying electronics, he kept on fantasizing about computers.

Since he wanted to support his parents financially, he checked the past records of campus placement cells to find the highest paymasters. 'RiverRun — that is the interview I need to crack,' he said to himself and started preparing for it.

'Computer is the machine whose intelligence equals 50 people. One person with a high IQ can equal five people, but not 50 people. So, combined intelligence is always vital than individual's intelligence. Hence, every organization requires computers to increase its output.' Vijay was answering the question posed by technical panel of RiverRun during his job interview. Though Vijay was not a programmer, he still managed to qualify for the job.

He had achieved his ultimate goal of getting a high-paid job. However, bitten by the entrepreneurial bug, he could not hold onto his job as he lost interest. After a six-month stint in RiverRun, he quit the job, assuring his family that he would be sending Rs. 10,000 every month till the time his sister got married.

~

'Harinder, I think we can make money not only by developing websites but also by bringing traffic to the website.' Vijay was discussing with Harinder over the phone. He had quit RiverRun and wanted to do more than just creating websites. 'Why don't we start something again?' Vijay suggested.

Again, Harinder and Vijay were in the same boat. They dreamt of developing something like an Indian version of Yahoo!. Hitherto both of them were designing websites for others. But now they thought of making money by increasing traffic to their website. They named this venture www.indiasite.net. It was a search site that focused on content and links related to India.

'Every link related to India will be shown on our website.' Vijay shared his plans about search engine optimization and website development.

'You know, while I was monitoring the Internet traffic, I found out that over 40 percent of the data traffic was received by Living Media,' Vijay told Harinder while returning to the office after delivering a project. Suddenly, Vijay saw the Living Media signboard at Connaught Place. 'Let's go and meet them,' he said in an instant.

Both Harinder and Vijay agreed and went to Living Media office to fix an appointment with company's top officials. The receptionist connected the line to Arun Katiyar, who was heading the Internet-related business wing of Living Media.

'Hi, I am Vijay Shekhar Sharma from www.indiasite.net and he is my colleague Harinder. We are here to ask you to provide us news and ads for our website. We will share the profit with you from the money we generate through your ads. And you must know that indiasite.net is already ranked number one by various websites,' Vijay said as he introduced himself. He blurted out nonstop while standing in Arun's cabin.

Arun smiled at his naïve confidence and said, 'OK, we will discuss, but first please take a seat.' As they sat, he asked, 'Now tell me, what is the strength of your sales team?'

Vijay wondered what to reply as he was clueless. He and Harinder were running a two-man show, so he decided to ignore the question and asked, 'First, tell me whether you are interested or not.'

'OK, we will discuss that. Do you want something, tea or coffee?'

'No, thanks,' he said and handed over his business card of XS Corp. The card read: Vijay Shekhar Sharma EO, Harinder Takhar EO.

It was first time that Arun came across the designation EO; he wondered and asked, 'What is this EO?'

'None of us is CEO, so we both are EO,' Vijay replied, raising his eyebrows in style and clasping his hands, brimming with overconfidence.

Arun could not stop laughing at their immature joke. 'Interesting, I like it, and what is this US address on your business card.'

One of Vijay's classmates worked in US and provided small projects to XS Corp. So they started flaunting his US address with their card, strongly believing that a US tag on their business card would bring more business than exhibiting their college degrees.

'This is our VC's address. You know VC — venture capitalists?' Vijay questioned Arun, assuming that nobody knew about VCs in India except him.

Arun smiled at them. Such immature and funny encounters were a rare sight in a plush office of Living Media.

'Oh, great, so tell me what can we do for you?' Arun asked humbly.

'Basically, we know that you update and post the news articles on your website, just give us your news content and we will increase traffic to your website,' Vijay told him point-blank.

Arun, a seasoned media professional, knew that he was trying to negotiate for a news syndication deal. 'How much will you pay?' Arun asked him.

'Pay? You give us news and we generate the traffic, that's it,' Vijay explained.

'We won't give it for free.' Arun made his decision clear-cut.

'Well, I can do it anyways. I will not even come and ask you, I can just link it online,' Vijay asserted his opinion.

'Do you think you can do that?' Arun was taken aback by his audaciousness.

'I am already doing it. I thought you will be interested in making a business deal with us. That is why we came.' Vijay, without knowing that there can be legal issues, especially with a media company, continued with his ignorance, coupled with confidence.

Thankfully, Arun was impressed by their innocence and did not bother to press charges against them. Instead, he gave them an opportunity to start business with Living Media.

In 1999, they partnered with Living Media India Pvt. Ltd. to establish a website called www.indiadecides.com.

'Arun, see we are working with and for you. Could we use the Living Media office during nights for my other official work?' Vijay was never shy of demanding. To meet the growing demands of his business, he now needed an office and some resources, like computers and Internet connection.

'OK, what will Living Media get out of that?' Arun, being an astute professional, enquired.

'We will do some of your work for free.' Vijay cut a deal. He had planned his move, and fortunately, it materialized, so he asked some of his college juniors to come and work for him from 11 PM to 5 AM. During that time, they were running their site and doing lot of other stuff. Vijay was very happy with the optimum utilization of resources that were provided by Living Media!

Later, Vijay sold his shares of www.indiadecides.com, along with www. indiasite.net, to Living Media India Ltd. for cash by striking a deal for more business prospects during the election coverage.

Meanwhile, XS Corp. received a buyout offer from Intersolutions India Pvt. Ltd. for cash and equity valued at a few crore rupees. Vijay was offered a monthly salary of Rs. 1 lac to be the company's technology manager, and he readily accepted the offer.

His parents were relieved as their son had a high-paying job and that too with a multinational company (MNC).

With so much money, all the debts were paid off in one go. His home in Aligarh got a new colour TV. For the very first time in his life, Vijay was experiencing luxury.

'I need *golgappa* shots without vodka,' Vijay ordered.

To celebrate his new riches, Vijay took his friends out for dinner at the Punjabi by Nature restaurant. All his friends had ordered beer, but Vijay, a nonsmoker, teetotaler, and vegan, placed a unique order. He asked for their signature dish '*golgappa* shots with vodka', but without vodka. Puzzled by the order, the waiter stared at him for a moment, wondering if the gentleman in front of him was a sage or a fool.

~

In April 2000, his younger sister got married, and once more, Vijay became restless to get into business.

'Sir, please accept my resignation,' Vijay said, handing his resignation letter.

'Are you crazy? Just stay for a month more. By the end of June, you will get your yearly bonus of Rs. 16 lacs and shares in the company,' Rakesh, his immediate superior, said, thinking that Vijay was unaware of the bonus details.

'I know, boss, but I want to leave,' said Vijay, aware of the fact that the job was nothing but a golden handcuff, and he thought the comfort zone of job environs might slacken his pace of achieving his entrepreneurial dream in the long run.

Meanwhile in India, telecom and Internet industries made rapid growth, and attracted VCs who wished to capitalize on the emerging market. With a dream of achieving big and, in the process, leaving his own stamp, he wanted to try his luck in this flourishing segment.

'Should I send a mail to the US office telling them that you are stepping down? Think again. It's just one month,' said Rakesh, hoping that Vijay would ponder on the issue.

'I have made up my mind,' said Vijay, with firm conviction. 'Leaving Rs.16 lacs will push me to create something bigger and better. If I stay today, it will mean that I am shifting my priorities towards money. It is not about money, it is about creation.'

'You drive me nuts!' Rakesh remarked.

~

Life was no more a bed of roses for Vijay. For the next six months, he did some random work on ISP, broadband, and so on and so forth. One day, while cleaning his room, Vijay came across a *Fortune* magazine (October 1997 issue) which carried an article 'Yahoo! Inc. acquired Four11 corp — an online communication and directory company'.

'People search! This is it!' That was his eureka moment! And he started working on the business plan.

One day, Rakesh Shukla, Vijay's boss in RiverRun, called him.

'Hi, Vijay, how are you?'

'Hi, I am fine. How are you doing?' asked Vijay.

'I am doing fine. What are you up to these days?' asked Rakesh.

'Actually, I am busy setting up a new business. Till now I was doing some stuff related with Internet, website, and so on, but now I have decided to get into people search. I want to create a directory in which one can find people, local business listings, phone numbers and addresses, driving directions, and more. I am also working on incorporating in reverse phone look-up facility — that is, if you have a person's name or phone number, either way.'

'Oh, it is like phone directory!' Rakesh commented.

'Yeah, more or less, but with focus on both landline and mobile phone numbers. No directory offers mobile phone numbers.'

'Interesting! You know, I am also considering doing something new. I want to quit my job,' Rakesh said.

'If it interests you, you are welcome to join me,' Vijay said.

'OK then, let us meet someday,' said Rakesh and hung up.

~

'What is your value proposition?' Rakesh asked Vijay while sipping tea at a roadside eatery in Nehru Place.

'What does value mean? The clients and customers look for phone numbers and other data which I provide via an online directory. From where did "value" come in?' Vijay was bit confused.

'First of all, why should anyone pay you? Aren't they looking for some value out of it? If not, then how will you make money?' Rakesh was trying to explain the basics of business dealings.

'What is value?' Vijay probed with a puzzled look on his face.

'People don't buy computers or services. They buy *value*. They buy the value a computer or a particular service can bring to their life. For example, when you go to a fine-dine restaurant, you pay much more for the same food that you get on a roadside *dhaba* (diner). You pay extra for the service, the hospitality, and the ambience that they provide,' Rakesh tried to explain in a layman's language.

'Oh, it is like that.' Vijay nodded in approval at Rakesh with his poker-faced expression, trying to understand the hard meaning of a soft word like 'value'.

'Yes, support too has a value.' Rakesh gave another example.

'Support? Who needs support?' Vijay looked at Rakesh with a bland expression, ignorance written all over his face about these new-age business jargons.

'Various support services offer convenience to a customer and thus save time. That is value.' Rakesh looked at Vijay and realized that Vijay wasn't able to understand a word.

'All right, I guess that's beyond my comprehension as of now. Coming to the point, you handle technology; I will look after the business development. That is the value we can offer to each other.' Vijay was smiling at his own value addition.

As a result, Rakesh and Vijay started their entrepreneurial venture and One97 Communications was born. The choice of name was inspired by BSNL's information query number 197. But their path was fraught with difficulties. To make a telecom directory, name and numbers of telecom customers are a prerequisite. For three months, both of them toiled to reach telecom operators to gather the relevant data, but had no such luck.

'Hey, I am going to Bangalore. If you strike a deal with any telecom operator, then I will return,' Rakesh informed over the phone.

'Oh, OK. I will keep trying,' Vijay answered while browsing through his monthly bank statement with depleting balance.

Even before One97 started its services, Rakesh had started looking for a new job.

~

'Clearly, the people search idea will not work,' Vijay was thinking while waiting to meet a senior manager at Airtel. 'Maybe I can ask for anything else they might have to offer. At least, something is better than nothing.' He thought of asking for any other value-added service (VAS) Airtel can provide.

'Hi, Vijay. Good to see you. I have some work for you,' greeted Sumeet, an officer in Airtel.

Vijay's heart skipped a beat. 'At last, I'll be receiving the data. I was giving it up too early. Maybe people search idea will work.' There was a glint of hope resurfacing in Vijay's mind; he sensed a possibility of working on a project for a major telecom service provider.

'Sir, tell me. I am here willing to do anything you have to offer,' said Vijay, hopeful that he would not return empty-handed.

'Do you have an office, few computers, and seating place for four to five people?' Sumeet enquired about the basic setup.

'Yes, I have.' Vijay was glad that he had rented an office last month. Though he had financial constraints, he had no choice. After all, this time around, he didn't have the infrastructure of Living Media.

'So do one thing. Get a few *panditjis* (astrologers) in your office. We will give you an astrology-related VAS (Value Added Service),' said Sumeet and explained that Airtel was launching a new VAS, wherein customers could call and check on their horoscope and other astrology-related queries through their mobile phones.

'Oh, it is not people search. The offer is regarding *panditji,*' he replied dejectedly. Vijay was shaken out of his slumber, and his optimism about his people search project vanished like last night's hangover. He was disappointed, but nonetheless, it was an opportunity.

'I should grab this opportunity. Until now, they were not even ready to meet me, but if I accept this work, at least I will get a chance to communicate more often with them. Since telecom VAS is a growing business, I might be kept fully occupied. Also, on the other hand, I may get a regular customer who can give me a repeat business order. It seems to be a profitable deal,' thought Vijay.

'Profit will be shared on a fifty-fifty basis. Infrastructure, phones, and even *panditjis* will be on your payroll. We will just market the service. In prepaid, the charges are Rs. 4 per call while in postpaid, charges are Rs. 5 per call. So you will get a commission of Rs. 2 on prepaid call and Rs. 2.50 on postpaid call. Is that fine with you?'

'Sure, sir, it is OK.' Vijay nodded eagerly. His priority was to establish a good working relationship.

'Kaam to le liya, par ab panditji kahan se laau? (I have taken the work, but from where will I get astrologers?)' thought Vijay, as he stepped out of the office premises. He wasn't sure of the road ahead — all that he could think of was recruitment ads in the newspapers.

Finally, Vijay did find a few *panditjis,* but there were other roadblocks on the path.

'You need to sit here in the call center from 8 AM to 6 PM, answer the calls from customers, and give them guidance about their future. Everything is same as your regular work, except that the person is on phone and not in front of you. And your *dakshina* (fee) will be given on a monthly basis rather than on per customer basis,' Vijay explained the *panditjis* about the dos and don'ts of the job.

For a traditional *pandit,* it was too much of technology. Knowing astrology was not enough, Vijay had to train them their phone etiquettes, tone, pitch, and voice modulation.

'Hey, Vijay, I heard that you have become a senior *panditji.* Shall I come to show my *janampatri* (horoscope)? After all, you can predict future events,' teased Harinder when he came to know about Vijay's undertaking. Harinder had taken up a job after XS Corp. was sold out.

'Kyun nahi yaar...Teri to main janampatri zaroor chapwaunga. Kundli milan bhi karunga. Apne business ko chalane ke liye main sab kuch karunga (Why not buddy...I will print your astrological chart. If need be, I will do every work to run this venture successfully)' said Vijay, with his usual enthusiasm. 'Telecom VAS can be really big game changer, Harinder. Why don't you join me?' he invited.

'OK, I will think about it,' said Harinder.

Harinder knew Vijay since college days. Vijay had grit — the one essential quality that made a successful businessman. Such people are born to win; he had left a well-paying job in an MNC, started his own company, sold it, took a job again in an MNC, left the job and shares, and then started One97 — his brainchild. Harinder was confident that sheer passion would make Vijay successful. He had faith in Vijay's ability to achieve things.

'I will join One97,' said Harinder.

Finally, 'Live Astrology' service became operational in 2001 with four astrologers on One97's payroll.

~

'How many *panditjis* can we afford?' asked Harinder. One97 had the workforce of eight — Vijay, Harinder, and six *panditjis.*

'Even I am worried about that. A call center is very expensive and inaccessible.' Vijay agreed with Harinder's concern.

'Why don't we install interactive voice response (IVR) systems?' Harinder suggested.

'IVR technology will not work for astrology-related services as every customer has different queries. It would have been great if everybody had the same future, same like Bill Gates's,' said Vijay with a smile.

'What if Bill Gates's destiny is same as ours?' Harinder winked at Vijay.

'I don't think Bill Gates would mind. It will surely be a brighter one,' Vijay grinned. 'On a serious note, if we cannot employ IVR technology for astrology, then we have to find services which have predetermined answer for every user with no human interaction.'

'Maybe, how about something like cricket score updates? For instance, if somebody asks for a live cricket scores, then IVR or automated SMS can be put to better use,' Harinder contributed.

'Yup, or we can have music, jokes, and the like. In the next meeting with Sumeet, I will push this idea,' Vijay suggested.

~

'Sumeet, now that we have started with astrology services, we should also think of offering VAS related to music and cricket. These are two hot-selling items,' said Vijay, trying to sell the idea. The stint in indiasite.net taught him that cricket and music were two fixations for Indian consumers. Even though content related to cricket and music was available in Internet for free, monetizing content on mobile phone was easy because people paid for on-the-go services.

When Vijay went overboard, explaining about his ideas and discussing about consumers' expectations, Sumeet, who was in his early forties, felt a blow to his ego because it was he who was supposed to dictate terms, not Vijay. So he brushed off Vijay's suggestions and said, 'Do you have infrastructure for it? Who sits in your office currently? *Panditjis,* right? How are you going to create contents on cricket and music? Kid, go slow, focus on the work at hand.'

Vijay wasn't able to identify whether it was a sarcastic remark or a genuine concern.

'Sir, please give me a chance. You will not regret it,' Vijay pleaded, as he was in no mood for giving up.

'Listen, I don't think you are ready for this. Get in touch with Harish. We are starting operations in Punjab circle. Harish is looking for astro services there. Go meet him,' said Sumeet. Though Sumeet did not agree to cricket and music VAS, he gave him a lead.

After three months, Vijay called Sumeet and requested for immediate clearance of his cheque. 'Sumeet Sir, please push for clearance of our bill with the accounts department. It has been three months now and I haven't received the payment.'

Starting 'Live Astrology' service had consumed most of Vijay's savings, and he was now running short of cash.

~

'You have *Rajyog,* Vijay. Your star positions and planet movements are at their peak. You will be famous one day,' said one of the *panditji.*

'Didn't you receive any customer call since morning that you caught hold of me?' Vijay retorted in a vexed tone.

'I am serious. You really have *Rajyog,* a great future,' he insisted.

'Then, I guess I should clear your payment in *Rajyog,'* Vijay said sarcastically. He did not believe in astrology.

'Ha-ha-ha, I am not saying this for my payment. I am just telling you that it's what you are destined for,' he laughed at Vijay's sarcasm.

'I don't have money to go to Chandigarh for the meeting. I am not getting payments on time, and you are talking about *Rajyog.* Not in this lifetime,' Vijay remarked in frustration.

Both Vijay and Harinder were not drawing any salary. Vijay had invested all his savings in setting up 'Live Astrology'. They had work, but no working capital. They needed the VAS contract from Punjab circle but did not have enough funds to start the work.

'Harish Sir, I will deliver "Live Astrology" service for the Punjab circle, but I have another business proposal,' said Vijay. 'There is a huge scope in cricket and music VAS. Please allow me to do it. We will surely make a lot of money.'

'That's quite interesting,' said Harish. After a pause, he continued, 'Can you explain the business model?'

'Sir, the model is the same. The only difference is that instead of astrologers answering the calls, we will have IVR machines to answer the calls. Customers can get updates on cricket scores or choose a song they want to listen to from a list of prerecorded songs. We will have the same service charge for calls and SMS as we had for the Live Astrology service,' explained Vijay.

'Good, actually very good,' said Harish, encouragingly. Harish's response enthused Vijay.

'How much will the server for this VAS cost?' Harish came to the point.

'If he is discussing about commercial aspects of the business, then it means that the deal is done.' Vijay with his usual impatience started counting the chickens before they hatched.

'It's Rs. 16 lacs only,' said Vijay quickly, having done his homework. The machine would cost Rs. 12 lacs, and Vijay added an extra Rs. 4 lacs as annual maintenance cost.

'We don't have money for all this,' Harish flatly declined the offer, thus pricking the balloon of hope that Vijay was blowing in despair.

'Then why the hell did you call me from Delhi? I wouldn't have spent money on my train tickets,' Vijay blurted, desperately trying to underplay, but with little success.

'You are working on a fifty-fifty revenue-sharing model in Delhi circle. Let us do the same here.' Harish maintained his stance, without getting perturbed by Vijay's reaction.

'This requires a huge investment. I don't have enough money,' Vijay explained his situation.

'OK, but you are telling me that this plan can be a big success. If you are so convinced about it, why don't you invest in it? What is the problem? The ball is in your court,' Harish stated.

'OK, let me check with my partner,' said Vijay and called up Harinder.

'Harinder, Harish is willing to offer cricket and music VAS, but it requires an investment of Rs. 16 lacs and tech support. What do you say?' Vijay wanted Harinder's approval on this deal.

'Honestly, what type of question is this? Do you really need my approval? Let's take it,' said Harinder, stating the obvious truth of start-ups — a big no to no; a big yes to every work that comes your way. 'Don't worry. I will manage technology-related things and you focus on business and content development,' Harinder assured.

'Even I was thinking along the same lines. We shouldn't say no to this. We will figure out the investment part later.' Vijay just wanted to focus on opportunity and not on problems he might face. He disconnected and turned to Harish.

'OK, Harish. We will take it, but can you give us some advance to buy the server? You can deduct from my payment.' Vijay took his chance.

'Nope, the only deal is fifty-fifty sharing on revenue. Server, staff, content, and all the rest of it is your headache. I will just market the service. Take it or leave it,' Harish made it very clear. With a job in his hand but no money, Vijay returned to Delhi empty-handed.

~

In the scorching heat of Delhi, they paid homage to almost every shop at Nehru Place in search of a secondhand server at a throwaway price, in hope that their prayers would be answered.

'Do you have any secondhand server?' Vijay and Harinder were negotiating with vendors to get the cheapest server available.

'Yeah, I can get you for Rs. 6 lacs,' said Shyam, a computer dealer, finally quoting the day's lowest bid.

One97 could not afford to pay even that. 'Can you give it to me at a monthly rental?' Vijay asked, knowing that Rs. 6 lacs was impossible to manage. He was looking for ways to save his initial investment.

'OK, the rent would be Rs. 50,000 per month and the server will always be my property,' quipped Shyam, a typical street-smart vendor of Nehru Place. 'No transportation and installation services will be provided. All arrangements have to be made by you. Any further application development, software updates, and so on, will be provided at extra charge.'

'OK, Harinder, let's take it. We will install it on our own.' Vijay and Harinder picked up the server and set it up in their small office.

They started with the 'songs on demand' service, where a subscriber could listen to the song of his or her choice. Soon this service became a major hit in Punjab. By the third month, they were able to make Rs. 55,000 per month.

'Harinder, we have already reached the breakeven,' said Vijay.

~

Vijay and Harinder went to one of the operator's office for some work. Instead of going to reception, they headed to the coffee vending machine spot.

'Harinder, we should buy this coffee machine for our office,' said Vijay, as he was fond of hot chocolate from the vending machine.

'It is better here, it's free. We cannot afford it, bro,' Harinder replied while filling his cup.

'From today, our mission is to get business from every potential telecom operator in India and to emerge as a leading player in VAS market so that we can install this coffee machine in our office.' Vijay blinked at Harinder and took a long sip of coffee, as if a toast had been raised to his vision.

'What a noble cause! This vision of yours will fructify when we start our cricket score updates and ringtones VAS from next month, and more importantly, we are going wherever Airtel is going,' Harinder said while finishing his coffee.

'Why only Airtel? We will approach other operators too. I am sure our strategy of having a 'no up-front cost' and 'fifty-fifty revenue sharing' will work well with everyone. Telecom operators want to spend their money on infrastructure and not on software which can play SantaBanta jokes!' said Vijay. Vijay was a dreamer — in a minute, he changed from going wherever Airtel was going to offering services to other operators to becoming the leader in the VAS market to becoming a business model for a Harvard case study.

'Yeah, but that means we invest in the SantaBanta software ourselves. At present, we have no money. Shyam is demanding his monthly payment while telecom operators are not paying on time.

How do we deal with this situation? We have insufficient funds,' Harinder pulled Vijay back from his utopian vision to reality, where everything wasn't as perfect as he had imagined.

'Insufficient funds! Actually, even the bank has the same problem. Yesterday, I went to ATM to withdraw cash. Once I inserted my card in the slot, the message read: Insufficient Balance. I was just wondering how come a bank doesn't have enough balance,' grinned Vijay, flaunting his sense of humor.

'Stop kidding, this is serious. It is not the bank but your account that doesn't have any money in it, and that is exactly what I have been trying to tell you,' said Harinder in one long breath.

'Don't worry, Harinder. Ours is a business which will eventually generate profits, and sooner or later, we will receive our payment and will pay off all our dues,' said Vijay.

~

'Vijay, it has been three months now. I will take all my servers back if you don't pay my rental fees,' said Shyam, threatening to put Vijay out of business. Even after regular follow-ups and providing extensions, Vijay was unable to pay him his monthly rental.

'Shyam *Bhai,* just give me one more week, please as soon as I get my payment, I will pay the money back.'

Vijay called up one of the telecom operators asking for a payment.

'Sir, it has been almost six months, please settle my payment.' Vijay was begging for his own money.

'Oh, no problem, your cheque is ready. Please collect from the accounts department,' one of the officers from the operator's office told him the good news.

Vijay rushed to the telecom operator's office, but his excitement turned into utter disbelief when he saw the amount printed on the cheque.

'There must be some mistake. This is not my cheque. I was supposed to get Rs. 2.5 lacs, but the amount printed here is just Rs. 37,000,' Vijay exclaimed.

'Please check again. I have generated revenue of Rs. 5 lacs. As per the agreement, I should get Rs. 2.5 lacs,' Vijay claimed anxiously.

'No, sir, as per our records, you have generated revenues worth Rs. 80,000 only. After TDS, and other deductions, this is your final amount,' insisted the accountant.

Vijay realized that all his potential receivables may not necessarily translate into actual receivables. The telecom operator's records may differ, and there was no way he could prove them wrong. He had to accept the telecom operator's data as absolute data, and there was nothing he could do about it.

'No problem, I will speak to the telecom people and find out the ideal way to track the business as per their records. Right now, I will pay this amount to Shyam and cajole him to give an extension for a few months,' thought Vijay, a go-getter. He was not really bothered for this one-time problem. But delays in payment became a frequent occurrence, so Vijay started borrowing money from friends to manage the payment cycle.

'Vijay, we are doing a lot of work, and yet we aren't receiving our payments. We haven't drawn salaries for the past four months,' said Harinder, apprehensive of his future.

'I know, but I am quite hopeful that we will receive our payment by next week. That will release some of the pressure,' said Vijay, convincing Harinder. Both Harinder and Vijay were under tremendous pressure — their families were worried about their future, career, and marriage.

'I hope we do get the payment because if Shyam didn't get his payment this week, he will take back his servers and we will be out of business,' Harinder said in a strained voice.

~

'Sir, the outstanding amount is Rs. 12 lacs. Why are you paying me only Rs. 6 lacs?' Vijay asked the marketing head of a telecom operator. Due to a cost-cutting measure, he was paid half the due amount.

The marketing head gave a smirk and said, 'You should feel happy about it. You are lucky that you are getting at least half the amount. What can you do if we don't pay you at all?'

'But, sir, you are such a big listed company, how can you slash my dues? This is unethical,' Vijay demanded a proper response. He was clueless of what was happening to him, and he was sure that whatever was happening wasn't very encouraging for his business.

When Vijay tried to reason further, the manager said, 'Take it or else you will not even get this,' and asked Vijay to leave.

Vijay realized that it was not a one-time accounting error. Telecom companies were growing rapidly and they had no ethical standards and behaved indifferently towards the concerns of their vendors.

Payment delays completely jeopardized the cash flow for One97. A profitable business model was getting into the doldrums because of inadequate working capital.

To add to their misery, OnMobile, backed by Infosys, started gaining prominence in Indian telecom VAS sector. Operators wanted to centralize all the VAS services. Hence, major clients of One97 transferred their accounts to OnMobile. That was the first major blow One97 faced, competition-wise.

Vijay was affected from both sides — intense competition and heavy budget crunch — leaving him with very little breathing space. He was doubly burdened. He feared that his business would crumble if the situation didn't change for the better.

Vijay was so engrossed in his thoughts that he did not realize that Harinder had entered the office.

'Vijay, I want to talk to you. I have to move out. I know I am leaving at a crucial juncture, but I hope you understand,' said Harinder, well aware that it wasn't the right time to leave, but he was under tremendous pressure from his family since last few months. After months of waiting for things to take a turn, he finally gave in.

After Harinder announced that he was leaving, there was a pindrop silence in the office. Words stuck in Vijay's throat, refusing to come out. He finally mustered some courage and said in a soft voice, 'Yes, I do understand.'

This news was a real shocker. After all, Harinder had a vital role in One97's growth. They were each other's support system during difficult times. Now in the battleground of One97, Vijay was the lone warrior, the only survivor, and the battle wasn't over yet.

~

At 10.30 pm, at Moolchand Paranthewala, *ghee* and oil *dabbas* were lined and the cooking pan was hot and ready. With the aroma of mouthwatering delicacies floating in the air, the setup needed no ambience.

While observing the crowd flocking to Moolchand's, Vijay recalled his days of extravagant spending when he used to order *golgappa* shots without vodka at Punjabi by Nature. Each plate was priced at Rs. 250, but he never thought twice before ordering it. And here, he was waiting for half an hour for a simple *aloo paratha* that costs a mere Rs. 15.

Vijay had a tough time as the cash flows had dried up. Shyam had taken all his servers back as Vijay still owed him Rs. 8 lacs. His only saviour now was 'astro service', but that alone was not enough to pay his mounting dues. He started taking computer classes and other freelance work for survival. For Vijay, life was a struggle and going back home was a battle. Every day, he had to play a wait-and-watch game to enter his house as he had not paid the rent for the past two months.

His furious landlord kept a round-the-clock vigil to catch him. It became a routine with Vijay to enter his home like a thief. It was a game of cat and mouse between him and the landlord.

Vijay was angry and disappointed with himself and the way things had turned out. He felt like throwing and breaking everything under the sun, but there was nothing in his room to do so. Eyes, which were once full of dreams to outshine Bill Gates, were now filled with tears and remorse. 'Could life get any worse than this? I am alone. I have no money. To top it all, I have to repay a loan. There are no servers to work with,' he yelled at himself, tears trickling down his cheeks. For the first time in his life, he cried a lot.

~

'*Kaise ho, beta?*' his father's call woke Vijay up on a Sunday morning.

There was an undertone of anger in his voice. He decided to maintain his peace. 'I am fine. How are you?' Vijay knew that this conversation was not going to end the right way.

'*Bahut ghode dauda liye, beta, ab aur gadhe na bano* (You have run many horses. Now don't be an ass),' his father spoke sarcastically.

'*Ji,* I don't understand what you are saying.' Vijay played innocent, even though he knew that his overconfidence and *badbolapan* (loudmouth) has already backfired.

'*Lagta hai hamara naam roshan karne ki than li hai tumne.* (It seems like you have decided to make us famous.) You left your job, stopped sending money to home, and suffered losses in your business. But this wasn't enough for you. You decided to take a loan from your sister's father-in-law. Have you lost your senses?'

'Please give me some more time, I am sure I will revive my business,' Vijay pleaded.

'Please forget about reviving your business. It will be better if you wrap up everything immediately and find yourself a suitable job. As it is no one is ready to marry their daughter to you. If you continue like this, you will never get married,' his father said. He had enough reasons to be angry.

'Why are you in a hurry for my marriage? I am just 25. Give me some more time.' Vijay was not ready to give up.

'More time for what? So that you can swindle more money from relatives and embarrass us?' asked his father in a fit of temper.

'I will pay it back. Anyway, I am paying 24 percent interest,' Vijay informed as if this piece of information would placate his father.

But it further aggravated his father's anger, and now he moved from his sarcastic gibes to direct scolding.

'Paying 24 percent interest! Oh my God, now I am even more worried. How will you sustain your business by paying such a high interest? How many more years you want to waste with *panditji? Khudke bhavishya pe grahan laga hua hai aur dusro ka batane chale ho!* (Your own future is in dark and you are predicting others' future!)'

In Uttar Pradesh, where Brahmin societies always acted conservatively, a bachelor with a good job was considered a prized catch in the marriage market. Instead of being a source of family pride, Vijay was putting family's reputation at stake. Also, with Vijay's failing business venture, marriage proposals were hard to come by.

The pressure exerted from his family forced him to look for an alternative plan. 'I probably need to look for a job, but what kind of job should I look for? I'm neither an MBA nor a software engineer, and I have even forgotten programming. Who will hire me? Where will I fit in?' Vijay was clueless as he had not prepared himself for such an uncertainty. 'Maybe I should look for some administration jobs' thought Vijay.

~

A navy blue BMW 5 series sedan stopped at a busy Indian Oil petrol pump in Noida. The window pane slid down. 'Full tank,' he said and handed over the credit card to the attendant. While waiting for the attendant to fill the tank, he admired the interiors of his car when the phone rang.

'Waah, Vijay Babu, naya office, nayi gaadi, badhiya ho,' (Wow, brother, new office, new car, that's nice) said a voice from the other side, imitating the Asian Paints' advertisement. It was Harinder congratulating Vijay on his new acquisition. 'So, Vijay *Babu,* how does it feel?'

'Thank you very much,' Vijay just couldn't thank enough for his best wishes. 'It feels amazing. You know, I am at the same petrol pump where I used to bring my secondhand Maruti 800, with no

AC and locks. You remember, I bought it from Shruti for Rs. 20,000, and I feel that it was a more expensive deal than this BMW,' Vijay continued, reminiscing about the days that had gone by.

'*Kabhi pachas se zada ka petrol dalwaya thha usme?* (Did you ever fill petrol for more than Rs. 50 in the car?)' Harinder taunted.

'That's true. Today, I got a full tank. How times change!' Vijay couldn't help thinking of the struggle he had been through for nine long years and how that one car had been with him during his struggle.

'You deserve every comfort you are getting. Your struggle is finally paying off.' Harinder was genuinely happy for Vijay.

'Maybe, but I think it's just the beginning. We still have a long way to go. You tell me, how is BlackBerry treating you?'

'Hmmm, going fine. I never thought that BlackBerry would be such a bitter fruit.'

'Thank God, we are living in a world in which BlackBerry, Apple, and Orange are not only fruits but also networking devices. Otherwise, I would have been eating bananas from a roadside shop and driving a non-AC Maruti 800,' Vijay exclaimed. After many days, Harinder and Vijay had a good laugh over a friendly chat.

Vijay parked his BMW in front of his office, a seven-storied building with a navy blue glass façade. He stepped out of his car and stood in front of the building and craned his neck to take a good look at it — after all, it was a reflection of ten years of sheer hard work. He was jolted out of his reverie as the security guard saluted Vijay, the founder and owner of One97.

'What happened, sir?' the security guard asked.

'No, no, nothing,' Vijay replied and entered the office.

As he entered, he sensed a different kind of excitement in the air. All the employees were happier than usual.

'Good morning,' greeted Sonia with an ear-to-ear smile.

'Good morning. What is the occasion? Why is everyone so excited?'

Vijay kept his briefcase in his cabin and walked towards the newly installed coffee machine. He pressed the button and poured some coffee in his mug and said, 'It tastes better when you drink it in somebody else's office for free.' He remembered the day when, few years ago, he and Harinder stood near the coffee vending machine in a client's office, where he articulated his vision and mission of his company.

'Everybody is excited about our Goa trip, sir. How many companies hire a charter plane and take their employees to Goa for an outing?' Sonia blurted out in one breath. The chatter over the charter flight was unending since the time Goa trip was announced.

'Don't thank me. Thank the finance guys who have approved the budget for it. Our chief financial officer (CFO) must be getting a heart attack by now. I must go and thank him.'

He took his coffee mug to CFO's cabin and knocked the glass door. 'May I come in?'

'Hi, Vijay. Come in, come in,' said the CFO and got up to greet Vijay. The early morning visit of the managing director (MD) of the company took him by surprise.

'Actually, I came to thank you for approving the trip to Goa,' Vijay sparkled with a childlike innocence.

'You put a gun to my head.'

'There was no other way,' Vijay smiled.

'But I still don't think it's a good idea. Do we really need to spend the money in this unproductive way?' For him, it was an unnecessary expenditure.

'Waste! No, it is an investment, an investment in the happiness of our employees. Happy people work the hardest and perform better because they don't spend time on sulking over petty disagreements. The focus and priority is on getting the work done, and that is what any company wants: minimum unhappiness, maximum output.'

Vijay knew that the CFOs were frugal and conservative.

'I understand that we need to invest in people and that is what we always do. That's why, on the very first day, they get a new BlackBerry and a laptop. We have the yearly outstation picnic as well. Last year, we went to Dharamshala. I am all for employees' happiness and welfare, but hiring a Kingfisher Airlines flight and going to Goa isn't investing; it is needless spending without thinking. It is sheer financial recklessness. Why are we showing off so much? What is it we want to prove?'

'You must be aware that Rohan from the sales department put down his papers last week. He had been with us for the past three years. When I asked him about his sudden decision, he said that he wasn't getting married because he wasn't working with a known brand,' said Vijay. The last sentence surprised the CFO. Vijay continued, 'You tell me, how are we going to create a brand name for our internal customers, our employees, so that they don't leave us? How are we to create a perception where they feel happy and content working with us? Rohan is not a one-off case. We have lost many people just because we aren't a brand yet. That's why we need to work harder and do things which only the likes of Amazon and Google do. We need to create a grand brand image,' said Vijay, clearly stating his point with a purpose.

'Is there no other way of doing it?' asked the CFO.

'Maybe there is, but right now, I am not concerned about the way. I am focusing on the results. We are competing in industry which is full of big players like Bharti, Spice, OnMobile, and so on. We cannot afford to lose some of our special talents to them. We need to create our own niche, our own name. We have to make One97 the coolest company to work with,' said Vijay, echoing the words of Larry Page.

'Whatever, I still don't think that the Goa trip is something that we should be spending on,' the CFO frankly expressed his disapproval.

'No, that isn't the only reason why you don't agree with the Goa trip,' said Vijay. With a naughty twinkle in his eye, he continued, 'You know I am going to ask you to do the monkey dance after two bottles of vodka.' Vijay laughed as the CFO blushed.

It was a satisfying conversation for Vijay; he was happy that he was able to instill a culture of honesty, transparency, and democracy.

After all, the tagline of One97 was 'Let's get talking!'.

With the ideology of 'Let's get talking!', there was no communication gap at One97.

'Hi, Vijay, I want to discuss an important issue. Can I come to meet you in the evening?' asked Pooja, the HR head.

'Well, if it is important, then come now,' said Vijay. He believed that if something is important, it should be attended to immediately.

'Yes, madam, tell me,' Vijay greeted Pooja with a bright smile when she walked to his cabin.

'Vijay, we have recruited a batch of professionals for our application development team. This is the first time we have recruited such experienced and qualified people for that department...there...'

But before Pooja could complete her sentence, Vijay said, 'This is the first time that experienced and qualified people were willing to join us. Our strong media presence has helped us to build up a cool start-up image.' Vijay smiled at Pooja.

'OK, whatever, but the point is that I see a conflict. Ravi, who has been with us since the beginning, is not qualified enough. He started as a data entry operator and has grown since then. I don't think it is right for IIT graduates to report to him, as it would lead to ego clash,' Pooja expressed her apprehension.

'Hmm, I agree. Actually, now we're able to recruit people with domain expertise. Earlier, those who were struggling to get a good job anywhere else were working with us. Then, our criteria of employing people were based on intent, sincerity, and skills, in that order. In Ravi's case, he scored high on intent and sincerity, so we compromised on his skill level. Now we are more organized and so we need more domain experts. Well, you are right in pointing out the issue that may creep up. We are going to face this problem in the future too, but as of now, I won't let Ravi down. He has given his best years to One97,' Vijay replied, understanding the issue.

'Yes, but how do we manage this?' Pooja was concerned.

'No worries, I will speak to the new joinees. They work on computers doing R & D because they have got the formal education and expertise; Ravi will do the execution part because he has got years of experience. Then there will not be any conflict. Righto?' Vijay looked at Pooja to get her consent.

'Perfecto...' Pooja nodded with agreement.

~

When Pooja left, Vijay delved into retrospection. The type and scale of problems had changed so much in the last few years. He remembered the time when he was struggling to get a server and the promise he made to himself. 'The worst is happening with me. *Mujhe isse bahar nikalna hai, par is tarah se nahi ki sab kuch khatam ho jaye, is tarah se ki kuch bacha reh jaaye aur phir mai use aage badhau.* (I need to get out of this situation. Not in a way that I finish everything, but in a way that I save something and rebuild it).'

He remembered the day when he bought the server again and made a new start. For that, he went through considerable hardship: worked day and night without break, took odd jobs in several companies, borrowed money from friends and relatives, took loans from banks, and convinced his parents to cope with him in this testing time.

Finally, in mid-2006, he once again arranged for the server. With renewed enthusiasm and vigour, Vijay started again; this time around, he was more cautious regarding outstanding payment.

Along with the astrology services, he decided to diversify. He understood that he couldn't grow if he kept working in the same segment. To compete with the big fish, he needed to create his own niche market. With the knowledge that he had gained by reading about Silicon Valley and about the developments in telecom field in other countries, he was able to read the market.

While other companies were working on content, One97 worked on creating a sales interface. Soon One97 shifted its focus from being a content provider to a service provider.

His relationship with Airtel came to his rescue, and One97 started managing back-end services like 121, 111, and so on. With these services, customers could check their balance, know about various offers, and the like. One97 also started offering services for prepaid telecom subscribers and expanded their portfolio through mobile marketing services.

Being a small-time player worked to their advantage. At one point One97 was so small that the bigger players never perceived it as a threat. When the big players were busy making new ringtones, Vijay was busy creating a platform where he could sell that content. He became a retailer who had direct rapport with the customers while big-time players were working like wholesalers.

Since Vijay was working in a space dominated by giants like Bharti Telesoft, OnMobile of Infosys, and so on, he made sure that he put extra focus on his service standards. Slowly, he gained reputation in the market as well as with new customers.

Vijay's financial condition started improving gradually by 2007. The issues concerning with working capital were dealt with extra caution, and as a result the billing cycle improved substantially. There was a synergy in the method of billing calculations between telecom operators and One97 and things became more transparent.

In late 2007, he started getting buyout offers from various companies. One company made a very persuasive offer. Along with a valuation of $55 million on the company's assets, Vijay was offered a majority stake in the company and salary with CEO designation.

It was a tempting offer but Vijay was keener to get VC funding. It was a difficult task, but that did not keep him from trying.

~

'One97 has many firsts to its credit. A few would include short code SMS service, 3030, and so on. One97 is the pioneer of the revenue-sharing model, which the telecom industry follows today. We have been operational since the last seven years, and with an interesting transaction-driven model, we have started making profits. With the investment that we hope you would bring to the table, we would expand our horizons and offer a broad range of integrated service offerings across voice and data platforms not only to global telecom operators but also to retail customers. The investment would serve as a catalyst for us in achieving a higher growth phase,' said Vijay, thus concluding his presentation for Series A funding from SAIF Partners.[1]

With ample money in his bank account, Vijay got intellectual firepower to scale up the business. He succeeded in hiring seasoned and skilled professionals and developing a subscription-based content model.

'When I call you guys, your "tring, tring" sound bores me. Spend just Rs. 30 per month and get a good Hello Tune,' said Vijay, setting the tone of the weekly meeting. He was encouraging everyone to try what their company was offering.

Everyone smiled.

'No, let us make it better. I have a liking for Kishore Kumar songs. So the guy who has a Kishore Kumar song as his ringtone will get a higher increment,' said Vijay. Everyone laughed with delight.

'Well, there is some good news. Soon, we will be starting PayTM, a mobile-based payment solution, and...' Vijay paused, before he gave them the big news, 'our next destination is Africa, but there is one warning,' said Vijay. Everyone looked at him with suspense written all over their faces. 'All of you have to work harder,' he could see some relief in their eyes. 'Keep up the good work.'

~

'Don't you feel bad about it?' asked Harinder. They were meeting after almost two years, but, in the meantime, their bond had grown deeper.

'Bad? About what?' asked Vijay as he sipped his coffee.

'I mean Piyush Aggarwal sold his stake in One97 to Reliance for Rs. 87 crores. He had bought the stake for just Rs. 8 lacs.' Harinder was referring to the deal that had been signed the previous week.

---

1 SAIF Partners was a venture capital fund that catered to the South Asia markets. It had a few big names in its Indian portfolio, including National Stock Exchange, IL&FS Investsmart, MakeMyTrip.com, TV18 Group, JustDial.com, and Slash Support to name a few. They agreed to invest $8 million in One97.

'Oh yeah, I feel bad about it. He should have waited. He sold it too early,' said Vijay, feeling truly sorry for Piyush Aggarwal.

Harinder looked at him, trying to gauge Vijay's emotions, but he knew that Vijay was an optimist. He always saw hope of victory in every failure, but at that moment he saw restrospection on Vijay's face.

'It is not that bad, you know. Today, it seems like it happened just yesterday. Remember, my father was after my life forcing me to get into a job so that I can get married. At that time, I met Piyush, who came as a blessing in disguise. I did some work in his software company for a while. He then asked me to become its CEO. But at that time I was running my own business, One97. I was not in a position to take up the offer,' said Vijay as if he was living those moments till Harinder's nod shook him out of his trance.

'I know it does not sound logical today, but at that time, he offered me Rs. 25,000 per month as salary for half a day's work. It worked for me because then I could devote the other half to my own business. This arrangement worked for me, and I informed my father that now I had a job,' said Vijay with a smile.

'That is not the point. The point is why you gave Piyush 40 percent equity share in One97?' asked Harinder.

'After some time, he offered to invest in my company. The high interest rate on the loan that I had taken from my sister's father-in-law was adversely affecting my profits, and I had been desperate to pay it back since a long time. So I took up his offer,' said Vijay.

'But why did you give him a 40 percent stake?'

'Then, I was not aware of all the complexities of 10, 20, or 40 percent. My entire focus was on building and developing my business. Before that, I had worked only with you as my partner. So, you know...' Vijay couldn't complete the sentence. He assumed that Harinder understood the story.

'And, by the way, he gave not only Rs. 8 lacs but also office furniture,' Vijay laughed, trying to hide the pain of his company's shares being sold.

'Yes, right. For an investment of secondhand office furniture and Rs. 8 lacs in three years, he is getting a massive Rs. 87 crores! How can you make a joke out of it, bro?' Harinder was not amused.

'You should always laugh at life, *bhai,'* Vijay became philosophical. 'Maybe, if Piyush would not have invested in One97, I might have been working somewhere. Things have changed now. We have already raised some money from private equity. This year, our revenues are going to be approximately Rs. 120 crores. It was not the case then. I was fighting for survival. So it is OK. I have no regrets.'

~

Vijay was sitting in his cabin and staring at the calendar. 'Let's make a dent in the Universe,' it read. He smiled. One97 marketing team had made this calendar with the objective to reach the desk of every decision-maker in Indian business community.

One97 had 1000 employees with operations in India, Africa, Middle East, and China and reported revenues of Rs. 183 crores in the year 2011.

'The agenda for today's board meeting was to announce One97 Mobility Fund backed by SAIF. The fund will invest in pre-revenue start-ups in mobile space.'

'Hi, Vijay.' Vibhor peeped into Vijay's cabin. Vibhor was on the board of directors of One97 and worked at SAIF Partners.

'Hello, sir, how are you?' Vijay replied politely.

'Good, so ready for the meeting?' he asked.

'Yes. I hope our fund helps young guys to overcome problems which I had faced,' Vijay became nostalgic about his journey.

'It surely will. You are doing a good job,' complimented Vibhor.

'Thanks, sir. Our next target area is to focus on mobile Internet. We now need to get into mobile apps for iPhone and Android platforms. We need to develop M-commerce applications. We will grow 100 percent year on year for next few years. I want to create a $1 billion company,' Vijay was beaming with confidence.

'Oh sure, you are already on your way, Vijay.' Vibhor patted his back.

'Yes, I am on my way, and this has been a fantastic journey. It is just 11 years, you know. In fact, even three years back, I was fighting for survival. But I never lost hope.'

'In business, it just doesn't matter from where you start, what matters is where you want to go and if you have the courage for the same.' Vibhor was a firm believer in Vijay's ability to make it big.

'Yes, we need no thought controls. One needs freedom, and one needs to fight for that freedom. Power is not gifted; it has to be earned through hard work, conviction, and persistence.' Vijay was looking at the various posters across his office through his glass door. One of the posters read: 'We need NO thought control' painted in red.

'I think we should move to the meeting room,' Vibhor reminded about the schedule.

Vijay looked at his watch and smiled. 'Yes, let's get talking!'.

Vibhor sat up from the chair and looked at the calendar which read: 'Let's make a dent in the Universe'.

ONE97
KEY LESSONS
VIBHOR MEHRA

Vibhor Mehra has over 12 years of professional experience including 7 years in private equity and has been associated with investments in companies including Makemytrip.com, JustDial, One97 Communications, and PayTM. He has worked with SAIF Partners, Boston Consulting Group and Hughes Software Systems. Vibhor is a Gold Medalist, MBA in Finance from IIM Bangalore and secured top rank in Computer Engineering at Delhi Institute of Technology.

The views expressed here are his own.

~

'Vijay reminds me of my youth'. This was a remark by Andrew Yan, Managing Director of SAIF Partners in 2007. Back then, Vijay was only beginning to make his mark in the industry.

Work Hard, Party Harder

There is never a dull moment with Vijay around. The rate at which he spews and processes new ideas is amazing. More importantly, he is at his happiest doing so. To have maintained his creative streak despite the rigmorales of running a large organisation, is no mean feat.

Raise your Benchmarks

Many would have been caught up and satisfied with creating a successful VAS company, but not Vijay. PayTM — a venture incubated within One97's alleys — was no more than an idea a few years ago, but has fast emerged as a game-changer today.

Embrace Diversity

Knowing what he doesn't know is one of Vijay's strengths. Not only has he invested in bringing complementary talent on board, he has worked at honing his personal skills as well.

Keep Learning

Vijay continues to be as sharp as ever on product design, sales and team building; at the same time he engages in a highly nuanced discussion on shareholder value creation, financial performance metrics, control systems and procurement policy. Whether it is his zeal for learning or love for One97, his personal growth through the entrepreneurial journey has been on steroids.

Focus on Solution

Just like any growing company in India, One97 and Vijay had their set of operating challenges. Many others would have got frustrated but he focused on finding a workaround. Sounds simple, but when confronted by an unreasonable detraction, it takes character to implement this simple principle.

Share and Contribute

One of the most important aspects that sets Vijay apart from other entrepreneurs is his knack for giving back. Perhaps because his journey hasn't been easy, he wants to ensure that the ecosystem is fairer to budding entrepreneurs. Vijay contributes time and capital — not just through One97 Mobility Fund and other institutional funds, but also gets associated with many startups in his personal capacity.

Nurturing Talent

There is an ever-growing population of ventures floated by ex-One97 employees. Some of them will be successful, while others will fade away. However, all of them would cite Vijay as their inspiration to keep striving.

~

The extraordinary story of Vijay Shekhar Sharma and One97 is an inspiration for all of us. The limited resources cannot limit the infinite power of dreams.

EKO/-

Bill Gates pays a low-key visit to tech start-up pilot project.
— *Mint, Nov 5, 2008*

Even today less than 500 million of India's 1.25 billion people have bank accounts, but there are about 900 million mobile connections. In 2007, Abhishek and Abhinav Sinha decided to attempt extending banking services on mobile phones to those without bank accounts...

Thus began Eko India Financial Services Pvt. Ltd.

EKO enables about 2,00,000 of its customers to save and transfer money through mobiles. It also provides payments, merchant transactions, bill payments and cash collection services.

In 2010, it was chosen amongst the 'NASSCOM EMERGE 50 — The League of Ten and was amongst the startups chosen as '50 Emerging companies redefining the benchmark of excellence for the next generation of SMEs.'

Providing mobile banking solutions for SBI, ICICI Bank and Yes Bank.

2

EKO

ABHINAV SINHA
ABHISHEK SINHA

'Even a worst case is not bad,
If you choose entrepreneurship as an option.'

'LISTEN CAREFULLY, THERE IS A BOMB in the flight to Delhi,' warned a suspicious voice from the airport terminal's PA system.

'W-w-what? W-w-who are you?' the operator at the airport's information desk stammered in the receiver, but the line had already gone dead. She became numb with fear, and was sweating profusely, because the plane was about to take off within the next 20 minutes. All passengers had checked in and were waiting to board the flight. Terrified and scared, she ran and informed her seniors about the bomb threat. Within minutes the airport staff was put on red alert and the flight to Delhi cancelled. While security was beefed up to check the CCTV video footage for any suspicious activity the bomb squad, with the sniffer dogs, was called on to conduct a thorough search of the plane. After all, Dr. A. P. J. Abdul Kalam, one of India's most prominent scientists, was travelling on the plane.

Unaware of the bomb scare Dr. Kalam, clad in his trademark grey safari suit, was observing the people around him, when a young man in his mid-twenties approached him. Adjusting his specs and T-shirt anxiously, the young man, unsure of how to introduce himself, said in a low voice, 'Hello sir, how are you? It is an honour to see you here. I am a fan of your work.' Unable to contain his excitement on meeting such a great personality, he was on cloud nine.

'Oh, I am fine. How are you, young man? What is your name?' Dr. Kalam greeted him with a smile.

'Sir, my name is Abhishek,' he introduced himself.

'Where do you work? Tell me more about yourself,' said Dr. Kalam.

'Sir, I work at Satyam. I am into software development.'

The conversation gained momentum as Abhishek gave a brief introduction of his family and his educational background. Abhishek was the eldest of his three siblings. Born to an IAS officer (from Bihar) and a professional school teacher, he finished his schooling from different schools in and around Bihar, completed his engineering from BIT Mesra and, finally, landed a job in Satyam, Hyderabad.

Dr. Kalam listened intently to what Abhishek said and then said, 'You have been extremely lucky to get this kind of an education. Why are you working for someone else? Why don't you start a factory or a company of your own and contribute to build the nation in your own way?' After a brief pause, Dr. Kalam continued, 'Actually, there is an Indian mindset that earning money is a sin, but actually it is not. If you read Swami Vivekanand's *My India: The India Eternal*, he says that being prosperous as a nation is very important because we would be remembered in the long run only if we hand over a prosperous and safe India, blending prosperity with cultural heritage, to our next generation.'

'I agree, sir, but with so many government regulations and licenses, starting a business in India is tough,' replied Abhishek.

'Difficulties are necessary to enjoy success,' Dr. Kalam smiled. 'We are not alone. Look at the sky. The whole universe is friendly to us and conspires to benefit those who dream and work towards realizing their dream. Of course, we will have problems, but the point is to not give up. We should not allow the problem to defeat us either.'

Meanwhile a few airport officials approached Dr. Kalam. A senior airport official said, 'Sir, your flight has been delayed by an hour due to a bomb scare. Please come with us, we have made an arrangement for your lunch in the VIP lounge upstairs.'

Before bidding adieu, Dr. Kalam gave his last piece of advice, 'Abhishek, remember one thing: you have to dream before your dreams can come true.'

Inspired and enthused, Abhishek nodded in agreement.

~

With a smile on his face and a dream in his eyes, Abhishek boarded the flight. He couldn't wait to tell his parents about his chance encounter with Dr. Kalam.

Once he reached his home, Abhishek told his mother about his meeting with Dr. Kalam, 'You know, Mom, Dr. Kalam said, "young people should work towards making India a better country and build something of their own." '

Abhishek's mother gave him a rap on the knuckles, saying, 'You can't even get more than 60 percent in your engineering exams, how will you be able to make India a better nation?'

Abhishek's father added, 'You will do something on your own? For all your admissions, from school to college, I have worked harder than you, and after years of run-of-the-mill performances, you got a job in Tata Steel, but you gave it up for a stupid venture of your own. Did you tell Dr. Kalam that it was closed within six months? I have a humble request: stay put in your job at Satyam.' His words were harsh but true, reality at Satyam was even harsher.

'Abhishek, what have you done in your four years of engineering life? Can't you even work on a simple program?' he remembered the reprimand he'd received from his team leader in Satyam.

Abhishek's initial months in Satyam were an intense struggle. Though there was no dearth of training, he couldn't cope with coding. Gradually, his discomfort turned into phobia, and he soon discovered various ways to avoid any task that involved coding. However, a software company doesn't provide a beginner with much choice. Soon, Abhishek's underperformance and incompetence was visible to everybody, especially his team leader. He saved Abhishek from further humiliation by transferring him to the testing and support department for an off-site project with Shyam Telecom in Jaipur.

Since Jaipur was nearer to Delhi, Abhishek thought of spending enjoyable time at home on weekends. But his wish for pleasant stay turned unpleasant as Abhishek's father grew very worried about his future and was even more concerned about the influence of Dr. Kalam's meeting on his son's career.

Abhishek always had great ambitions. Though an average student from a typical middle-class family, he always dreamt of starting his own company. For his parents, it was no less than a nightmare, and they used to pray for him to get settled.

But Abhishek was firm in his resolve, 'If I don't do something now, my life will be worthless. It is a do-or-die situation. If I don't leave Satyam, they will throw me out. I have to do something on my own and prove a point to myself. I can't take this burden of non-performance anymore.' With determination to start his own company, he left for Jaipur.

Abhishek and his colleague — Abhilash, an engineer from Cochin, who was sharp at coding — had long been contemplating on a start-up, but had not got past the planning stage. But this unexpected meeting with Dr. Kalam inspired him to plunge into action.

~

While one brother was fighting the failure on professional front, the other was accepting it on the academic front. Abhinav, Abhishek's younger brother, a twelfth grade student at Delhi Public School (DPS), was sitting in his room, disappointed and disgruntled. Everyone in the family, his cousins and their parents, had been invited to the annual felicitation program of DPS, barring him and his parents. This felicitation program is a yearly ritual conducted by the school where only parents of the toppers were invited and the toppers awarded different coloured jackets and badges, which had to be worn by them for the rest of their academic session. Abhinav looked at his green colour uniform; neither had its colour changed nor was he ever been awarded a scholar badge by the school.

Considering his family background, where schooling from DPS was a tradition, it was humiliating for Abhinav; he was surrounded by cousins who, unfortunately for him, were toppers.

Abhinav's frustration turned into acceptance as he consoled himself, 'What a way to humiliate mediocrity! Anyway, this too shall pass; I have been facing it for 11 long years. I at least hope things turn out to be better in college.'

For some, disappointment turns into depression, but for Abhinav, the disappointment in school turned into a decisive mantra to meet future challenges in college.

Abhinav soon developed a knack of hanging on. He lived by the example that when an airplane flies, the flight is not always smooth — at times, there is little turbulence; at times, it's prolonged. In both cases, just stay put and soon the ride will be smooth.

Once Abhinav realized his potential, he devised a new strategy to accomplish his mission in college.

'I will spend my time and focus on three most difficult subjects and make sure that I master them while the toppers will study all six subjects in the same amount of time. In the remaining three subjects, I will only aim for pass marks,' Abhinav decided. 'I should know something of everything and everything of something,' he thought to himself.

Finally, the second-year university results were declared. Abhinav got excellent grades in the three toughest subjects, while barely clearing the other three subjects. After looking at his results, he smiled. He had fared well in the target subjects he'd set for himself. With this achievement, he had learned a valuable lesson of life — focusing and achieving mastery in the chosen goal will surely yield success.

~

'I think we can start by developing "location-based services and applications" for telecom operators. If you can sell it, then I can make it, and we can start our own business,' said Abhilash. Abhilash and

Abhishek were given the responsibility to handle the off-site project with Shyam Telecom in Jaipur.

They decided to continue working at Satyam for a few more months, take a loan and arrange capital, as the Satyam brand name provided a strong backing to raise a bank loan!

'Abhilash, I got the money from the bank. I think now we can make a move from Satyam!' exclaimed Abhishek over the phone. It was the culmination of their planning to move out of Satyam and start their own venture. With a loan amount of Rs. 2 lacs, two credit cards with a limit of Rs. 50,000 and savings of Rs. 35,000 as his seed capital, Abhishek embarked on his journey of entrepreneurship.

Thus, Abhishek and Abhilash were captains on board of their ship called 6d Technologies. Though people do a lot of research and thinking while naming the company, Abhishek didn't. At times, when people like Abhishek are involved, gut takes over rationality, and it works. At Birla Institute of Technology (BIT), his room number was 6d, and to him, it was his lucky charm, and had an emotional value.

Gradually, their team expanded and two more partners stepped in. Though the new partners assured them of their full commitment to 6d, they didn't quit their current jobs for the sake of 6d Technologies. This arrangement was agreed to by the partners till 6d could find its exclusive pool of clientele and generated sizeable revenues.

Soon, a small office in Kalkaji, Delhi, became 6d Technologies' address. A chartered accountant was appointed to take care of the legal requirements, and soon afterwards, 6d had four partners. A small office with two computers and a phone stood in stark contrast with the glass palace of Satyam.

6d Technologies started off its business by approaching major telecom players of the country, but its first break came with Shyam Telecom. Its first project was on an SMS center (adding SMS center details).

~

'Hey, Abhilash, we are going to a party tonight. Guess what I have got!' Abhishek handed him the envelope that carried the cheque of their first payment. 'Rs. 14 lacs, can you imagine! That's our first income. Abhilash, why are you so blank? *Shock lag gaya kya, mujhe bhi laga thha* (are you shocked, even I was).' Abhishek was super excited.

'I am not shocked about the cheque, I am shocked about our stupidity.' Abhishek gave him a quizzical look; he was too happy to think of anything that is negative, but Abhilash kept on fretting. 'How are we going to redeem this amount? Do you realize we don't even have a bank account? Damn! We are running a business without a bank account, and it never occurred to us. How can we be so dumb?'

Though the situation was messed up, Abhishek replied patiently, 'Cool down, Abhilash. Let's open a bank account, okay?'

Abhilash retorted, 'Abhishek, ignorance is bliss, but sometimes it's also a bane. When we started a company, we had two partners who never worked with us, but legally, they are our partners. How will we open an account, with one partner working in US, and the other not in touch with us for over six months? We need all four signatures to open an account.'

Abhishek sank into his chair; it was surely a terrible way to learn the lesson. It took them two solid months to locate the other two partners and arrange for their signatures. Once all four signatures were made the account was opened. Though they corrected their partnership deed, they did not correct the way they operated the company. Therefore, they were destined to learn the next lesson soon.

~

'Abhishek, can I get some cash to fill the fuel tank?' asked Sameer in utter desperation. In his early twenties, Sameer was doing a three-month internship with 6d.

Abhishek, unable to comprehend his anxious tone, looked at him and suddenly realized his blunder. Sameer had agreed to join them without expecting any compensation, but 6d did not even reimburse the travel expenses he'd made on behalf of the company.

'Yeah, sure. You please give me the details of all the other expenditures you did for the company, I will clear that as well,' Abhishek said hesitantly.

Sameer's request was a moment of realization for Abhishek that he is an employer who is now accountable for his team. Though there were not many employees, expansion was always on the cards.

Soon, various processes were set up and employees' needs were taken into consideration. But Abhishek and Abhilash were still not drawing their salary from 6d and were using the company's debit card for their personal expenditures, as and when required.

In the first year, with the number of assignments they had, Abhishek was expecting revenue of around Rs. 75 lacs. With this, Abhishek and Abhilash wanted to recruit new members to their team. Soon Saurabh an IITian, was referred to them by Harish, a colleague who had joined 6d from Satyam. Both Abhishek and Abhilash were elated that finally someone with IIT pedigree had joined them.

Abhishek was so overwhelmed by Saurabh's qualifications that he made him, still a rookie, the CEO of 6d Technologies. Even Abhilash gave his consent, and both of them didn't think much about it till it was too late.

'Abhilash, did you check the bank statements? They have made a mistake. Who had breakfast at InterContinental, lunch at Le Méridian? What's going on?' Abhishek hollered.

'Did you do it, Saurabh?' Abhilash looked at him in disbelief as Saurabh nodded. 'How can you spend that kind of money in five-star hotels? We are a start-up, and don't have money to waste. We lead an abstemious lifestyle and you are splurging in five-star hotels? Don't you have any ownership for the company?' asked Abhilash when he found out that Saurabh was misusing the company's debit card.

'All of you too use the company's debit card for your personal expenses. I am the CEO. I have to maintain my lifestyle,' said Saurabh rudely.

'In that case, you go your way and we go ours. We cannot afford an expensive employee like you,' Abhishek bluntly asked him to quit.

'Abhishek, I am also putting down my papers,' Harish said, handing over his resignation. This wasn't expected from Harish, but since he was the one who had introduced Saurabh, he felt responsible for the loss. With two out of four employees gone, the smooth ride became bumpier. Their bank account was almost empty and their confidence had been badly shaken, but there were lessons to be learnt. They recruited an accountant to manage their finances and to set up new processes. The worst was yet to come: Harish and Saurabh started their own company and were competing for the same business as Abhishek and Abhilash.

~

'Why? Don't you know that your brother Abhishek is in a financial mess? Last week, three people came home to recover the money. You have given money to Abhishek many a times. Why do you want to leave such a well-paid job in Oracle? People aspire to join Oracle. For a middle-class boy, Oracle is a dream come true and you want to leave it and for what? 6d?'

Abhinav's mother couldn't understand her younger son's newfound passion. Abhishek wasn't doing well. Recently, he got married and was struggling with the household expenses.

'*Maa,* I can get a job anytime. My friends have joined 6d. They all are saying it is more fun. They are doing some excellent stuff. Their exposure is much higher than mine,' Abhinav was determined to join 6d. Realizing that she didn't have much choice, Abhinav's mother withdrew herself from the debate.

'I think our peaceful days are over now, courtesy the entrepreneurial dreams of both my sons. One is Rahu, one is Ketu, and that 6d is sitting like Shani on my head. Do whatever you want,' finally his parent relented.

6d now had its offices in Delhi and Bangalore. In February 2005, Abhinav joined the Bangalore office under the leadership of Abhilash, while Abhishek travelled across India to give presentations about their products and solutions to various telecom operators.

With the company's rapid expansion, the expenses increased. So it was Abhilash's turn to dive deep into debt. He took a personal loan to fund the salaries and other operational expenses.

If taking a loan was a sign of commitment, then both Abhishek and Abhilash were outdoing each other.

~

'Abhilash, I have to travel to Muscat for a day. Nawras, a new telecom operator, requires a customized telecom solution. This deal is crucial for our survival,' said Abhishek.

'When are you planning to travel?' asked Abhilash.

'Next week. But do we have enough money to book tickets? Our travel agent has invested more in our company than we have,' Abhishek said with a smile. 'He won't let us enter his office.'

'We owe him Rs. 12 lacs already. I think now we can only get away with a begging bowl. He is our one and only hope,' said Abhilash, reminded of the debts that required immediate attention.

To their luck, despite the hefty outstanding, Biswajeet, their travel operator, booked the tickets for Abhishek. Sometimes, one strikes a chord with the right people who believe in the future potential. Biswajeet had faith in their potential and goodness, hence despite the delayed payments he continued lending money.

'Where will you stay?' Abhilash inquired.

'I plan to honour Muscat airport,' he replied with a smile.

'As if you have an option! What about food?'

'I hope I can manage that, and if not, then fasting is always good for health,' Abhishek said.

A few days later, Abhishek left for Muscat with a mere Rs. 2,000 in his pocket. He was praying for a cheap transportation in Muscat. To his relief, the company had sent a car to pick him up.

This was his most unexpected business trip. 'When you keep striving hard, you do get lucky by chance,' he thought. He reached Nawras office. He wasn't sure of what awaited him in the boardroom, but he was sure that he won't wait to say yes to whatever they asked for.

'Our expertise is in these four telecom solutions. Let me explain to you about our products,' Abhishek started his presentation.

'Hang on please! We are looking at customized services as per our specific requirements. We have already approached Bharti Telesoft, but we are looking at a better offer than that,' interrupted one of the board members.

'I am aware of your requirements and your expectations,' Abhishek said confidently.

'At a competitive price!' one of the members asserted.

'Yes, we can. We are India's leading telecom solution providers. We are confident that we can fulfill your requirements at an unbeatable price,' said Abhishek assertively, but there was something on his mind. 'I have to seal this deal or else we will be in trouble. Let me focus on getting the work first, I will figure out the specifications later,' he thought. Soon, he was signing papers for the project.

~

They got their first overseas project from Nawras. Was it a moment of celebration or of concern? There was still a scene of confusion.

'Abhinav, you have to go to Muscat after two days. You remember, I briefed you about that Nawras project?' said Abhilash over the phone.

'Yes, I remember, but that's such an important project for us. Why don't you send someone senior? Why me?' asked Abhinav.

'Because your English is good,' said Abhilash. 'See, you are fluent in English, so you can converse with them and understand their requirements better. It's very important to have clarity of thought on information before going ahead on any project.'

Abhinav had never thought of a weirder reason. 'You mean to say, we don't know the specifications yet. Then how did we get the project?' Abhinav was shocked.

'They wanted software for their customer service department. Once we know their specifications, we will make it. That's it. You just need to get the information. Remember, we are a small company and can't afford to lose any opportunity. We need projects, big or small doesn't matter,' Abhilash gave a pearl of wisdom.

'OK, if knowing English is all that is required then I will do it,' said Abhinav, clueless about what he was supposed to do, but then he thought, 'If Abhilash thinks I can do it, then let me do it.'

Abhinav landed in Muscat where his job was to gather complete information on the software within 21 days. Owing to his affable nature, it became an easy task. He spoke to people from various departments, understood their requirements, came back and explained it to his team. By the end of the month, the software was up and running. Abhinav was glad that he had made a significant contribution to 6d's revenue and, consequently, to its survival: it was the brightest feather in his cap.

Easy Recharge, a point-of-sale (POS) based electronic voucher distribution system, was the easiest way to recharge a prepaid number from any of their retail outlets. This technology had become a popular medium to recharge in most parts of India and South Asia due to lower pricing and distribution charges. However, no one had thought that this medium would work in other areas too.

Soon Abhinav took complete ownership of the Easy Recharge system and pitched it to various telecom operators, both in India and abroad. He stood by his philosophy of 'focus on few' and pursued it with the goal of maximizing revenue for 6d.

~

While everyone in 6d was striving hard to include every telecom operator in their client list, they forgot or overlooked certain basic and essential legal formalities.

Only after a legal notice was received from the income tax department did they realize their blunder. The notice warned them that failing to pay the taxes, which had been due for the last two years, within the deadline mentioned, might land them all in jail on charges of tax evasion. They realized that the amount of tax dues had surpassed the amount of earnings. There was no way they could pay back the arrears unless they took loans, or a messiah came to their rescue.

Luckily, a messiah did come in the form of a venture capitalist (VC), who proposed to invest a sum of Rs. 2 crores in 6d for 20 percent equity. Bearing in mind the company's future prospects, they agreed. It was a much diluted figure, but considering their desperate need for liquid cash, it was a sigh of relief. Once they received the amount, they cleared their debts worth Rs. 80 lacs.

After discussing the future plans for 6d, Abhilash said, 'Abhishek, with this load of Rs. 80 lacs off our shoulders, I think we should start drawing salaries. With Satyam, we had said goodbye to salaries, but now we have the luxury of choosing to go back to it.'

'You are right. I had drawn my last salary two years back. It has become a long-lost dream, but now let us put the processes into place and transform this partnership firm into an organization to reckon with,' Abhishek replied.

For the first time since its inception, everybody in 6d, including Abhishek and Abhilash, began to draw salaries.

With high-paced growth achieved by aggressive pitches and follow-ups, the business development team was outpacing the project development team, which was finding it difficult to meet deadlines. So 6d needed more people to deliver the projects that they had in hand.

'We have to get more people working on the back-end. Saying no to business is foolish. And we will lose our credibility in the market if we don't deliver our projects on time,' said Abhilash in a worried tone.

'I understand that but to hire people we need more working capital, which looks difficult especially considering our current payment arrangement with our clients,' said Abhishek.

'We should approach a few VCs. That would be the best thing to do as of now,' Abhilash suggested.

While one half of the team set about making presentations, the other half was in talks with VCs, but every VC rejected their proposals.

'Your offerings are just the same as your competitors. There is no product differentiator in your business model. Your success lies in your lower pricing, but lower pricing means lower return on capital employed (ROCE). We will not invest in this kind of business whose future is bleak in the face of tough competition,' replied one of the VCs.

Everyone was disappointed, but this was the ideal time for the 6d team to put on its thinking cap and come up with something innovative, something that would give them a competitive advantage.

~

'Abhishek, don't you see an indifference in our team regarding a new business idea. From every VC, we are getting the feedback that we have to come up with something new. But no one is working in that direction,' said Abhinav over a cup of morning tea.

'Maybe they are not able to visualize the difference it can create. I think we should work on it and then present it to them. Our next idea has to be business-to-consumer (B2C) product. That's where the numbers lie,' Abhishek was already mulling over the issue.

'In fact, you must have read about the Vodafone-Hutch deal for $22 billion. They paid a huge amount: $776 per user.'

'It's a value a company commands if it has consumers on its side. That's what we need to build, a B2C product.'

Abhishek and Abhinav, together, worked on the new idea, which could give a quantum leap to 6d's future. They christened it as Echo, as they were contemplating on a small name which could be used as a verb. But later on, they styled it as EKO.

Finally, they were ready to unleash EKO. But before presenting their idea to the 6d team, they wanted an external validation.

'With EKO, people can use their mobile phones for money transfer. It is another form of mobile commerce,' chorused Abhishek and Abhinav, who participated in the TiE-Canaan Entrepreneurial Challenge — a national level business plan competition for early stage entrepreneurs to get platform and funds for their novel and pathbreaking ideas.

'Through EKO, a secured financial transaction can be completed using the simplest of mobile phones. Ease of use and low cost per transaction is our differentiator,' Abhishek added. The concept was simple: use mobile phones for financial transactions.

'With this technology, the mobile phone would become a common man's wallet. One can shop articles, book movie tickets, transfer money,' said Abhinav as he explained the details.

Their low-cost mobile commerce concept won the TiE-Canaan Entrepreneurial Challenge award in 2006, but funding still remained a challenge. The VCs said that their team was not suitable to venture on such a big idea. Nevertheless, just winning the competition was itself a big validation for their idea.

Once they won the award, both Abhinav and Abhishek decided that now was the time to break this news, of winning the competition, to their team. Excited and thrilled, Abhishck and Abhinav presented EKO to 6d team. They were expecting a big applause from their team members on their effort, but seeing the blank faces they slowly sank back into their chairs.

'Abhishek, please understand that we are a telecom software company. We operate in the B2B space. Getting into consumer-facing business is not our expertise. We have so many projects right now that we are not able to deliver on time. Why should we even touch a new idea?' said Manish, Abhishek's classmate in BIT who was designated as COO at 6d.

'Abhishek, I don't think we are ready for it. We should focus on our core; we already have plenty of projects in the pipeline. I don't understand why you are doing random things for 6d without involving and consulting us,' said Abhilash. He was tired — it was their third meeting and Abhishek and Abhinav were not willing to give up on EKO. Their persistence wasn't helping.

'It was probably easy to convince the judges in TiE-Canaan competition than my own team,' said Abhishek, sensing the growing differences between him and his team. Abhishek was unable to convince his core group at 6d to warm up to EKO. His insistence on continuing to work on the idea of EKO without involving others in his vision and lack of communication caused irreversible damage that he had not expected.

'Look at it this way. We need income to run 6d. The VCs have already said that our business model has no product differentiator.

Trust me. This project will give us that edge. We can raise funds through this project and use the funds for supporting other projects.'

'Then why hasn't anyone funded your award-winning idea yet, Abhishek?' Manish retorted.

'The judges said that we neither have suitable skills nor the expertise to run this project. Then why should we put our energy into it? Anyways, even if we invest our time and money in it, there is no guarantee that we will be able to raise funds,' Abhilash said, pointing out the obvious. The discussion had long crossed the lines of being friendly — tempers ran high, there was tension on both sides.

Each side stuck to its guns. No one was ready to budge. Abhishek and Abhinav seemed to speak a language that no one understood. Suddenly, everything changed. The team had broken up into two.

~

The hopes of reconciliation faded further when Rajat Mehta, who held only 20 percent stakes in 6d, offered to acquire 6d. It became another contentious issue between Abhishek and Abhilash, who were the founding pillars of 6d Technologies.

'I think it's a good offer. After all, how long will we keep slogging for such paper-thin margins? If we accept this offer, it will give us money for diversification and expansion,' reasoned Abhilash.

'Abhilash receiving funding from VCs and selling a company are two different things. What will happen to the projects that we are working on? In fact, we can deliver those projects and come out of our financial stress. Now that we have built a name in the telecom industry and know the sector is booming, we should hang on for another six months. We should not sell now,' said Abhishek.

'Abhishek we are a young team. Some of us are already married and others about to get married. It makes sense to sell 6d. He is offering good valuation plus enough cash. We may not get a similar price in the future,' Manish voiced his opinion. The entire team agreed.

'But, Manish, it is our business. If we sell we will become employees. As an independent entity, we will have freedom to work the way we want. I still think we should give the EKO idea a chance. With that we can raise money from VCs,' said Abhishek.

'Abhishek, we are tired of your obsession with EKO. We are not interested in EKO and on behalf of the 6d team, I can't make myself clearer. We have created this company. We have slogged day and night and now when we have a chance to monetize our efforts, you are saying no. Majority of us want it to be sold. I am done for today. The meeting is over.' With that, Abhilash stormed out of the room.

Slowly, one by one, each member walked out of the room. Only Abhinav and Abhishek remained. The conclusion of the meeting ended their stint with 6d Technologies. The ambition to pursue EKO alienated them, making them strangers in their own family.

~

Abhinav wasn't able to cope with the thought of leaving 6d. After all, he had grown with it. It was an ironic twist of fate that he had to leave 6d Technologies on the same day that he had joined it: February 7. Till this day, he had considered February 7 as the most auspicious and promising day, but it turned out to be the gloomiest one.

He glanced at his cabin and his heart sank. His workstation had photographs of the team. He reminisced about how every project and every night out to meet deadlines was more fun than work. And today, all lines of communication between him and his friends were dead.

Even Abhilash, who had been his pillar of strength, who encouraged him to take on new challenges, had turned his back. In the past two years, Abhinav had spent more time training under Abhilash than under the tutelage of his own brother. But now things were different: he needed to muster courage to speak to Abhilash. Finally, he entered Abhilash's cabin to bid a final goodbye.

'Abhilash, thanks a lot for all your support. It was great working with you,' Abhinav extended a formal handshake.

Even Abhilash was going through an emotional turmoil. Questions like 'Is it right? He just has a different opinion.' 'Have things really gone bad?' 'Can't we do something to correct things?' 'Is it really irreversible?' were taking a toll on him.

'Good luck,' Abhilash said softly. He knew that he was losing much more than just a partner.

Eventually, Abhishek and Abhinav sold their stakes in 6d. While it was tough for them to give up the company, it was even tougher for Abhilash. Not only did he lose a confidante and colleague in Abhishek, with the 'buy out' deal not coming through, 6d had to struggle to stay afloat without funds and broken morale.[1]

~

After quiting 6d Abhishek was home. 'Mekhla, this sofa looks so old. It doesn't even match with the curtains,' Abhishek complained to his wife.

'Abhishek, am I dreaming or are you actually saying it? Finally, after so many years you have noticed something at home,' said Mekhla. Her remark pierced him and he realized that he had left the responsibility of managing the house to Mekhla far too long. He resolved to fix the loose ends at his personal front.

Abhishek was about to declare his decision to participate actively in the household when Abhinav came in and sank into the sofa. He was wearing a morose expression. Abhishek knew what was coming.

'I don't think it should have happened,' Abhinav moaned.

'What happened was unfortunate and beyond our control. I agree, but we need to move on. Let bygones be bygones; we will not sulk over it for a minute more. We believed in EKO and we still believe in it. Now the point is to work towards making it real,' said Abhishek.

'You are right, but in EKO, our model revolves around the financial sector. We are engineers, with no knowledge or experience of the financial sector. We have to find people who have both experience and expertise in this field,' said Abhinav, regaining his long-lost spirit.

---

1 Under Abhilash's leadership 6d is today a profitable and successful telecom value-added-services company.

'But before that, we should put all our learnings from 6d to paper so that we don't repeat the same mistakes,' said Abhishek. This time, Abhishek chose to be more organized and structured.

Abhinav got a pen and a paper, and the brothers sat down to jot down the key learnings. They zeroed on the following:

1. We will build a consumer brand where price is not the only differentiator.
2. We will hire people only if they have the right skills and can gel with us, not because they are branded from IIT, IIM, etc.
3. We will build transparency in the system. All crucial decisions and new ideas will be discussed among the core members.
4. We will define the roles clearly and set up a more organized HR policy and framework.
5. We will also define a vision for company and for ourselves and will review it from time to time.

'Most importantly, we will not use company's debit card for our personal expenses!' Abhinav said with a smirk.

Experience and learning has its costs; some people incur it in B-schools, while people like Abhishek incur it otherwise.

~

Though the differences had put an end to their partnership, it did not put an end to their friendship. Abhilash, Abhishek and the other core team members were mature enough to respect their contrary viewpoints. After a few months, their relationship returned to normal.

'Hi, Abhishek, I need a favour. One of my friends, Manoranjan, wants to start something of his own. See if you can invest in his business or work out something together,' said Manish Chandra from 6d. 'I will ask him to get in touch with you.'

Abhishek had received a lump sum from selling his stake in 6d and that was the seed capital for his new company: EKO India Financial Services. Manish knew that Abhishek was always open to new ideas. Soon, Manoranjan called and they scheduled a meeting for the next day.

'Abhishek, I am planning to start a venture, and I am looking for funds,' said Manoranjan. 'Manish informed me that you may be interested in funding the business.'

'What is your idea? What business do you want to get into?' asked Abhishek.

For an hour, Manoranjan explained him the business idea he was working on. It was still a half-baked idea, which required further research and feasibility study. But what appealed to Abhishek was Manoranjan's passion and sincerity.

'Why don't you join our start-up as a co-founder? We already have an idea and we can work on it together,' said Abhishek. He thought Manoranjan, a dropout by choice from IIFT, had the guts, so, instead of funding his idea, Abhishek made an offer that he could not refuse.

With Manoranjan joining in, EKO became a team of three non-bankers who wanted to build a mobile commerce company.

'The first thing that we should do is to get a banking and finance professional to come on board, otherwise, we cannot think of taking a step further,' said Manoranjan.

'Even I have been pondering on the issue. We can check with Alok, if he can suggest a suitable candidate,' said Abhishek.

'Who is he?'

'Alok is the founder of JobsAhead.com. He sold his stakes and now works with Canaan Partners, a private equity firm which sponsors the TiE contest, where we presented our EKO business plan and won. I had met him there,' said Abhishek enthusiastically and called Alok.

'I think Sanjay Bhargava will help you. He has rich experience in the financial sector. He has worked with Citibank, PayPal, etc. In fact, Sanjay was one of the main architects of the back-end of PayPal. He can certainly be great asset to the team. I will connect you with him,' said Alok and scheduled a meeting with Sanjay for next week.

Dressed in formals and wearing a serious look with a nervous smile, the trio — Abhishek, Abhinav and Manorajan — entered the restaurant, where a lunch meeting with Sanjay had been scheduled. After friendly handshakes, Sanjay came straight away to the point.

'Alok told me about your business plan. It is workable and scalable, no second thoughts about that. But do you really want to be in the mobile payment space? It is hard to digest, considering your engineering background. The business you want to get into is hard-core banking. It is not an Easy Recharge for a mobile, it is branchless banking,' said Sanjay, unable to contain his amusement.

'I agree, but it is largely a technology-driven product, and that is how we as engineers connect to it. What is the big deal in understanding finance? Isn't it pure logic?' said Abhinav, beaming with confidence.

'Oh, great! Tell me one thing. If a bank takes a savings deposit from the customer, will it be a liability or an asset for the bank?' asked Sanjay, wanting to bring Abhinav face-to-face with the reality by showing him that their knowledge of technology wasn't sufficient to operate in payment space.

'Asset. It is the bank's property now,' Abhinav replied.

'Not really. The bank has to pay it back when the customer asks for it and that makes it a liability,' said Sanjay, hiding his smile at Abhinav's ignorance and over-confidence.

Sanjay started briefing them about the nitty-gritty of the sector. He believed in their passion and commitment towards their dream and eventually agreed to be a part of EKO.

Sanjay was aware that the product had to go through a lot of changes before it would fit in with RBI regulations and be accepted by banks. But the biggest challenge was to develop the financial acumen of his team of non-bankers. He had to sit with Abhinav, Abhishek and Manoranjan to explain the basic concepts of accounting.

~

While Sanjay's classes were the pillars, lessons from 6d became the foundation stones of EKO's inception. By putting the learnings into writing, Abhishek lived his promise of not repeating his mistakes.

The four co-founders started working together on making EKO a reality. The partnership deed specified that none of the founders would draw salaries. The agreement defined the role of each partner clearly and explicitly stated their exit terms. Everything was structured and transparent.

Apart from being the chairman of EKO, Sanjay gladly assumed the role of a mentor for the three novices.

'There has to be one lead entrepreneur in the company, who will also be the face of the company. Abhishek, you take on the role. You will have a larger share of the company, but if anything controversial or negative happens, you will also have to bear the lion's share of the blame,' Sanjay was guiding everyone on the founders' agreement.

So, Abhishek was nominated as the CEO of EKO, though he was assisting Sanjay to a large extent. With Sanjay's financial connections and experience in the banking sector, they undertook the task of developing a good working relationship with banks. Manoranjan was entrusted with the job of managing the operations and building the retailer network. Abhinav was given the responsibility of handling the technology back-end.

The first success for EKO came early as Sanjay got his act right when Centurion Bank agreed to try their product.

~

Centurion Bank had only 200 branches. The only way they could have scaled up their operation was through branchless banking.

The pilot project with EKO was in the same direction. The agenda was to develop a mini savings account, where a customer could save and transfer money through his or her mobile phone. A customer didn't need any documents, only a mobile phone to open the bank account. All that was required was to approach retailers who were working as agents for EKO. The cell phones of customers would act as debit cards and POS (Point of Sale) devices for retailers. EKO would get a commission on every account opened.

Meanwhile, the EKO team's manpower also increased. Now the ten-member team started working on product development and technology integration.

Abhishek and Sanjay started approaching various banks by explaining the EKO project. Convincing them was their biggest challenge. All their stakes lay in the successful deployment of the Centurion Bank project that could work as the tipping point.

'It will be much easier to convince others once we go live with one project. We just need to work hard for the first client, others will follow suit,' Sanjay explained.

'Bankers are not taking us seriously. We don't have any background in banking,' said Abhishek. He had sent emails to every banker in the country seeking an appointment, but no one had responded.

'For them branchless banking is uncharted territory. Their skepticism, assessment and appetite for risk are different from that of a telecom company. Mobile commerce or PayPal may be big in US and Europe, but in India, it is still new. Don't worry. It will take time, but keep trying. By the time you manage to get an appointment, we would have rolled out our Centurion Bank project. Then it will be easy for us to convince other bankers. Till then, just try to reach them, find the right connections,' said Sanjay.

'Why are you so keen to get these unorganized retailers to become our agents? They are not reliable. Also, how will we manage the operational complexities?' asked Manoranjan, when he was given the task to convince retailers to be EKO's sales point in Uttam Nagar market in Delhi.

'They are far more reliable than our own outlets. It will be easier to run banking operations through them. We will never achieve that kind of number by ourselves; look at all the major telecom players.

Airtel has at least 1.5 million sales points. How many outlets do Airtel run?' said Abhishek.

'Not just that, they have stability and credibility in the local markets. Our customer will feel secure that his or her money is going through a known person,' added Abhinav.

'That makes sense, but why Uttam Nagar?' asked Manoranjan.

'Well, your father-in-law's house is in Uttam Nagar. We can set up a temporary office without paying any rent,' smiled Abhishek, while Manoranjan was taken aback by Abhishek's bluntness.

'Don't get zapped. Of course, that's the secondary reason, but the primary reason is that Uttam Nagar has a high mobile penetration rate and a large percentage of rural, under-banked population. A large percentage of Uttam Nagar population is made up of migrant workers; they don't have any formal address proofs; hence, they cannot access normal bank facilities. If they have to send money to their home, say a village in Bihar, they give money to a broker who charges an unreasonable commission. Uttam Nagar fits rightly as our target audience. In addition, I am sure we would be welcomed in your father-in-law's house,' said Abhinav with a wink.

Soon, a new office was set up in Uttam Nagar. Manoranjan carefully identified reliable and progressive shop owners and started approaching them one by one, teaching them how to open a bank account and how to remit money using their mobile phones.

Sumit Gupta, a young college pass out, owner of a medical shop in Uttam Nagar, was bowled over by the idea, but was discouraged by his father. Manoranjan, with Gupta's example, learned that he should approach the young shopkeepers as the old shopkeepers were not open to trying out something new. He started meeting and selling the idea to them.

Finally, after two months of continuous and rigorous follow-ups, he was able to appoint 16 shopkeepers as EKO's customer service points (CSP). They were ready for the Centurion Bank project now.

Next day, the Centurion Bank project, their first ever project, was to go live. The trials had been successful, and everyone was banking on it. But to Abhishek's dismay, when he was browsing through the newspaper, the headline 'Centurion Bank of Punjab, HDFC Bank to merge' made his heart skip a beat.

He called Sanjay, 'Did you read the news about the merger?'

'Yes, I did.'

'What will happen to EKO project under new management? Will they continue with us?'

'They may not proceed with the project,' said Sanjay. Abhishek's heart sank at the thought of cancelation. They had put their blood, sweat and money in the project. It was their hope for a brighter future. All they could now do was to pray for a better turn of events.

But in the first week of March, EKO received a notice from banking authorities stating that the company had to squander the 2,000 accounts they had made for the project by June. Thus, all their efforts and money had gone down the drain.

Abhishek realized that they needed to start all over again and that too without any sustainable funds. They had exhausted all the money they had got from selling stakes in 6d. Denial and dejection made them feel completely down and out, but they kept on moving.

~

'Good morning, Ashish,' Abhishek and Abhinav greeted Ashish, a young manager in his mid-thirties working in Citibank. He got the directive from the senior manager to assess the possibility of a tie-up with Citibank.

'We are the pioneers of branchless banking in India,' Abhishek started. They wanted to communicate the ease of use and the relevance of the product.

'At EKO, banking can be done using mobile phones,' said Abhinav and picked up the phone to explain the model.

'What is this?' exploded Ashish, even before Abhinav could finish the sentence. 'What are you doing with this phone? Don't waste my time. You should come with a proper presentation. You don't know how to present your idea.'

'Ashish, the product is all about—' Abhinav tried to explain with the phone in hand but was cut short by Ashish.

'Cut the crap. I am not sitting here to see how you play with cell phones. Do you have something sensible to show us?' Ashish was humiliating them single-handedly.

'But the product is about mobile phones. There is no better way to explain than with a demo,' said Abhinav.

'What the hell! You are wasting my time. I don't see anything worthwhile in your product,' Ashish passed the judgment and left. Out of the 15 minutes meeting they had, team EKO was generously humiliated for 10 minutes.

'Today was even worse than yesterday,' said Abhinav, wiping sweat off his forehead.

Abhishek had become thick-skinned. He understood that banks were large institutions and, more often than not, would find people who were not open to new ideas.

'What happened yesterday Abhinav? Why were you so livid?' Abhishek was curious.

'Yesterday, I had a meeting scheduled with a top-level manager, a lady, in Airtel. Instead of a face-to-face meeting, she wanted that I should explain the model over the phone, which I attempted sitting in their office reception area. Midway through the conversation, she said that she didn't want to hear anymore and that I should leave. Even today, Ashish was barely polite,' Abhinav was frustrated with disappointments they were facing from all directions.

Abhishek smiled at him and said, 'Don't be disheartened. Rejections are very important because they prepare you for the future. Probably, two years down the line, that lady would still be a manager in some circle, but you would have become a VP of EKO.'

Abhishek had developed the virtue of patience and maturity to deal with such discouraging and annoying situations.

It seemed that difficulties had become his destiny.

'It has almost been a year since the Centurion Bank debacle, but we have not achieved anything credible yet. We are going nowhere,' said Sanjay. He had lost his patience.

'We are trying. What else can we do? We have to wait and not give up,' said Abhishek patiently. Abhishek knew that this was impending. It looked as if Sanjay had made up his mind. The discussion soon turned into a heated argument.

'It is not working. I am quitting EKO,' said Sanjay bluntly after 15 minutes.

Abhinav and Manoranjan were shaken with the news, but Abhishek was unperturbed.

It took EKO two weeks to regain its momentum. Sanjay had contributed immensely to their initial set-up. He brought the soul of banking into what was largely a telecom company.

~

'The representative of the Bill & Melinda Gates Foundation will visit your office,' Mike called from the Consultative Group to Assist the Poor (CGAP) Technology Program, housed within the World Bank. The group is co-funded by the Bill & Melinda Gates Foundation. CGAP was assessing branchless banking technology across the globe. EKO had been on their radar for the past six months.

'Somebody from Bill & Melinda Gates Foundation is going to visit our office next week,' announced Abhishek.

'Who will be coming?' Abhinav was curious. He browsed their website and checked on all the senior people working in the Bill & Melinda Gates Foundation.

'Don't worry about who is coming, worry about what we will show them. We don't have any active tie-up. How will we show them the power of our product?' said Abhishek. He was anxious about the visit, and rightly so: if the visit went well, they might get funding.

'We can show them the dummy transactions. We have our network ready. Gupta Medicos in Uttam Nagar could give them a demonstration of our product,' said Manoranjan, trying to work a way out.

'Right, we don't have any other option,' said Abhishek.

Once they decided how they would go about demonstrating the usability of the product, they stopped worrying about the impending visit and resumed their work. Towards the evening, they received a call again from Mike of CGAP.

'Tomorrow morning at eight o'clock sharp, Mr. Bill Gates will come to your office,' Mike told.

'What! Are you serious?' Abhishek was bewildered.

'Yes, I am serious. Prepare well and best of luck!' said Mike.

Abhishek informed the team about Bill Gates's visit; none of them could believe their ears. 'Oh my God, that "somebody" is none other than Bill Gates himself!' exclaimed Abhinav. He had butterflies in his stomach.

Nobody in the entire team of EKO slept that night in the excitement of meeting the legendary Bill Gates himself.

Bill Gates, accompanied by his father and two sisters, visited the EKO office and Mr. Gupta's retail outlet. Gates asked Mr. Gupta a few questions and took notes in his diary. He was impressed with EKO's usage of technology. He believed that the EKO model could contribute significantly to society.

'Gates pays low-key visit to tech start-up pilot project' read the headline of *Mint,* a business newspaper, on November 5, 2008.

In March 2009, EKO received a 'grant funding' of $1.78 million from CGAP, which came as a huge relief.

At the weekly meeting, everyone in the team was charged up.

'Now we can focus on providing services to State Bank of India (SBI). We have enough money to sustain ourselves,' said Abhishek proudly.

'It took us a year to crack SBI, Manoranjan. Now the onus is on you. Make sure that we create enough agents (CSPs) to service them,' said Abhishek, clearly explaining how the success of this project rested on its successful execution. SBI had appointed EKO as its business correspondent and launched a no-frills 'SBI Mini Savings Bank Account' for those who earned less than Rs. 5,000 a month.

'Don't worry, Abhishek, we will make this opportunity work,' said Manoranjan. 'I just have one concern. Will the people who are making less than Rs. 5,000 understand our SMS messages in English? One of our retailers brought this issue to my attention.'

'In that case, we must send the SMSs either in Hindi or in the local language,' said Abhishek.

'That would increase our costs. We are already working on wafer-thin margins, and we cannot afford to increase the cost,' said Abhinav.

'We don't have any other choice, Abhinav. If they don't understand the SMS, our entire model goes for a toss,' said Manoranjan.

'We must think about this and come back with some solution in the next meeting,' said Abhishek.

Manoranjan and Abhinav interacted with some of the account holders and came to know that those who can't read understood the message through the numbers given at the end of the message. The numbers acted as a sign that their phone was recharged.

In the next meeting, it was decided that they would do the same. The format of the message would be similar to that of the telecom operators — the amount would be placed in the end. So, after a lot of discussion, a small yet crucial operational glitch was resolved.

~

Though SBI was a big catch, things were still progressing at a snail's pace in EKO. Despite a growth in the number of customers and retailers, a critical mass had not yet been achieved. By this time, Manoranjan had lost his patience.

Manoranjan had always dreamt of building his own company. He started introspecting, 'Did I ever want to create EKO? Should I stay here or pursue my dream?' The love for his initial business idea was reviving back in his heart, so he decided to move on from EKO.

'Abhishek, I am planning to quit. It has been a great experience working with you, and I know EKO will have a great future, but my calling is different. I want to give a shot to my own business idea. I have a different vision, and my vision is not in sync with what we are doing in EKO. I think it is time for me to move on,' said Manoranjan.

Abhishek accepted Manoranjan's decision with respect and understanding and thanked him for the hard work he has put in for EKO's growth. After all, Manoranjan was the backbone of EKO — he had created many CSPs single-handedly.

'Abhinav, Manoranjan has put down his papers. The money from CGAP will last till May 2010 — that is, another six months. We will not be able to survive with the SBI account alone in our kitty,' said Abhishek in a matter-of-fact way.

'You are right, but we need to find the missing link. I strongly feel that we are missing something in our business model. We must review our business model,' said Abhinav.

'We need to reach more people and make them learn to use mobile for banking,' said Abhishek. He went to the board and started writing.

~

On a bright Friday morning, Mangal Bazaar in Sitamarhi, Bihar, was buzzing with activity. Fruits and vegetable vendors were busy negotiating the rates with the shoppers.

Suddenly, there was a loud drum beat from a corner of the street. Everyone turned and saw four boys in white T-shirts. The boys started talking to each other in a very loud voice.

'Pyaar ka darwaza. Tujhe pata hai pyaar ka darwaza kya hota hai? (Do you know what the door of love is?)'

The street play *Pyaar ka Darwaza* was being enacted by two men with EKO's poster, held by another two, as their backdrop. Everyone stopped whatever they were doing and started looking at the play. A group of women stopped bargaining and joined the crowd to see the *nukkad natak,* a common tradition in Bihar.

'Kya bhaiyya, hume kaise pata? Hamari to abhi shaadi bhi nahi hui? (No, how would I know? I am not even married)' said one of the boys, blushing.

'Kal jab tumhari shaadi hogi, bacche honge, baccho ki padhai hogi, to yeh sab kaise karoge? (When you get married, have children, how will you manage their education and everything else?)'

'Ye to maine socha hi nahi (I had never thought of it),' he said and sat on the street, worrying about his future. Then, the other guy came with the solution, '*Arey khata kholo, bachat ka darwaza kholo, apne parivar ke liye zimmedari ko nibhane ka rasta kholo.* (Open an account with us, open the door of savings, and start fulfilling your responsibility towards the needs of your family.)'

The play was woven around a character who was in love. The story was narrated by a 'wise guy' (representing EKO), informing people about the responsibilities that will increase in the future — marriage, kids, school, health — and to deal with them, through teaching the character in love to open a savings account.

'Arre bhaiya, pehle apne dimag ka dhakkan kholo, phir soch samajh ke bolo. Padhna likhna aata nahi, gaon main bank koi jata nahi. (Open your eyes. People don't know how to read and write and so no one goes to the bank in our village.)'

'Arre jab EKO hai saath, to darne ki kya baat. Bas mobile phone lao aur lallan bhai ki dukan pe jao. Woh kholenge khata tumhara, yeh wada hai humara. Bank jane ka jhanjhat nahi, padne likhne ki koi tension nahi.' (With EKO around, why worry? You don't need to go to bank, just go to Lallan *bhaiya's* shop. He will help you open an account. No need to go to the bank and bother yourself.)'

EKO had also set up a stall at the bazaar. They were asking people to play Snakes and Ladders, a board game where players rolled dice and navigated through the squares. Ladders represented the good that an EKO account could do — that is, allowing the player to jump squares; while snakes represented the problems and set the player back by several squares.

EKO turned the routine market place into a place buzzing with the new idea of saving money for the future. Many people actively participated in the game and even inquired about the products.

'We were able to open 100 new accounts from the Mangal Bazaar activity,' Mughda exclaimed. Mugdha Bhargava, vice president, marketing and communication, had very little funds allocated to create awareness about EKO's branchless banking through mobile phone among a less educated target audience. She rose to the challenge, and soon she was organizing street plays in line with the tradition of Jatra, which became an option for EKO.

'That is not all! There is more!' exclaimed Mugdha. 'Diamond Comics has agreed to print comics in which Chacha Chaudhary will teach customers on how to use EKO products.'

'Wow! That's great! We can distribute a copy with every new account,' remarked Abhinav. After all, he had grown up reading Chacha Chaudhary and Sabu's adventures.

With a plethora of marketing and PR activities, EKO started its operations in Bihar. It enabled a migrant from Bihar to transfer the money from Delhi to Sitamarhi, a district in Bihar. It was important to create awareness about the use of the product, and *nukkad natak* did the trick.

~

'Abhinav, we have to start EKO operations for ICICI in the next seven days,' said the voice from the other side.

'What, in the next seven days, are you serious?' Abhinav wanted to confirm.

'Yes. By August 1, we should be up and running. Today is July 23, and that leaves you with precisely seven days.' The official did not leave any scope for negotiation to increase the time.

ICICI Bank, an account that the EKO team had been chasing since the last one and half years, got converted now, but Abhinav was not excited. They were running out of working capital. The CGAP money had been exhausted even before one and half years. The loans from friends and family had been used to pay the last month's salaries. The ICICI account meant they had to invest more.

'We will do it. The next few months will be tough, but this is probably the last battle for survival. We have already partnered with SBI. If we can cross this block, we will be winners in the long run,' Abhishek motivated the team in the weekly meeting.

For the next seven days, everybody in EKO worked 24/7 and ensured that they went live with ICICI.

The transaction volume started increasing. EKO did a few pilot projects for other banks too. It was a new thing for the banks in India. Even they were learning something new. With the increasing pressure from government of India and RBI for financial inclusion of poor, banks were experimenting with various ideas. Finally, the banks realized that the only solution for sustainable business was to charge customers nominal fees for every transaction. Post offices were charging 5 percent while money transfer fees by banks were around 2 percent. So, banks decided to charge 0.50 percent per transaction and agreed to pass on 0.15 percent to EKO.

Finally, after four years, EKO started making money with a scalable idea. It proved the point that their efforts did not go in vain. They had tried everything they could, and it was finally reaping the benefits.

~

The sight was stunning and breathtaking as they reached the entrance of the Umaid Bhawan Palace. Abhishek and his family, had come to Jodhpur to spend a weekend over the palace. As they checked in, all of them were in awe. The magnificent structure stood tall in the midst of verdant gardens. While kids were running around, brimming with excitement Mekhla had a strange smile on her face.

'Abhishek, this is just divine, the ultimate luxury. Do you remember our first date, when you took me to lunch at Pizza Hut?' Mekhla reminisced.

'Oh, don't remind me of that. On their first date, people are full of excitement, but I was full of anxiety; people are lost in romantic dreams, but I was lost in a bunch of credit cards; people can't take their eyes off from their partner's face, but I was only thinking of saving mine. None of my credit cards worked,' Abhishek reddened at his recollection.

'And we had to return home without eating. I hadn't even brought my lunch that day. It must have been very embarrassing for you,' added Mekhla.

'That was still OK. I have a long list of embarrassing moments, the first of which is when your dad checked my bank statement. I was going to Malaysia. That time, I had asked him to mail me a few documents for my visa. He got the glimpse of my horrible financial status, so he offered to arrange the tickets through a travel agent.'

'You never told me about the incident?'

'How could I? I was ashamed. What would he have thought of me? Even for your pregnancy and the birth of our child, I did not have money. Thankfully, we had some good friends who made sure that we sail through those precious moments happily.'

'That's true. I will always be grateful to Abhilash. For our first child, he took a personal loan to meet the expenses. That was very thoughtful of him. That was really a tough phase. You messed up almost everything, Abhishek,' she teased him with a smile.

'To tell the truth, I am glad that I did. That's why you are spending a weekend here. Actually, I had no idea of the complexity of the future. Had I been aware that funding business with personal loans and credit cards is the worst strategy, I would have never done that. If I had even the slightest clue that I may not get a job again, I would have never left it,' said Abhishek.

'You were really so naïve.'

'I was, and I think it's good to take advantage of being naïve. It's so important to experiment in life, challenge the status quo and try out wild things, at least for a few years in life,' Abhishek said passionately.

'Yeah, yeah, so they should open a company without a bank account, live hand-to-mouth and have no money to take one's wife for a honeymoon, right?' she pulled his leg.

'Come on, now you cannot complain as I am providing you the best of everything. In fact, now you should acknowledge me by saying, "Even the worst case is not bad, if you choose entrepreneurship as an option".' Abhishek smiled proudly.

EKO
KEY LESSONS
PROF. S. SUNDARARAJAN

Professor Sundararajan is Director of ICMA (Institute of Cost & Management Accounts) in Oman. He was Professor of Finance and Entrepreneurship at IIM, Bangalore for 18 years and was instrumental in establishing NS Raghavan Centre for Entrepreneurial learning. He is serving as Director and consultant at many companies in India and abroad.

~

The old proverb 'Success has many fathers but failure is an orphan' sums up the entrepreneurial experience of Abhishek. Failures often cause conflict within a team and threaten the very purpose for which the members get together.

Abhishek's entrepreneurial story is about how conviction, grit and determination eventually triumph over back-breaking series of failures and the consequent conflicts within a group.

Conflict: An Inseparable Part of Business

In their entrepreneurial journey, Abhishek and Abhinav have experienced difference of opinion and conflicts with their loved ones, friends and partners, but these disagreements did not affect their personal relationships.

It is important to see conflict as an engine of creativity and innovation rather than shying away from it or suppressing it. Some of the most creative ideas come out of people in conflict remaining in conversation rather than flying into their own corners or staking out entrenched positions. So one needs to appreciate and accommodate different perspectives and viewpoints.

Mistakes are OK

In his entrepreneurial journey Abhishek committed some very foolish mistakes. He was on cloud nine when he received his first cheque for Rs 14 lacs, only to realise that he had been dumb enough not to have opened a bank account! It took him months to track his partners and get the account opened. This was his first lesson in business.

His next lesson was from the hasty reversal of recruitment of a high flying IITian as his CEO, who turned out to be too big for his shoes. But his mistakes were never too big to stop him. He learnt from his mistakes and kept moving ahead.

Execution the Key

When Abhishek and Abhinav started EKO, their B2C pioneering idea for providing low cost mobile banking, the Indian banking was unable to grasp this idea, let alone appreciate it. This was accentuated by the fact that the idea came from two software engineers without any banking or finance background. When everything looked doomed only their conviction and energetic perseverance took them ahead.

Persistance

It is not about how many times one falls down but it is about how much time one takes to stand up again. We fail when we say 'quits', not till then. So, never say 'quits' to anything you consider important in your life to achieve.

The entrepreneurial story of Abhishek and Abhinav is an example of this philosophy so vividly portrayed by their undaunting spirit of conviction, passion and focus. The brothers show how ordinary mortals can achieve the impossible dreams — provided they dream and then pursue it relentlessly.

3

COLOSCEUM MEDIA

AJIT ANDHARE

AJIT WALKED THROUGH THE TILED corridor with steps that could not be mistaken of a man on a mission. He maneuvered his way towards the glass door on the far end, which proved much difficult than he had expected. The unopened cartons and unwrapped furniture were strewn all around the room.

See the cartons, a wave of nostalgia swept over him, remembering the mess he and Kamal had made while working on their science project. He revisited his childhood. He now realized that he was destined to be an entrepreneur.

~

'*Is baar* science exhibition *mai kya kamaal dikhaane wale ho?* (What amazing thing will you show in the science exhibition this time?)' enquired Mr. Gupta, a research scientist in CSIR (Council of Scientific and Industrial Research). At the CSIR residential compound in Pilani, Kamal and his friend Ajit had been winning the annual science exhibition for the past three years. Their candidature for the first prize seemed to be granted as no one could ideate like them. Others had no choice but to bet for the second position. The senior scientists at CSIR were awestruck by Kamal's and Ajit's out-of-the-box thinking and experiments; they both were only 15 years old.

'We are building a robot with an optical vision. We plan to have a light-dependant resistor in its "eyes" so that when it nears an object, the change in light intensity will signal the stepper motor, which in turn will change the robot's direction, preventing it from colliding with the object,' said Kamal. Inwardly, he thought, 'Why is he so interested in this child stuff?'

'Brilliant! I am looking forward to the exhibition, just to see your model. The life-size model of an "unmanned railway crossing" that you made last year was really impressive. From where do you get such ideas?'

'Uncle, news of fatalities at railway crossings made us think about automatic crossing gates which would make crossings safer, plus the design was simple. We hope it will save some lives,' Kamal said in one breath, but Mr. Gupta was taking his own time.

'Great, I am proud of you guys,' Mr. Gupta complimented.

'Uncle, can I go now? Ajit is waiting for me.'

'Oh yes, your *jodidar* (partner) in scientific discoveries? You two make a dashing duo. Andhare *sahib ka ladka bhi bada smart hai.* (Mr. Andhare's son is also very smart.) Carry on and good luck for your experiments,' said Mr. Gupta before leaving Kamal to his business.

Ajit's father was a respected research scientist at CSIR. The group comprising of Kamal, Ajit and few others were known as the 'Golden Batch' of CSIR, Pilani. They focused on innovation and gadget-making without any mentoring from the scientific fraternity in the campus.

The experiment room was two blocks away from the campus. While running to reach their experiment room, Kamal slowed down as he saw Ajit coming from the opposite direction. Both reached their spot simultaneously. They then opened the door of the room and clapped together. The light turned on along with some music playing. Two years ago when they were in Class IX Ajit and Kamal made clap switch. It was a sound-based electronic circuit which sensed the clap and triggered a relay, which was connected to the power supply.

The shelves in the room were filled with all sorts of books: electronics, Leonardo da Vinci, Einstein and Faraday. It was really an unusual room considering their ages; they were only 15 years old. Kamal turned to the desert cooler as he was sweating.

'From where do we arrange the stepper motor that we need for the robot project,' rued Kamal, scratching the top of his head.

'No problem!' exclaimed Ajit. 'I have found the company which can provide us the stepper motor for the robot, but its cost is Rs. 1,200.' He was excited about the motor but anxious about its cost.

'What Rs. 1,200! *Kya baat kar raha hai?* (What are you saying?) Is it that expensive?' Kamal was shocked. It almost equaled his school fees for an entire academic session, in 1984-85.

'I have the catalogue and other details. It perfectly fits our experiment, but it is expensive.' Ajit handed the catalogue to Kamal.

'So what should we do now?' asked Kamal, turning the pages of the catalogue. Buying a new motor was beyond their reach. Suddenly the desert cooler shrilled.

'Kamal, I guess it's running out of water, switch off the cooler or else the motor will trip,' Ajit said.

'First, let's get rid of this problem. We should find a solution and make sure that cooler will switch off automatically once the tank is empty. Then we will figure out the problem of arranging Rs. 1,200,' said Kamal.

Ajit grinned. 'You already did. We will solve this problem and sell the circuits to others in the campus.'

'Wow, Ajit the businessman. That's really great!' Kamal exclaimed.

Thus, Ajit and Kamal started work on their ancillary project. After three days of hard work, the duo was able to create a circuit which, if connected to the motor, would stop the cooler automatically once the water emptied in the tank. This also saved motor from tripping or burning. They named their first ever commercial innovation as Sigma — after their favorite sci-fi TV series *Space City Sigma,* which was aired every Sunday on Doordarshan in 1986.

The circuits were priced at just Rs. 99 to lure maximum customers. Within 15 days, Ajit and Kamal were able to sell enough units to earn Rs. 1,200, scoring their first entrepreneurial success unknowingly.

~

Snapping back to the present moment, Ajit smiled to himself, grateful that he had finally reached his room, and then slowly pushed open the glass door. The room before him was occupied by the lone grand mahogany desk. The nameplate on the desk proudly read 'Ajit Andhare — CEO'.

Ajit was about to set up his own company in the very office he was standing in. He had also decided the name for his new company. Ajit remembered his last day at Hindustan Lever Limited (HLL). He was about to put down his resignation papers, when his friend Kedar dropped in.

Kedar was working with Lowe Lintas, an advertising agency.

'Hey, Kedar, you came in at the right time. I just got the confirmation that the term sheet for funding has been signed by Raghav Bahl. I will put down my papers tomorrow,' Ajit said.

'That's great! Congratulations!' Kedar was happy for Ajit.

'Thanks. I hope I have taken a right decision.'

'Now don't doubt yourself. You are playing to your strengths. You are a creative person, and I am sure you will do well,' said Kedar encouragingly. 'So, what's the name of your company?'

'Well, we are still thinking. Initially, I thought of *Pitara,'* said Ajit.

'Oh, *Bhanumati ka Pitara?'* Kedar added, but he did not quite approve of the name.

'Yeah, I mean it is about entertainment. When we switch on the box, there is entertainment for everyone. But somehow no one gives a go-ahead on it,' Ajit lamented.

'Thankfully, there is some creative sense left in people. C'mon, Ajit, it just doesn't sound like a name of a professional media company,' Kedar strongly put across his view.

'Everyone gives their opinion, but no one gives any options. Suggest something related to entertainment.' Ajit wanted to finalize the name of the company as soon as he could.

'OK, think of places where people go for entertainment. Maybe we will be able to,' Kedar said, trying to figure out some relevant name.

'Theater, park, circus, *nautanki,* what else?' asked Ajit.

'No, some other places. Let's go back to ancient time, medieval age or Roman era.'

'How about Colosseum? Colosseum was the largest amphitheater built by the Romans where gladiators displayed their prowess. It was the most glorious stage in the world. In those times, reality shows took place in a Colosseum, where people got the freedom to perform.' Ajit was excited, suddenly realizing how good the name was.

'Colosseum sounds grand. Perfect!' Kedar gave his consent.

'Yes...Hey, no. We cannot have this name.' Suddenly Ajit looked morose.

'What happened? What is wrong with it?' asked Kedar, perplexed.

'The spelling has "loss" in it, Co(loss)eum. I can't start my company with a word which has "loss" in it,' said Ajit, looking at the writing pad where he had written the word.

'So what? *Vaise bhi* media *mai* successful *hone ka ek* funda *naam change karna bhi hai.* (In the media industry, it is a trend to change spellings in order to be successful.) Some people believe that inserting or removing a few letters bring luck and prosperity to their business. You do it at the very start and ensure your success. Everyone will think it's appropriate according to numerology,' Kedar smiled mischievously.

'I didn't think of this angle. Then, it is Colosceum,' said Ajit enthusiastically.

~

In the beginning of 2008, Colosceum started its operations from a business center run by Stylus Office Services located in Logitech Park in Sakinaka, Mumbai. It was hard to believe that such posh office spaces were available in Sakinaka.

Colosceum was aiming to bag *Wheel Smart Shrimati* as its first project.

Ajit was talking to Rajeev. 'Tell me, do you think we will be able to get *Smart Shrimati* project?' asked Rajeev. They had been pitching to create content for Unilever. *Smart Shrimati* had already completed its third season on Doordarshan. Now the contract with its current production house was up for a review.

'Why do you think we will get it? Is it because I have worked for Unilever?'

'Well, yeah, of course. You know people there, so...' Rajeev paused.

'Oh, in that case, we should get that dating reality show for MTV since you know people there.' Ajit smirked, putting the ball in Rajeev's court.

'What I meant was since you have conceptualized *Smart Shrimati* and was instrumental in creating intellectual property (IP) for the program, you must have known the ins and outs of how it will work.'

'We will get this contract only on our own merits. We can't get any undue favours from Unilever. It is known for its fair, transparent and professional assessment, but we may have the upper hand if we can own *Smart Shrimati* as our property for the next three to five years,' said Ajit, determined to guide the team to its first victory.

For Ajit, *Smart Shrimati* was important for two reasons: First, if he led the team to their first ever contract, he would be able to instill confidence in his leadership. Second, it would be relatively easier for them to crack an advertiser-funded programming (AFP) than getting broadcaster-commissioned programming.

Rajeev nodded. 'Hmm, what do you think of competition?'

'Well, every big player in the industry will be there: Endemol, Miditech, Show M and so on and so forth. All of them will be competing to get this show. We will handle them. Don't worry,' said Ajit. He was confident that he had just the right idea to win. It is the execution they needed to focus on. 'What about the MTV's brief?'

'They want another program which can be aired for multiple seasons. Currently, they have *Roadies,* an adventure reality show, in their bouquet. The brief is to come up with a concept-based dating reality show like Flavor of Love, an American dating reality show, transformed to suit the Indian audience, environment and mindset.' Rajeev knew what worked best, and this was his forte. In Colosceum, every individual always had some proposals on the table.

'Hmm, let us crack that one. It is already three in the morning,' said Ajit, looking at his watch. 'Let me make a move. I have to go to Kriti's school for the annual function.' Ajit had promised his daughter that he would attend the annual function.

'Yes, please go. Otherwise who will save you from the reality show that happens at each one's home every day.' Rajeev winked.

~

Ajit had a long association with *Wheel Smart Shrimati* even before Colosceum's inception. He had worked on it while working in Hindustan Lever as brand manager for Wheel. It was the very thing that gave Ajit the idea to enter into entertainment business. He remembered about the meeting at Hindustan Lever the board conceptualization and presentation of *Wheel Smart Shrimati* by him.

The meeting room was packed in Hindustan Lever's head office in Vashi, Mumbai. The agenda was to discuss the impact of last quarter's advertising spends on brand measures on the country's largest detergent brand, Wheel.

The two representatives from Indian Market Research Bureau (IMRB), began by explaining their research methodology. When they showed PowerPoint presentation with the competitive comparison graph, the calm and quiet mood of the board members turned skeptical.

'Yet again, after three quarters, your research says that Ghadi's brand recall continues to be significantly ahead of Wheel. Our absolute spends are nearly twice as them as reflected in higher share of voice. However, our mind measures are not moving up. If you compare the advertising gross rating points (GRPs) of both brands, we should perhaps conclude that we can safely stop advertising and save precious money,' the marketing manager said.

'Are you sure there are no data pickup issues as pointed out last time, especially from the smaller centers? What's the frequency of data collection? How reliable is this process?' the media agency representative questioned the researchers.

'What is the sample size of the households? Is this representation enough for the kind of population in Lucknow, where you have conducted the research?' queried other team members.

This time the IMRB team was at the receiving end; they were hardly painting a happy picture.

Ajit, having newly joined the brand team, whispered, to the product manager, 'Aren't we shooting the poor messengers? They are simply telling what is what from the stats available, but we expect them to answer why it isn't what we want!'

The marketing manager turned around to the whispers and said, 'Ajit, do you have anything to comment? Why don't we all hear it?'

Ajit began, 'Well, if we were to take the data on face value, it seems to suggest that our advertising effectiveness isn't very high, and we need to rethink our decision on communication instead of maintaining these levels of ad spends. Possibly, it's not cutting through the clutter, given that detergent is a low-involvement category. Perhaps we need to engage with the consumer in a novel way.'

'I think you have a point, Ajit. The last time we had celebrity who cut through was in the Govinda era. We need to look for ways to truly engage with consumers. Of course, we should use a celebrity to cut through and promote our product,' said the marketing manager.

This marked the beginning of a series of activities: consumer home visits, brainstorming sessions to find a way to communicate the brand Wheel in a more engaging way, etc. The brand activation team spent many hours visiting smaller towns and meeting low-income group housewives — the target consumers for brand Wheel.

'Our target segment — the low-income women — does the most thankless job, rarely gets appreciated for what she does and reprimanded for what she doesn't. The most honest way to reach out to her is to appreciate her and make her feel valued,' Ajit explained while briefing the creative team. 'She has very limited resources, but she has infinite resourcefulness, and that is why our activation platform will showcase her resourcefulness. If we can project her as a smart homemaker, then we will not only connect with her but also capture the positioning of Wheel as the smart shopper's brand.'

'Well, we have Wheel Active as our new variant coming up for a re-launch. If we can organize Mrs. Active contests, based on her household knowledge, this might provide an opportunity for our brand to engage with her,' a team member suggested.

'Great idea! Not just a quiz contest, but a bigger competition, in the likes of a poor man's beauty pageant that can equal a Miss India title for an average housewife,' voiced another member of the team.

'But we need a title that connects with the common housewife. Mrs. Active is great, but something that has a wider appeal would be catchier. Besides, Active is a variant. We should think of a name that can be associated with Wheel, our core brand,' said Ajit, encouraging everyone to propose names.

After half an hour of discussion, everyone seemed to agree on one name: *The Smart Homemaker,* and thus was born the moniker *Wheel Smart Shrimati.*

'We also need a ritual to felicitate her, like the winner of Miss India contest being decorated by a sash and a tiara. Why not use *tulabharam,* a ritual in south India, as a metaphor, or what the politicians do, weighing themselves in currency or gold, with a slogan *"Wheel Smart Shrimati ko sone main tol denge",'* said Ajit as he turned towards the marketing manager for his approval. 'And the icing on the cake is it will be done by their husbands to appreciate their spouses, in line with our activation platform.'

'What! *Sone mein tol denge!'* The marketing manager was flabbergasted.

'I mean we will give the gold equivalent to the grams of their weight. For example, if their weight is 85 kg, we will give them 85 grams of gold.' Ajit did his best to keep the conversation sane.

The pilot events of the program were carried out in the small towns of western UP. And soon the *Wheel Smart Shrimati* events became the talk of the town with print partners flashing front-page pictures of women being weighed in gold by their husbands. The activities were so engaging and rewards so exciting that everyone wanted to be a part of the program.

'See, one point is very clear: it is working, and as per the dipstick study, the mind measures are moving up,' said Ajit to the marketing manager describing the success of *Smart Homemaker* contest in UP.

'That's great, Ajit! Now your next challenge is to find a way to scale this up. We cannot do the on-ground activities for the entire country,' said the marketing manager, wondering how to make the event a household name.

'We need to think of something that can be a televised event to ensure a higher reach among our target audience,' Ajit replied.

'And what would that be?' asked the marketing manager, wanting to know the next move of Ajit.

Within a few months, the entire Wheel team was set for the review of their latest experiment on television. Everyone was seated around the table. Ajit began presenting the recent success story of *Wheel Smart Sunbai,* a weekly program broadcasted on DD Sahyadri, a Marathi channel with strong reach in Maharashtra.

'Having learnt from below the line (BTL) events in Uttar Pradesh, we launched *Wheel Smart Sunbai.* After being on air for two months, the television rating points (TRPs) of the program have moved up, and dipstick study suggests positive changes in the perception of brand Wheel,' said Ajit.

'This is indeed working, and the proof of principle is there. How do we take this to national television?' asked the category head, equally enthusiastic about the prospects.

'Yes, that would be the next challenge, as we cannot broadcast the program at national level with this format, which is native to Maharashtra. To air at national scale, it has to have a mass appeal, entertaining yet delivering the core brand message of *Smart*

Homemaker.' Everybody nodded in agreement. 'We will revert with a plan in few weeks,' Ajit acknowledged.

~

As promised, the presentation, in a few weeks, started on an interesting note with Ajit drawing a checkered board headlined by the word *chausar.*

'Do you remember *Mahabharata?*' Ajit asked the brand head. Everybody looked at one another, trying to decipher how it was relevant to the current issue. Suddenly, he turned the future of Wheel to the past. No one could guess what was in store.

'What is the relation between *Mahabharata* and Wheel?' All the brains in the conference room were busy solving the puzzle.

Ajit smiled on seeing the inquisitive faces all around. 'Well, in a male-dominated society, what if wives play *chausar* and put their husbands at stake? What if we reverse this metaphor of *Mahabharata?*' Ajit paused, trying to gauge each one's expressions. Some smiled, while others were still confused.

'The point is if we reverse this metaphor and put a woman at the center of the game, we give her a chance to showcase her resourcefulness to save her husband. That will be the USP (unique selling proposition) of this game show. *Wheel Smart Shrimati* will be a light entertainment focused on housewives and yet deliver the precise brand message on prime time. The winner will be felicitated with the title "India's *Wheel Smart Shrimati*".'

It was decided that *Wheel Smart Shrimati* would be telecast on Doordarshan and would be hosted by Annu Kapoor, the anchor of *Antakshari,* the most popular musical show on Zee TV.

For Ajit, it was an unparalleled experience of working closely with both television industry and content development companies through various stages of production, from conceptualization, to promotion, to brand marketing this program. The entire journey of imagineering and bringing to life *Wheel Smart Shrimati* gave a creative high, and his innovative mind raced ahead with new concepts that could be tried on Indian television platform.

~

After *Smart Shrimati,* Colosceum was running full steam ahead. The new projects kept Ajit busy in the office. *Meera,* a historical fiction drama series based on the life of Meera Bai, was aired on NDTV Imagine. He was working on a bunch of other TV programs also. Meanwhile, Ajit had a meeting with Mr. Kapoor, the programming head of Channel 2. The meeting was scheduled at 2 PM. A punctual and disciplined professional, Ajit reached their office at 1.55 PM only to be told that Mr. Kapoor was not in the office. He called Mr. Kapoor and reminded him that they were supposed to meet at 2 PM.

'Oh yes, Ajit, I am sorry. I am running late by 40 minutes. Please wait in the office. I will come and join you in some time,' said Mr. Kapoor and hung up the phone.

'Not again! Somebody please teach them the value of time,' muttered Ajit under his breath. Waiting long hours at every broadcaster's doorsteps had become a routine for him, and every minute of wait reminded him of his days of comfort at Unilever. Coming from a disciplined background, the chaos and indiscipline rampant in the media industry infuriated Ajit. He picked up *Outlook* and started turning the pages before the cover story caught his eye.

'How to Sack Your Boss' read the cover-page title. Ajit smiled at the paradox. The word entrepreneur translates for many as dynamism, action and the power to control. On the contrary, a large part of being an entrepreneur is about patience. The article which was about being your own boss — that is, an entrepreneur, was ironic. 'Actually, I was a far more influential boss in Unilever. Those were the days when at one call the whole system was ready to roll, and now, to even move a stick, I need to move heaven and earth.' Ajit was engrossed in his thoughts when an office boy came and asked, 'Sir, *chai lenge ya coffee?*'

'No thanks,' Ajit politely refused and returned to thinking about the days that had gone by.

'One day you will be sitting at broadcaster's office's receptions and drinking sorry coffees and trying to convince people. You will be convincing people at their free will and wish. That would be terrible. This is not a job for a person of your stature. At your level, you should be the head of a channel. Don't do this. You don't know what you are getting into.' Ajit could not but think about the prophetic words of Rishita Bhatia.

Ajit had worked with Rishita while developing the concept for *Smart Shrimati.* She had cautioned Ajit, and she was right in so many ways. In a large corporate house, life was filtered, only people with certain stature could meet the bigwigs and senior management. But being an entrepreneur, one has to sell the ideas and concepts to any prospective customer be it a small company or a large corporate house. Some of the people might not be qualified, and one may not hold them in high esteem, but still one needs to please them as they hold the trump cards now.

'Hey, Ajit, sorry to keep you waiting,' said Mr. Kapoor, finally reaching the office after an hour's delay. 'So tell me, how can I help you?'

'Sir, I wanted to enquire about *Kaalchakra?'* Ajit had been chasing Mr. Kapoor for the past six months. Colosceum had developed a concept for the show based on spiritual Indian concept of rebirth and named it *Kaalchakra*. They developed the program in the form of a debate, with rationalists, sitting in the audience, questioning the anchor about the authenticity of the whole idea of rebirth. They wanted to do it with a channel that had more credibility. They did not want their program to be presented in a sensationalized manner.

When they presented a few episodes of the program to the team of Channel 2, everybody was excited and gave their approval. Subsequently, the negotiation hit an impasse due to IP ownership deal. In the Indian television industry, the broadcasters pressed upon owning the IP rights, while internationally, it was the side that developed the concept who owned the IP rights, and rightfully so. Since the concept was developed and shot by Colosceum Media, they wanted to own the IP rights for the program.

'See, Ajit, we are discussing the same story again. I guess we have made it pretty clear that we want to own the IP, and frankly, I don't understand why you are insisting on it. You give us the IP and let the program go on air. We will make sure that Colosceum gets the commission of the program every year promptly,' said Mr. Kapoor, offering a consolation prize.

'You want us to be at your mercy. If you own the IP, every year we will be begging to get the program which we have developed,' Ajit thought. Maintaining his calm, he requested, 'Sir, we have developed the whole concept and shot the pilot episodes as well. It is our property, and we will make sure that we broadcast this program through your channel. Don't you think that is the right approach?' Ajit came back with a counter-offer, but to no avail.

'Well, right approach! You guys work like corporates,' Mr. Kapoor smiled sarcastically.

'Sir, I hope it only means that we are more disciplined and professional in our approach,' Ajit said.

'Well, yes, but maybe the word cooperate will work better... You guys think about our offer, and we will also discuss it in our meeting next week,' Mr. Kapoor gave him a fake assurance.

'Following these guys is a real task! Now, I think it is better that I jump on the corporate bandwagon than to cooperate with these guys,' Ajit thought looking out of the window. Rajeev called Ajit.

'What happened in the meeting with Mr. Kapoor? What did he say?' asked Rajeev.

'Same old IP battle! They said they will revert by next week,' said Ajit.

'Ajit, there is no use of pushing the issue. We will lose everything — our concept, time and energy. By now, don't you know how these channels work? Why are you hell bent on convincing Mr. Kapoor?' Rajeev said in desperation.

'Why should we not want to own the IP rights? After all, we have put our heart and soul into it? How can we give it away?' retorted Ajit.

'Fine, as you say, but you will regret later.' Rajeev had no choice but to conclude the conversation.

'Maybe he is right, but then we all agree to disagree,' thought Ajit. With a conscious effort, he had created an open organization where employees need not give in to conformity. Instead, they had mutual respect for each other and valued each other's opinion.

Unlike the culture of a typical media house, where the boss is kept on a high throne, Ajit did not let the hierarchy weigh down upon creative thinking.

'We are not an army trying to show unified command. We are a bunch of people who have their own views, and we all must have the ability to listen to each other,' he believed.

~

'I agree, Mr. Adhikari. I am also a big supporter of research before taking the plunge, but some decisions have to be taken based on gut feeling. Everybody can see the potential of this concept,' Ajit vociferously attested to make his case for a biopic on Phoolan Devi, the infamous dacoit. Her life was full of bizarre events, and that is what made it perfect for a television soap viewing. In fact, they had signed the letter of intent with the channel to make the program, but things got stuck.

'It seems like not everyone is able to see the potential,' said Mr. Adhikari. Ajit could feel the sarcasm in his reply.

'Sir, we have the signed copy of letter of intent, which means everybody did approve it. Now when we are running short of time and have already started the groundwork, you are asking us to wait,' said Ajit, a little apprehensive, that this concept did not share the same fate as *Kaalchakra:* some other channel carried out a similar program on the lines of past life regression, and Colosceum felt the pinch.

'I know that, but we also have our limitations. We cannot give you the green signal unless our research team confirms it. You will have to wait. We will let you know.' Mr. Adhikari shrugged his shoulder.

Ajit had no option but to leave. He felt powerless. It was symptomatic of what is the power he commanded in value chain. It had almost become a routine where his ideas were either rejected or lingered on in the hands of broadcasters.

'Office *chalo.'* He gave instruction to his driver. Sitting in his Fortuner and making his way through the narrow lanes of Mumbai, he felt as if his fortune had been squeezed between broadcasters and their budgets.

He received a call from Lalit just when he was entering his office. 'How was your meeting? Anything happening on the biopic front?'

'Not very fruitful. I think they will delay,' Ajit gave the usual reply.

'Maybe not. I heard from the grapevine that some other production house has picked up the similar theme and has already started shooting,' Lalit broke the bad news.

'Oh no! Another lost project! That's what I feared. Are you sure?' Ajit wanted to reconfirm.

'Almost. They have named it *Phulwa*. Once again, we lost time and, more importantly, the concept.'

'What choice do we have? Have we done anything wrong?' asked Ajit. It was hard to swallow that they had to drop another good idea. After all, they had the letter of intent from the channel and had been pursuing the concept for a couple of months.

Time tests the toughest of people. It was definitely a testing time for Ajit. The company had hit a rough patch. Ajit's leadership skills and decision-making abilities were being pushed to the limit.

'The TRPs of *Meera* are not up to the mark. The broadcaster is threatening to pull it from the schedule,' said Ajit. Usually, the weekly meeting started in gala spirits with some jokes, but this time Ajit's message and serious tone made everyone sit up in attention.

'How can they cancel airing a scheduled program? They don't have a clue how much money we will lose! We have done the costing and budgeting on the basis of 260 episodes. *Meera* has completed only 60 episodes till now. It is a historical show. We have made huge investments in the sets and costumes. How will we recover that cost?' Jayesh, the CFO of Colosceum, was taken aback by the news.

'I know we all are going through some tough times right now. Well, if a movie flops, do the lead actors pay back the money?' asked Ajit. Everyone in the room knew that power equation in the industry was such that the channel would not bear the cost for the sets and costumes. As agreed before, the channel would pay for all the broadcasted episodes.

'Yes, but at least actors don't give a minimum guarantee. An actor does not say that the film will do 100 crores, but channels give us that minimum guarantee, which in this case was 260 episodes,' said Jayesh. It was the first time that the finance team of Colosceum Media was going to face such huge losses.

'Yes, but everybody works with the assumption that the program will work well. If it doesn't, then somebody has to bear the losses. The TRPs of our show are not good, and that's the truth,' said Ajit, knowing very well that the impact of losses on their yearly balance sheet would be significant.

'TRPs are not the optimum benchmark. *Roadies* and *Splitsvilla* didn't have very high TRPs, but they are still considered successful. We can talk to the channel and put forth this point,' said Rajeev, still hoping against hope, even though he was aware that the media industry was like a ruthless jungle, where stronger animals prevail over the weaker ones. Producers had to follow the directives if they wanted to remain in business.

'Well, I agree that TRPs are just one indicator out of many in the entire gamut, and it may not be the optimum benchmark, but it is still a benchmark. It is the rule of the game, and we also need to adhere to the rules,' said Ajit, knowing that there was nothing they could do if the channel had decided to cancel the show.

~

'How come you are home so early?' Deepali, Ajit's wife, was surprised. It was just 10 pm!

Enervated and depressed, Ajit crashed on the sofa without answering.

‘What happened?’ she asked sensing by Ajit’s body language that something was wrong.

Ajit was too upset to say anything. With a frown, he opened an email on his BlackBerry and handed her the mobile. Deepali read the mail by Mr. Freeman — ex-CFO of a European company which had showed interest in buying out Colosceum Media.

‘It was so close. Even he knew it,’ Ajit said meekly. It was a mail with apologies for nonconclusion of the deal.

‘It’s OK. Everything will be fine. You will get another chance; it’s not the end of the world,’ she tried to console Ajit. She was aware that negotiations did not materialize with a European company for a stake buyout. His management was interested in Indian media space and hence was looking for Indian company for strategic investment.

‘I know it is not the end of the world. But I was so close to the glory that every entrepreneur dreams of.’ Ajit looked at his phone and read the same mail again. The management, including CFO, who was involved in negotiation, changed their stands just before finalizing the deal.

‘Everything was set, the term sheet to buy Colosceum was signed, but a new management came in with new thinking. They kept their focus on Europe, and in just a few months, India lost its potential for them.’

‘But you have not lost yours. You are talking as if you have gone bankrupt. Every businessman goes through ups and downs. Even fairy tale has a sad part.’

‘I agree, but when you see yourself taking the last step towards your dream, and suddenly you slip, it hits you hard, even more when you are not at fault. It is sheer twist of luck. I am the same man, Colosceum is the same company, but we are off their radar.’

‘Everything happens for the good, Ajit. Maybe, you are meant for something bigger and better.’ Deepali smiled with optimism.

‘Yeah, maybe.’ He smiled and looked at his watch. ‘Oh, I have to work on a concept note to give a presentation tomorrow. We will name the program *Luck by Chance,’* he said.

She smiled at sudden change of tempo. 'At times, setbacks could slacken the pace, but could not stop, Ajit. The show had to go on,' she thought.

Deepali knew about Ajit's never-say-die attitude. She was a big support for him when he decided to quit HLL (now Unilever) and start his own company. She remembered the day when Ajit had come home after a meeting with Mr. Raghav Bahl.

~

'I have an appointment with Mr. Raghav Bahl,' said Ajit to the receptionist in the Noida head office of Network18. Ajit was posted in Unilever's Bangkok office. He had come to India for this meeting.

'Mr. Bahl is in a meeting right now. He should be here any moment. Kindly wait,' said the receptionist.

Ajit sat on the sofa, anxious about the outcome of the meeting. He was looking for an endorsement and funding for a potential business idea that had been bubbling in his mind for the past few months. A friend had fixed his meeting with Mr. Bahl, co-founder and CEO of the Network18 group. Ajit had spoken to Mr. Bahl a couple of times before and shared the novel ideas he had in space of television programming.

'Sir, Mr. Ajit is waiting for you,' the receptionist told Raghav as he entered the office.

'Hi, Ajit, how are you doing?' Raghav shook hands with Ajit and said, 'Sorry for the delay. Come, let's get to my cabin.'

After a small talk, Raghav came to the point. 'Tell me one thing, for the past 12 years you have been working with HLL, a fast-moving consumer goods (FMCG) company. How did you become interested in developing content for television?' Raghav wanted to understand the motivation behind such a move.

'While working with HLL, I got an opportunity to conceptualize and develop IP for *Wheel Smart Shrimati*. I worked closely on all aspects of the show, and realized that being in media gives wings to creativity. That was the time of transition when I was really drawn to this industry. HLL is like a sophisticated jetliner, and I learned the controls of that complex machinery just by being in it. Now, I want to be the solo flyer on a hang glider.' Ajit paused for Raghav's response.

'That's very true. Being a solo flyer on a hang glider is interesting and fun, but it should be based on strong logical business thinking; otherwise, it may get lost in the stormy winds.' Raghav, a successful entrepreneur, shared his insight with Ajit.

'That brings me to my next and more important question. I don't see any correlation between FMCG and media. Then what makes you think that you will be successful in this field?'

'Actually, it all comes down to how one approaches it. From my viewpoint, I do not see any disconnect between FMCG and media. I have spent 12 years of my life thinking what will appeal to housewives, what makes them happy, what makes them sad, what are their dreams, what are their expectations, what emotions they go through, etc.

'I strongly feel that the core of both industries is same. The only difference is that while we are connecting with them through our products, you are connecting with them through your programs. In a way, it is soaps there and soaps here.' Ajit and Raghav shared a smile.

'Oh, I see. So, what is your plan?' asked Raghav.

'While working on *Wheel Smart Shrimati,* I did a lot of research on production houses based in India and abroad. I was surprised to find that there were just a handful of production houses. Also, a majority of them were either personality-driven businesses or one-man shows. Another limitation was that most of these companies were largely into fiction programs,' said Ajit.

'That's true. Production houses are fragmented and work like boutique shops rather than professionally run organizations. The trend now is skewed towards fiction,' added Raghav, an authority on Indian television.

'I see a dearth of content on reality, mythology and history. In fact, the very formats of programming, like we have in the Western market, are scarce here. There the companies are far more organized. I am really inspired by the way they operate — from idea development to production. They follow stringent processes of evolution of an idea. So I want to build an organization which will not be a one-man show. The domain experts will head their verticals and produce a variety of content,' Ajit said.

'How do you see yourself getting into this market at this stage of your career?' Raghav looked inquisitively at him.

'Well, it is a matter of perspective. You can see the glass half-full or half-empty. I see my glass as half-full, as all the industry reports — KPMG, FICCI or any other agency reports — suggest that the media market in India will grow in double digits for the next few years. Clearly, there will be demands from production houses to create programming of various genres for various TV channels,' Ajit put across his case persuasively. 'The number of channels has increased drastically. Overall, the market is not mature yet in terms of the content. I strongly believe it's the right time to enter the market.'

'Oh, I see. But the space is dominated by fiction-based programming. How do you intend to be different?' asked Raghav, who himself had been musing over launching a channel in GEC (general entertainment category).

'I agree that fiction is the dominant trend, but the trend is changing. Reality programs are making their mark. Shows such as *The Laughter Challenge, Voice of India* and *Sa Re Ga Ma Pa* are gaining popularity, and their success stands testimony to the changing trend. Internationally, reality programs are increasingly exploring newer domains such as cooking, parenting, matrimony, relationships and so on. Eventually, at some point, it will hit the Indian shores as well. Every big format, whether it is a talent hunt in dance, or cooking or celebrity-based shows such as *Big Brother,* are grabbing eyeballs in India as in anywhere else in the world,' said Ajit passionately. 'In general, there will be greater acceptance to new and bold creative approaches, and broadcasters will try new genres of programming. That's where I see the entry point.'

'Oh, I agree, the Indian audience wants to see a whole lot of new ideas. There is also the *Saas-Bahu* genre. Production houses and channels will have to try new genres and adopt international programming formats,' Raghav agreed.

'If we are able to create an operationally sound company, then we can bring in partners from overseas. They will have rights of international formats. Finally, if the market is worth Rs. 2,000 crores and growing, I am looking at a mere 5 percent market share in three years. I have already given the copy of the three-year plan to you,' concluded Ajit with flair.

'Principally I agree, but my only apprehension is you are just a beginner in this industry.' Raghav nodded.

'That's true. However, experienced hands can always be hired, and that's precisely what I will do. I plan to put together a team of people with expertise and sensibilities to produce a variety of content,' Ajit said confidently.

Raghav smiled and gave Ajit a thumbs-up.

~

'Thank you, Raghav!' Ajit's excitement was soaring high as he kept the phone down.

'Deepali, guess what! Network18 will fund our company! Raghav has signed the term sheet,' exclaimed Ajit. Deepali had always been by his side through thick and thin. She knew Ajit's ambitions and had always encouraged him.

'Yahoooo! Both of us gonna deliver our babies together!' exclaimed Deepali. Deepali was due with their second child...they had both been keeping their fingers crossed for this news. Finally, it became real!

'Yes,' said Ajit, and suddenly, Deepali felt the strain in his voice.

'What happened? Why are you so anxious?' She expected Ajit to be ecstatic.

'No, it is just that now I have to put down my papers at Unilever and make a move,' said Ajit, a little quieter than usual.

'This is what you have always wanted to do? Why are you sad now?'

'Till now, it was an effort of chasing a dream. Now that it is a reality, my next step will change everything for our family. Here in Bangkok, we are leading a very comfortable life. I have a great career, and our children will be going to international schools. We have this large house and all the comforts under the sun. When we move to India, life won't be the same for either of us.' Ajit was worried.

'I am sure things will fall in place sooner than you expect,' Deepali said calmly. She brushed aside his fear. 'If this is what you want to pursue, then why do you have second thoughts? Let's just do it. Honestly, apart from leaving a global career, you are not taking any other major risks. You have already got funding, and there is an ecosystem to assist you. Isn't it similar to new age explorers who have all the gadgets, GPS, phones, etc., to guide them?'

'What you do without doubting your dreams or vision, a woman can give the confidence and support you need to succeed.' Deepali's reaction overwhelmed him. It was Deepali who had to make maximum sacrifices, and yet she made it seem so effortless. She shared the vision he had for himself, and she was a sounding board for his ideas and actions. After moving to India, they were to live out of boxes for a good six months in guest houses with a two-month-old baby!

~

Ajit believed in start-from-scratch approach. He was selected from HLL for an MBA program at Indian School of Business (ISB), Hyderabad. At ISB Ajit learnt all the nitty-gritties and technicalities needed for the trade.

'This is one of the most prestigious "business plan" competitions in the country. Our team needs to present an idea which is really innovative and which addresses a need gap or an existing inefficiency in the system,' said Rahul.

Ajit, Rahul and Vinay were sitting around a round table at ISB campus in Hyderabad.

'I think we should focus on organized retail. After all, the industry is booming, and every booming industry has a scope to be taken to a next level,' said Ajit. After operating an animal feed business at HLL for two years, he wanted to do MBA. He applied to various colleges in the USA, but before the results could come, he was chosen as one among the four candidates who were sponsored by HLL to join the founding batch of ISB for their MBA program.

'Exactly. Organized retailers in India have horrible service standards. Yesterday, I went to a mall in Banjara Hills. It took me two hours to pick two dresses, and an hour more in trial rooms to try it. It was so frustrating. I felt like returning back immediately. An enjoyable experience turned into a disappointing one because of their poor customer service and inefficiency,' complained Deepali.

'My point is that this is a universal problem, not unique to India.'

'Can we ideate a solution for it?'

'Yes. Maybe we can make a virtual trial room, where the customer can feed the data about his or her sizes and retailer can upload the images of their products like shirts, trousers, suits, etc., on their webpage. The customer can drag the shirt he likes and check for the fit and look,' Ajit suggested.

'Sounds interesting, and very similar to Yahoo Avatar, where you can style it as per your liking and options,' said Vinay, excited about the prospects.

'Yeah, but here it is a more customized version where the picture will be of real person, and exactly as per the size, to understand the fits and style of actual look without even trying the clothes,' explained Rahul.

'We can even add light features, such as how the outfit will look in disco lights or in daylight so the customer can choose as per the occasion,' Vinay offered an add-on.

'Great, we will call the product Try-On. Now if everyone is convinced, let's start making the business plan,' concluded Ajit.

Eventually, their group presented Try-On in various business plan competitions and was adjudged the winners for original thinking. The ISB exposure helped Ajit to add a new dimension to his thinking, and he started writing business plans, which was his best head-clearing exercise.

Every time he sat to work on the business plans it excited him to think. 'How would it be to start something from scratch?'

~

'My friend, the show will be on air in 30 minutes from now. Can anyone tell me when is the master reaching?' the programming head of Channel 2 was now panicking. *Bandhan,* the new television daily soap produced by Colosceum, was going to be aired today.

'Let me check the issue,' said Ajit, the CEO of Colosceum Media, as a drop of sweat trickled down his face. With exasperation, he looked at his watch. Although last-minute crisis was hardly uncommon in television world, it was Ajit's very first crisis, and today, it was cutting just too fine. 'Rajeev, has the master reached? Mr. Swamy is calling me personally. We will be on air in next 20 minutes!'

'The delivery boy left half an hour back. He will be there any moment,' Rajeev assured Ajit.

'Mr. Swamy, don't worry. The master CD will be there in five minutes. We will not miss the slot,' Ajit assured the programming head.

'That better be the case,' said the programming head before the line went dead.

Breathing heavily, Ajit sank in his chair. He checked the 'received call' list in his mobile phone. In the last 15 minutes, he had received ten calls. His discomfort heightened when he saw the television promo running 'Next program — *Bandhan*'. Suddenly, he remembered that Rajeev was still on hold on his second phone.

He picked up the phone and asked, 'Rajeev, what caused this delay? When did we finish mastering?'

'In the morning,' Rajeev replied.

'Then?' Ajit enquired.

'They wanted to incorporate a list of last-minute changes, including adding some re-shoots.'

'Changes again, after the master was ready? Didn't the channel approve the final edit yesterday night?'

'Sania was here this morning, assisting the editor and keeping us from delivering the master. I suggested that this be delivered while we can work on another version as it will cut very fine, but she would have none of it. That's why the mess. I didn't tell you as I thought there was no point doing so when we are already in the battle.'

'So how are we to keep delivery deadlines if final approvals keep happening even post-mastering? And here is the programming head who is fully aware of what his team is doing but still questioning me on the delivery delay!' said Ajit, exasperated.

'Besides, we all were on the reshoot sets till 4 am, and our key editor Rahul fainted,' explained Rajeev.

'What?' Ajit was worried.

'Nothing serious, he was overworked. He had been on his feet for the past three days. He couldn't get a wink of sleep,' Rajeev explained.

'Isn't this true for all of us? This master better reach on time, the clock is ticking, only ten minutes left for the show to start,' Ajit said anxiously.

This was not happening for the first time. TV industry was replete with unsustainable pressures and clients driving deadlines while keeping on the boil through last-minute changes.

'Ajit, it is 6.50 pm. *Bandhan* is going on air in ten minutes. But where is the master?' the programming head was now livid with rage. There was desperation in the air.

Ajit could sense his pulse racing and his heartbeat triggering. 'Gosh, what a chaos it is! You are like a candle burning on both ends,' he thought. His mind travelled back to his Hindustan Lever days where he was expected to be fair to suppliers, agencies and business partners. 'We never put this kind of pressures on our agency, did we?' Ajit was thinking while his eyes were moving frantically between television screen, clock and mobile phone.

At last, the title sequence of *Bandhan* started playing, and Rajeev was audibly relieved on the phone. 'We were lucky. Master reached just in the nick of time.'

'Yes, I can see that on TV,' said Ajit while texting a message to the programming head.

'Now that everything is sorted, I am going to take a quick lunch and come back. Tomorrow, we have this presentation to a channel for our new show.' Rajeev was exhausted.

'Lunch at seven! You need not be crazy to work here...but being one definitely helps.' Ajit chuckled.

~

By 10 pm, Teesta, the hall in Hotel JW Marriott, was jam-packed with employees of Colosceum. After nights of drilling, finally it was time to celebrate.

Team Colosceum was celebrating the success of *MasterChef*, their cookery reality show. *MasterChef*, the highest rated show from their stable, was an international format cookery show. Colosceum had acquired full rights to broadcast it on Indian television. Akshay Kumar, the *Khiladi* of Bollywood, was anchoring the show. The team had burned the midnight oil to make the show a grand success. Creating and managing the reality show was a grueling task, and finally, their efforts were paying off.

'So, guys, let us have a party tonight,' shouted Ajit.

'Yay!' Everyone shouted and clapped.

'Hang on, guys; do you think you don't have to work to be in the party? I know there are people here who, despite my continuous reminders, haven't fulfilled all of their goals. So there will be no drinks for them today,' Ajit said with straight face.

Everyone turned quiet, wondering why Ajit had suddenly become so serious.

'Kamlesh, I told you to shed a few kilos, but all I see is few more kilos of flesh around your belly. You promised that we will run the Mumbai Marathon next month. You did not fulfill your promise. Now you just watch us drinking.' He winked at Kamlesh, the assistant art director.

'Come on, that's a ridiculous goal!' Kamlesh started laughing.

'I have heard that line before. Is it the dialogue that our team has patented? I guess I need to develop an IP for this as well. Do you guys remember, two years back, when I set up the goal of Rs. 100-crore turnover within three years, all of you said the same thing — this sounds ridiculous! Isn't it, Rajeev?' Ajit aimed his salvo at Rajeev.

'I agree I said that, but I am glad that we were able to achieve most of our goals and targets,' Rajeev, the idea machine of Colosceum, acknowledged the truth.

'I still remember the bewildered look on his face when I set the target to Rs. 100-crore in three years. Not just him, all of you were looking at me as if I had asked you to fight with Mike Tyson. Even then, I believed in the motto "given a greater challenge, one will develop the powers necessary to overcome them".'

'In that case, I don't want to develop powers to beat Mike Tyson.' Rajeev laughed, and everybody followed suit.

'Ajit, come here, let's cut the cake and open the champagne,' Lalit shouted. Everyone could sense the sheer excitement in his voice.

'Before that, I would like to address the team.' Ajit moved to the table which had the cake and the bottle of champagne.

'Manzilein unki hoti hai jinke sapno mein jaan hoti hai. Pankhon se kuch hota nahi, kyunki honslon se udaan hoti hai. (Targets are for those who dare to dream. Nothing can be achieved by merely having wings, one needs ambition to fly high.)'

'First of all, a big cheers for all of us! And a big cheers for Colosceum!' exclaimed everyone and applauded.

'All of you must be thinking that we are here to celebrate the success of *MasterChef,* our highest rated show till now, but that's not the only reason I am here. I am here to acknowledge something bigger than that,' Ajit continued. 'In 2007, when we started this company, it was not the best time. In 2008, due to the meltdown and recession, advertisers cut their advertisement expenditure and broadcasters slashed their budgets. We faced lots of issues. We did not have enough cash, and some of us went home with empty hands for months, and in addition, some of our good pitches bombed, but instead of giving up, we came up with innovative solutions. We partnered with other production houses, which, otherwise, would have been our competitors, so we expanded the pie for everyone. We convinced others that instead of being small, loose, fragment outposts of mom-and-pop shops, we should make something like the Federal Republic of India and not the small provinces. We were successful to certain extent, and hence we collaborated with Sagar Pictures for *Jai Shri Krishna*.

'Then *Splitsvilla* went on air. That was the first time our logo came on screen — we all rejoiced. With *Splitsvilla,* we explored the dating reality genre for the first time on Indian television. Since then, we have created our niche in reality shows, and now we are moving to other genres as well. As national broadcasters are moving to the regional market, we adopted the strategy to go regional. We are opening offices in various regions in India. Right now our reach is in four states, and that is sure to go up in times to come.'

Ajit continued, 'We have taken each show as a challenge and worked hard through our approach, challenges, competition and problems that we might face. We are very much aware and clear about our plans with our feet on ground. All this was possible because of you, every member of the Colosceum team. So, today I am here to celebrate the colossal spirit of Colosceum team. And I would want all of you to believe that we are just one idea away from greatness.' He moved to cut the cake. Others opened the cork of the champagne.

Kamlesh shouted, 'Three cheers for Colosceum! Hip, hip, hurray!' And the hurrays echoed across the hall!

COLOSCEUM MEDIA
KEY LESSONS
AJIT ANDHARE

Ajit Andhare is founder of Colosceum Media and currently the COO of Viacom 18 Motion Pictures.

~

Prior to taking the road to entrepreneurship my most professional decisions were governed by my career goals. However when I made the choice to take an uncharted path, that decision was governed not by a career goal but by a larger life goal.

Career wise I should have continued where I was doing very well. However deep down the desire to pursue something on my own made me take-off the career-lens and put-on life-lens instead. This helped me make a tough choice. Sometimes career-lens can be a bit limiting while a life-lens can be empowering; it lends clarity to what you are in totality beyond your CV.

Who am I?

I like to think about people who become entrepreneurs in two broad groups, one what I call the specialist and the other the generalist entrepreneur. The former is perhaps someone for whom the road to entrepreneurship is an outcome of what he or she loves doing. While a generalist entrepreneur is someone for whom entrepreneurship is the key motivation and thus he is usually domain agnostic.

I turned an entrepreneur for my liking of the creative domain. To build a creative enterprise was more important to me than building an enterprise. There is no harm in being either. Just that assessment provides a lot of clarity to who you are, what you wish to do and what really matters in the end.

It's a Marriage. Are you Ready?

What you are about to do might look exciting but honeymoon comes to an end sooner rather than later. Your startup soon becomes your life and consumes you 24x7. There isn't another thing to do. You need to be certain that you are ready for it; it takes a long time, seemingly forever, and to go without perks that might have been with you otherwise.

Plan and Trenches

I am a big believer in planning and worked on a detailed business planning before starting, but found out that reality in trenches was somewhat different from what I had imagined.

So you need instinct and course correction from that original plan. It's a bit like rock climbing. At start you see a broad path which will take you up, but once you start climbing, for every next move you will need to look around for the next rock that gives you a good hold to go further up.

Play out Sessions

As an entrepreneur, life at times can be tough and there may not be a solution in sight. This is something one is not used to as a manager. As an entrepreneur, you need to continue driving straight through till new possibilities and solutions emerge. This is not easy to internalize. You have to play sessions out like test cricket and take stock only at key milestones else you will quit at time when you should have persisted.

Where is the Value

One needs to be honest about where the value lies in the enterprise, in yourself, in your founding team, in an algorithm or in a technology or relationships or at the best in a unique combination of all of this. You cannot survive for long if value lies a place from where it can easily migrate.

The biggest challenge one faces is the DNA of the new enterprise — the founding team. I got this right and had my entire founding team intact even after 5 years of Colosceum. This has to be a must-win for a successful venture. Think very carefully about your founding team and whether it would survive when the waves get higher than the ship and have the ability to sail troubled waters.

The ease of Starting vs. Scalability Question

By design, ventures with low entry barriers are easy to start and tempting. However the ones that really go far are the ones that can answer the scalability question. Rewards are proportional to the size of the problem you solve. Never be tempted by the easier option of starting on the easy problem. You might succeed but the rewards may not be of the scale you wanted to achieve.

I started a content development studio. I was successful and scaled it up to nearly 60-crore within a few years. But how scalable beyond that a content business in 5 year period can be? Can it be global. How about a channel instead? What's the orbit you are aiming for? Your escape velocity needs to be proportional to that. Even if you start something to get the hands dirty, be clear that that's not really where you are aiming to be. Most successful entrepreneurs are able to move from the ante-chamber into the living room and eventually to the bedroom.

Not Everyone Succeeds. What's Your Safety Net?

If you are starting early — say in the mid twenties — I won't worry about this. But if you are starting late then you need to have a fall back plan. It could be as simple as your spouse will support the family. This is not to dampen the spirits but the success rate of new ventures is statistically low and you need to be prepared for a rainy day. Every venture that starts doesn't succeed. You just get to read about the ones that do! It's important to have an exit strategy in place. It only gives you strength to jump with belief.

Obsessed about customers not competitors

redBus.in, India's largest online bus ticket and hotel booking company. It offers around 80,000+ routes in India with over 1,500+ bus operators and reportedly has 70% of the market share in online bus ticketing.

In July 2015 redBus crossed the four-crore (40 million) number of tickets sold. It has over 2 million registered users and is rapidly approaching the $300 million GMV (gross merchandize value) mark.

redBus was acquired by the Ibibo Group, a joint venture of South Africa's Naspers and China's Tencent in June 2013 for $138 million (INR 800 crore).

The company is now looking to expand into hotel and taxi bookings.

Like all start-ups, redBus too has a very interesting story to tell. Read on...

4

REDBUS

PHANINDRA SAMA
CHARAN PADMARAJU
SUDHAKAR PASUPUNURI

CENTURIES AGO, AN APPLE fell from a tree and Newton wondered WHY and created the theory of gravitation. Similarly, few years back, a young guy couldn't get a bus ticket and wondered WHY and created a multi crore company.

~

The morning had started at lightning speed. Maneuvering his way through the small lanes of Bangalore, he felt like a Formula One driver. Never before had the traffic of Bangalore got on his nerves like this...but today he was getting unusually impatient, especially when he reached the Domlur flyover, where traffic was at a standstill. To get some respite from the honking of horns and helplessness of the situation, he turned on the instrumental *Buddha Bar* to calm his mind. He had to be focused for the board meeting at the corporate office of redBus. As he finally left the maddening traffic behind, he was all alert and active. Soon, he had parked his car at his designated space and locked the car to the familiar *beep-beep* sound.

Everyone in the sales and marketing team was charged up. There was an air of exasperation. A competitor from Hyderabad had sparked off total mayhem in the office. The fellow's newfound passion for marketing had brought him to Bangalore and spend huge sums of money on outdoor advertising and on the Internet. There was another offer floating on the Internet using the redBus offer code, directing customers to some other website.

'This is unethical; those buggers are trespassing in our territory,' Rohit, the head of marketing ranted. Rohit was one of the oldest employee of the company and had seen it grow from a half-baked idea to a well-known brand. A competitor, who had cropped up overnight, playing against the rules of the market made Rohit see red.

The entire sales team was fuming with rage at such unscrupulous tactics and was ready to take the competition head-on. And why not? They were the market leaders. Determined not to let others reap the benefit of what they had sown, they were already visualizing the whole city dotted with redBus billboards and hoardings. All that their power-packed marketing proposal required was the approval of their CEO.

Phanindra a.k.a. Phani was the CEO of redBus. His innocent, simple and next-door-guy look was a good façade for his calm, contemplative and intellectual personality. A bright smile played on his face as he browsed through the proposal. Just a poke from the competitor had revealed the commitment of his team!

Thinking of the competition, he wondered if there was any reason to get into a panic mode. To him, it was a completely wrong strategy.

After contemplating for some time, Phani finally addressed his team. 'I understand your concerns, but we should tread carefully. Now let us think logically.' He paused, looked at everyone and continued, 'If our competitor would have invested in a city untapped by us, he would have definitely scored on market share. But here in Bangalore, where redBus already has a very strong brand loyalty, it will not be easy. Even if he burns his money, the conversion rate would be very low. Clearly, the competition is not playing to its strength; his strong marketing skill will not bear enough fruits. We shouldn't lose our peace. Our focus should be on making our service offerings more robust.'

Phani sensed the need to alleviate the anger of his team. To handle the situation, he decided to take an assertive stand. 'I am overwhelmed to see your commitment, and I respect all your efforts, but we will not react, and certainly not in this way. The ideal way to compete is by serving the customer in the best possible way. We are here to solve the problems of our stakeholders. Kindly put all your energies in that direction. That's the way, I believe, we should answer.'

~

Phani, an engineer from BITS Pilani, was working with Texas Instrument in Bangalore. Happy and content with his job, he wanted to make a mark in the microchip industry, until the Diwali of 2005 changed it all.

At 5.30 PM, Phani rushed from his office and contacted travel operators all over the city to book a bus ticket to his hometown, but it turned out to be no less than a scene from a Bollywood movie — where the hero runs after the train the heroine has just boarded, frantically searching for his lady love in every compartment, and when unable to find her, sits on the platform, disappointed, disgruntled and devastated. Melodramatic as it may sound, that was the situation Phani found himself in when he was unable to get a bus ticket to Hyderabad. He was looking forward to celebrate Diwali in Hyderabad with his friends and family.

For about four hours, he contacted one travel operator after another but in vain.

Disappointed, he returned to his room. His frustration had a companion in the form of loneliness. His Diwali plans having been crashed, he could not stop himself from crying about the whole transportation system in the city, especially the bus services. But soon his crying turned into thoughtful curiosity. He wondered, 'What if one bus operator had a ticket and the other didn't? Maybe an enquiry with a few more agents would have brought me luck.'

Suddenly his 'Mr. Know It All' alter ego caught hold of him. He recalled his childhood days, when he had learnt to devote all his energies in one subject and master it rather than focusing on all subjects. This belief has been his guiding force since then. And this time his baits were 'Why couldn't he get the ticket? What if some bus had left for Hyderabad with a vacant seat? How on earth would he ever know?'

~

These questions clung to him like a leech. Next morning, he decided to visit Mr. Manohar Reddy, a local travel agent. Phani was a loyal customer of Mr. Reddy, an oldie in the market, sat in a 10x10' dungeon-like office. He had been in the business for 20 years and was always willing to talk. He could rant and rave about anything under the sun; was friendly and good-humored. With Diwali over, and having packed his customers to various destinations, he had ample time for people who had been left behind, like Phani. Mr. Reddy was in a relaxed mood and was as willing to talk as ever. Phani greeted him with a handshake and an ear-to-ear smile.

He was generous in reciprocating with sweets and tea. He enquired, 'How come you are gracing our office on the occasion of Diwali? Sorry, but there is no bus to Hyderabad now. How can we help you?'

'You have already helped me enough, *Anna.* I enquired with all the travel agents and bus operators you had referred, but I couldn't find a single ticket,' Phani sighed.

'So tell me, what should I do? During the festive season, there is a huge rush. Next time, inform me well in advance, and I will try my best,' Reddy empathized. But Phani wanted information.

'Why is it that when you don't have tickets the others you refer may have a few?' asked Phani, curiosity writ large on his face.

Mr. Reddy jumped at the chance to flaunt his knowledge, and that too to an engineer! He stretched himself, cleared his throat and, with a serious look, said, 'Basically, there are three parties involved: the bus operator, the travel agent and the customer. The bus operator allocates a fixed number of tickets to each agent, and once an agent sells his quota, he won't get any more tickets to sell. Because of this, someone who hasn't yet sold his quota may still have some tickets.'

‘Hmm...so that means there can still be a vacant seat in the bus if an agent has not sold the quota allotted to him?’

‘You are kind of right. Once I sell my quota, I ask the bus operator for extra allocation. The operator then cross-checks with the other agents for the seats allotted to them. If an agent still has seats, the operator calls me and tells me about the availability. Another option is to enquire directly with other agents.’

‘Seems like a long process. How much time does this take?’

‘Normally, it takes eight to ten calls to get one seat,’ said Mr. Reddy.

‘Oh! So when you don’t know which agent might have a ticket, how would a customer know? Is that the reason why you don’t sell return tickets, like flights or train, as you need to connect with the agents in that city and you probably don’t know them? Is that the reason why you don’t call them up?’

‘Even if I know them, what’s the use in making STD calls? My STD calls’ costs will be more than my earning on the tickets.’ The give and take of information ended there. Phani thanked Mr. Reddy for answering his questions patiently and started musing over the information he had gathered.

The engineer in him was already visualizing how a computer system could easily solve this never-ending problem. An idea flashed in his mind: to develop a software application wherein all bus operators would register the required seats which the travel agents would access and book on first-come-first-serve basis. Then the bus operators and travel agents would know the real-time status of seat availability of buses on the same route and would be able to communicate to the customers, thus making the process more transparent. Other issues such as departure locations and pickup points, bus type, return trips, seat preference, etc., could be addressed as well. According to Phani, seat preference was a major issue. It reminded him of his experience when he had booked seat 4, hoping that he would be occupying a seat in the front row; instead, the operator had started numbering the seat from the back. He had felt cheated: the last row was very uncomfortable. Like in a train or an airplane, why a traveller couldn’t choose a seat for himself or herself, he thought.

Questions galore haunted him. He wanted answers, but he wasn't getting any. He needed more information; he needed to talk to more people from the industry.

Lying on his bed, overcome with loneliness, he spent the evening wishing friends and family over the phone. But the conversation he had earlier in the day with Reddy echoed in his head.

Could a software actually be designed to bring every stakeholder under one roof? Will it work in the majorly unorganized market? He decided to meet a few travel agents and take their feedback.

Morning came with hope. Phani picked up the newspaper, but he didn't read it; he neatly folded and placed it on the table. He then went into the kitchen to make tea. While it was boiling, he was so lost in his thoughts that the tea spilled over. As he was cleaning the spilled tea, he felt more and more confident that his software could make the bus ticketing industry clean and free from the complexities of an unmanaged structure. Soon, Phani left home, feeling quite optimistic about his meetings with various bus operators and travel agents.

Seated across the table was a grumpy man who seemed hard to convince. He had been working this way since ages and had grown into his style of operating the business, but Phani knew better. Like a deft salesman, Phani confidently said, 'You just need to buy the software once and it will ease your work and make managing your bookings very organized. Your area of business will also increase.' After a convincing sales pitch, a few operators were willing to try the software. Not only were they willing to try the new software — in spite of not being competent in using computers — they were also willing to pay for it. Their positive feedback encouraged Phani to create a software which would serve the bus industry and consumers like him.

Returning home as he unlocked the door, he realized, that he had, in fact, found a key to open his locked ideas. After that, it was like burning the midnight oil...Phani locked himself in his room for countless hours to prepare the project note that explained the purpose, research findings, kind of software that needed to be build and the possible solutions that could be implemented on a nonprofit basis. He mailed the concept to six of his friends.

~

'Let's do it.' Sudhakar was the first one to reply. Sudhakar, popularly known as Su among friends, was Phani's wing mate in BITS Pilani. Both were state-rank holders in their higher secondary examinations and had bachelor's degree in electronics.

Phani's email set the tone for an intense brainstorming session over endless tea sessions. Weekend laziness was replaced by great camaraderie among friends who had come to set out on an interesting journey. Bustling with a feel of reunion at Phani's place, some sat on chairs, musing over the grave issue, while others formed a circle. While Phani took center stage, another was busy preparing tea. With hot *samosas* and *pakodas* laid out on the table, Phani started the discussion.

'Isn't it too off track? We don't even know the 'W' of web technology, how will we create such a software? Moreover, the bus industry is full of illiterates, how will we make them use our software which is in English?' Charan raised the issue while taking the plates inside the kitchen. Usually, during such get-togethers, no one would get up to keep the plates back in the kitchen, and inevitably the job fell on Charan, who was the most caring among the friends. Behind the unshaved face and messy attire lay a creative genius and a brilliant troubleshooter. This out-of-the-box thinker was the Rancho[1] of BITS Pilani.

Anecdotes recounting Charan's innovative thinking were narrated at BITS Pilani even after he had left the institute. Pilani, a small town in Rajasthan, saw freezing winters, and every time, it was painful to leave the warmth of the blanket when someone knocked the door. In order to find a solution for this situation, Charan tied wires that extended till the bed to the latch of the door. With the help of the wires, he could easily pull the latch and open the door from the comfort of his blanket. *Necessity is indeed the mother of invention.*

'The whole world is getting into outsourcing, bro, and we are in Bangalore, where every third company is an IT company. We can get the software made at a reasonable price. Why to waste energy

---

1 A character from *3 Idiots.*

in pursuing something that a software expert can do?' commented Sudhakar, in his usual style by wiping his wet hands while patting Charan on the back. Charan was too lost in his thought to notice; his mind was wandering somewhere else, figuring how they could learn the web technology.

Phani was listening to everyone patiently. He interrupted Sudhakar and said, 'Wait, guys! What are you saying? I think our biggest contribution in this project is technology; how can we outsource it? This is the core; we should learn it thoroughly and understand its complexities. It will help in visualizing the difficulties that we may encounter in the future.'

All of a sudden, Charan's thought bubbles exploded with a solution. 'We can learn it through "Hello World". Since it is a software development program for dummies, it will help us in learning the basics of web technology.'

Wearing the boots of the devil's advocate, Sudhakar questioned, 'OK, assuming that we learn it from scratch and even develop the software, what's the guarantee that the bus operators will buy it? I want to buy the IPL team till anyone asks me for money! Phani, I am telling you, *abhi jeb se paisa nahi jaa raha isiiye sab haan bol rahe hai* (no one has to shell out money from their pockets right now, that's why they have agreed). How can you trust bus operators?'

This time, it was Phani's turn to get into the boots of the rabble-rouser. 'To be, or not to be, that is the question,' Phani quoted Shakespeare. Everyone stared at him, wondering at his new passion for Shakespeare and bus operators. He continued, 'There will always be problems, but worrying about the unknown has not taken anyone anywhere. Our strategy should be to keep the goal in mind and address one issue at a time. Our first problem is to understand the Web. So our immediate priority is to learn the software.'

~

'Where is Charan?' Charan's boss Priya asked aloud. 'It has been three days since he has reported to work. No one in the office has any information about him,' she yelled.

Phani could sense anger in her voice. The entire week had gone by and Charan's behaviour was getting more unusual with every passing day. The 'Hello World' software had kidnapped their friend. His sleep, hunger and daily life had gone for a toss. He was so caught up in learning the software that he did not bathe for days. Phani decided it was time to rescue his friend.

As Phani was climbing the stairs, he heard the familiar voice of their landlord. He was talking to Charan. Phani overheard his name, so he stopped at the stairs and listened to their conversation. 'Charan, *aap log aaj kal kya kar rahe hai? Tum office bhi nahi ja raha hai? Pehle aap itna seedhe the, jab se Phani aaya hai aap logo ko bigad raha hai. Aapka naukri chala jayega. Aap Phani ke chakker mein mat pado.* (What are you up to? You are such a simple guy. Phani is spoiling you. Do not listen to him or else you will lose your job.)'

Charan didn't utter a word. 'I wonder why Charan is not defending me, but knowing him, maybe it is a strategy to calm down the other person?' Phani contemplated. He decided to climb up the stairs. The landlord saw Phani and gave him a look as if he was staying in the house without paying rent for the last three years!

The journey had just begun, and it wasn't going to be easy.

~

This was the fourth and final meeting for the day. After three unsuccessful meetings with bus operators, Charan was desperate for some luck. For Charan, things got off to an unpromising start as he sat in a corner of a small dingy shop and waited for the operator to attend to him. The operator was busy answering the unending phone calls. Half an hour had passed and the operator hadn't even looked at him.

The life of a bus operator was total chaos: people streamed in and out of the shop all day. Small shops were always buzzing with activity, and there was never a moment of silence. Amid all this, Charan had to make himself heard, but he was already exhausted. Though *exhaustion* was not usually a word in his dictionary, the thought of no light at the end of the tunnel was making him lose the zeal he had started off with.

He couldn't quit though; for five months, he and his friends had dedicated their evenings, weekends and holidays to create groundbreaking software for bus operators. He could envisage sleepless nights spent coding and testing in his mind's eye. Quitting wasn't an option for him.

However, coding is one thing and selling it is another. Charan and his friends were good engineers but, probably, not good salesmen. They had been trying to sell the software for the past two months, but to no avail. Those very agents who had initially seemed quite receptive to the idea of the software were now turning a deaf ear.

Charan's last hope lay on the operator who he had to meet today. After numerous rebukes and refusals, he did not have enough strength to face yet another rejection. He waited for two long hours; finally the bus operator had some respite from his customers and calls, and he apologetically said, '*Haan bhaiya bolo.* (Tell me, brother.)'

However, the moment he heard about the software, he was infuriated and said, '*Kitni baar mana karu, pehle bhi tumhare dost aake gaye. Kahan rakhu software, sir pe. Dikhta nahi saans lene ki fursat nahi, software kaha se lenge. Aur computer kaun dilayega.* (How many times do I have to tell you that I don't require the software? Your friends have visited me before. Can't you see how busy I am with my customers? Anyways, how will I purchase the computer? And where will I keep it?)'

Without uttering a word, Charan, took an auto and returned home. He had dedicated his life to this project at the cost of his job. He had been ignited with the passion of creating the software, but, after a streak of disappointments, realized why his other friends lost interest. When they had started, they were seven members, but now they were only three — Charan, Phani and Sudhakar.

~

When Charan reached home, Sudhakar had just finished his lunch. The moment he saw Charan, a big mischievous smile played on his face, and as usual, he wiped his hands on Charan's shirt. Charan didn't even protest.

The reason for Sudhakar's smile was manifold. As Charan settled comfortably in the chair and stretched his legs, Su showed him the advertisement of the Entrepreneurship Acceleration Program (EAP) conducted by The Indus Entrepreneurs (TiE) — a project that gave winners a chance to be mentored by industry experts. The advertisement proved to be the blessing that they have been praying for!

The two friends settled down, eagerly awaiting Phani's return to further discuss the idea with him.

After experiencing his rejections from the bus operators, Phani returned in the evening. On seeing Charan and Sudhakar smiling, his heartbeat increased. 'I think Charan has sold the software today. Wow!'

'What happened? How come you both looking so happy? Did you manage to convince someone, Charan?' Phani asked curiously.

'No, I made four calls today, and none of them even offered me a glass of water, forget about sales. One of them even yelled at me.'

'What?' Phani was puzzled to see the smiles on his friends' faces.

Sudhakar placed the paper displaying the TiE advertisement in front of Phani. It immediately brought a smile on Phani's face. 'Maybe this was the missing link. Mentors. Yes, this was it!' Phani thought.

~

Suddenly, he heard the sound of the school bell ringing for the next class. 'An atom is the defining structure of an element which cannot be broken by any chemical means. A typical atom consists of a nucleus of protons and neutrons with electrons circling this nucleus.' The seventh standard chemistry teacher was explaining the concept of atom. Most of the students were staring at the teacher blankly. While some were yawning and looking out of the window in search of something more interesting, others were passing chits to each other making fun of the teacher, only a few were trying to concentrate on the teacher's explanations, wondering how they could believe in such an erratic concept when their imagination was driving them crazy.

'Why is it that I am unable to imagine an atom?' thought Phani and decided to quench his curiosity by asking his chemistry teacher. Mustering up courage, Phani approached the teacher. 'Sir, when I cannot see an atom, how do I believe in its existence?' he asked.

The teacher smiled, happy that at least one student wanted to know, and answered, 'Do you see air? No. Yet you know it exists because you can feel it. Do you say there is no air just because you cannot imagine it? No. Same is the case with an atom.' Satisfied with the teacher's answer, Phani learnt a very important lesson that day: Trust in your teacher completely and you will be able to perform much better.

Little was he aware that it was a lesson that would be the strongest pillar of his future success.

~

Lost in his own world, Phani felt a hand shaking his shoulders. 'Hello, *kahan kho gaya?* (Hello, where are you lost?)' Sudhakar asked.

'Nothing. I was just thinking that if we can get mentors, we can learn a lot from their experiences. We need to do well in this presentation.'

It was September 2006. Phanindra, Sudhakar and Charan were all set for the big day. They were presenting the business plan to TiE under their EAP. A winning impression today could ensure that their project be guided by experienced mentors.

They reached the venue ahead of time. The place was buzzing; about 50 nervous participants were having last-minute discussions with their teammates before going to the stage for final presentation. After all, only three participants would be awarded mentorship.

Nervous, Phani wiped the droplets of sweat from his forehead as he practiced the opening lines in his head: 'We want to make booking bus tickets for intra-city travel easier and more transparent.'

The emcee called them to the stage. A panel of judges was seated in the front row.

'We can't afford to lose this chance,' Phani thought and could read the same thought in the eyes of Sudhakar and Charan.

They had prepared well: a 42-slide PowerPoint presentation for the ten minutes allotted to them. They wanted to be thorough, but they knew that a 42-slide presentation was just too much. So they compressed it to mere six slides. The 42 slides had, however, helped them prepare well.

Phani started, 'We want to make booking bus tickets for intracity travel easier and more transparent.' He paused to see the reaction of the judges. One of them seemed to be nodding, but the others were alert. 'I should go on,' thought Phani. 'I know we can.'

With renewed courage, Phani went on, giving the panel members the details of the project. 'The Indian bus transport industry is a highly unorganized sector. Some 2,000 private bus operators run about 20,000 buses on long-distance point-to-point routes. In these buses, the customer has to buy the ticket in advance.

'The buses are run by bus operators who own and run close to two to ten buses each, on various routes. They lack a countrywide presence. The customers buy the tickets through various travel agents who are pre-allotted a designated number of seats to sell. Every time a ticket is sold, the bus operator is informed, making the process very messy. While the travel agent knows the number of seats he is allowed to sell, he does not know the status of availability of seats. As a result, more often than not, the buses ply with empty seats while there may be customers looking to travel on that route.'

Phani continued, 'Since these regional players do not offer e-ticketing or e-reservations, they rely heavily on a network of travel agents to handle bookings. There is no provision for booking return tickets. Usually, the fares are not listed and the customer ends up paying whatever amount the agent demands for a ticket. Also, there is no standardized system of numbering seats, thus giving little importance to a customer's seat preference because the travel agent is at the mercy of the bus operator for seat allocation. The bus operators often have cash flow problems because agents usually pay them at monthly intervals. If all the above problems do not exist for the airlines and railways, why should a passenger availing a bus service face it?'

Having made a cogent argument, Phani paused to take a deep breath, letting the judges absorb his point.

'We wish to address these problems at Pilani Soft by developing inventory management software for the bus operators,' said Phani as he concluded his presentation.

Once the result was announced, the presentation made by Phani and his team was adjudged the best among the numerous other presentations. Their three-member team then got introduced to three mentors. This marked the official beginning of a company which they had never imagined they would build one day!

~

There prevailed a childlike nervousness in the air in their flat. The trio were like school kids arranging their bags and uniforms on Sunday evening for the next day. They revisited their presentation, made notes of questions to be asked, decided on what to wear — they were gearing up for the first meeting with their mentors. The dilemma of the first day, the first impression, was bothering them. All the three of them had a restless night. A hopeful morning was at their doorstep.

On the morning of the meeting, Phani, Charan and Sudhakar suffered bouts of anxiety. It was the first time they were being exposed to such a situation. 'The mentors come with a lot of experience, and I hope they will help us translate our dreams into reality,' said Sudhakar with hope. Both his friends also prayed for the same.

The discussion started on a pleasant note. The mentors ensured that the trio was comfortable enough to have an open discussion. There was no room for any inhibition, consciousness or nervousness.

'So what's the progress so far?' enquired mentor Sanjay Anandram.

'We have already developed the software, but we are stuck with its sales. For the past two months, despite trying hard to sell, approaching each bus operator four to five times, we haven't been able to sell the software to a single operator. Before designing the software, we had spoken to about 50 bus operators. We explained the benefits of the software in detail, and they too agreed to buy it. But now they are making excuses of all sorts. They say that they have neither a computer, nor the know-how to operate the software, nor well-trained staff. We are unable to progress,' answered Phani.

'Hmmm,' pondered the mentor, and said, 'tell me one crucial thing that the bus operators really want.'

'Increase in sales is all they want. It's a numbers' game,' replied Sudhakar.

'Then, if you want them to buy what you have to offer, you have to tell them how this software will increase their money flow. Show them how it works, then your software will sell immediately like hotcakes,' said Anandram.

The three shared confused glances. 'How would we demonstrate if they are not ready to buy? Once they start using it, they will know it how beneficial it can be for them...' Sudhakar wondered.

Seeing them perplexed, the mentor enlightened them with his fundas on consumer behaviour. 'It is a chicken-and-egg situation — they will not use it if they have not seen the benefits; they will not see the benefits till the time they use it. See, the bus operators have their own way of operating their businesses. They are running their businesses like this for ages. They will not buy any incremental product — or nobody will buy a product if they have not seen someone else benefiting from it, for that matter. Have you heard the Hindi proverb *'Kharbuja kharbuje ko dekh ke rang badalta hai?'*

Phani and Sudhakar could not help smiling. What he was saying made a lot of sense. They knew that their approach was obviously wrong. They had no clue which was the right method.

After a pause, Anandram continued, 'Basically, bus operators must feel a strong need to change. Show them that by using the software they can increase their sales, and the only way to do that would be by targeting the consumers. Shift your focus by selling your software to their customers, and soon the operators will follow suit.'

By the end of the meeting, all three were baffled but hopeful. It seemed as if a beautiful destination had been shown to them, but the location was unknown. Sudhakar and Charan were wondering how to move ahead, but Phani had a confident smile on his face.

'You can't connect the dots looking forward; you can only connect them looking backwards. So you have to trust that the dots will somehow connect in the future. You have to trust in something — your gut, destiny, life, karma, or whatever.' The lines Steve Jobs had once said at Stanford University lecture.

~

Phani reminisced about the internship in Noida at STMicroelectronics and sharing a room with Srinivas Rao, a senior at office. During this time, Srinivas was working towards opening his six sigma-based consultancy firm, while Phani was observing him in doing the initial legal work, which was an invisible hand of destiny that was now working in his favour. Though he could not connect the dots then, now he was aware that he would create his own company a year later, when all those experiences came in handy.

Srinivas was very passionate about his start-up. After office, Phani used to accompany Srinivas to his start-up office, where Phani got a chance to understand the basic legal requirements for starting a new company; from him, he acquired an insight into drafting of the memorandum of association (MoA) and articles of association (AoA).

Apart from this, Srinivas walked them through the initial difficulties and cumbersome legal processes in the initial phase of setting up redBus. He gave them the set of all legal documents from the HR offer letters to MOUs, and when it came to setting up the website, he directed them to www.net4india.com. The revelation that one can own a domain name just for Rs. 800 was exhilarating.

'Yes, guys, this is our domain email ID.' Sudhakar read out the mail which had come from Phani@redbus.in. It marked the starting of www. redbus.in, the outcome of the first meeting with their mentors.

~

Some people are fooled by randomness, some are blessed, and Phani was among the latter. *Losing my Virginity* by Sir Richard Branson had just hit the stands and was topping the best-seller list. His hands were twitching to buy something, and he picked up the book. The book was so riveting that he could not put down till he had finished reading the end page. Not only the book but also the vibrancy of the colour red had a deep impact on him.

So when their brainstorming was going on to decide the name of their website, Phani emphatically said *gimme red,* so the colour red was finalised. The spellings were short and simple. They did not want to take chance with other colours, like green or yellow, since it had two Es or Ls. If someone missed a letter, another webpage would pop up. Also, their engineer's memory was decoding some advertising funda stored in their brain cells from a long time ago that said 'if you associate a colour with a brand name, it has a very high recall value'.

'Yes, this sounds perfect; we will associate our brand with red,' Charan said excitedly. 'We should also have something like the *tilak* as in the ICICI bank advertisement, that red line at the bottom of the ICICI logo. What say?'

'Wow, Redline! Like the blue line and green line buses in Delhi, we will have red line,' Phani quipped.

Fortunately or unfortunately, the Redline domain was not available, so they settled with the next best alternative: 'redBus'. Even Redbus.com was not available, so they opted for redbus.in. Though '.in' extension was not the best thing in the Internet domain circle, but they did not have much choice.

Thus the site www.redbus.in was up and running on August 18, 2006. They had two-week quota allocations from bus operators as their inventory. Not that the journey so far had been easy, but the best, as they say, was yet to come. As hardworking salesmen, they had to sacrifice the comforts of their air-conditioned offices and embrace the shelter of trees in the scorching heat to sell tickets directly to their end users.

~

Positioned at Bagmane Tech Park, home to various prominent national and international IT companies, Sudhakar stood in the sun with the leaflets of redBus, vying for every passersby's attention. He wasn't the only one distributing leaflets — there were a few other people from credit card companies. There was a culture of taking a stroll after lunch in most firms, so in the afternoons, the roads would be bustling with employees from different companies.

Standing on the other side of the road, Sudhakar was thinking of the time when he used to shun such intrusion from people selling different schemes, but now, as fate would have it, he was one among them.

There are times you get into a situation you dread, but there is no escape. The redBus trio experienced the same, especially Sudhakar, who hated addressing people as 'sir' or 'madam'. Influenced by the corporate culture, where everyone is on a first name basis, it was a struggle for him to address even younger people as 'sir'. But there was no way out. They could not afford to hire people to distribute leaflets for them.

People didn't shun them outright due to their attire and manner of speaking. On being approached with the leaflet, most of them paused to read. Often, they even asked questions about how it worked.

This strategy worked in their favour. The leaflets were attractive and the trio slowly became better at their sales pitch. Sudhakar would approach strangers very politely and say, 'I am from redBus. My friends and I have started a new company where you can book your bus tickets online.' Then he would hand the person the redBus leaflet and his visiting card carrying his designation as the 'cofounder'.

'You are the founder and you are distributing leaflets!' exclaimed most of the strangers.

This was disturbing at first, but they kept their goal ahead of them and ignored the comments. This actually worked to their advantage because, even if it was to make fun, people talked about redBus, resulting in increased page views.

When you persist, even God can't resist helping you. Once, while distributing leaflets in a bus, Charan ran into a journalist; she was fascinated by their story and wrote an article about them in her daily.

That was their first media coverage, which got them a lot of traction. Soon, other media people followed, giving their site a boost.

Distributing leaflets and selling tickets were just a beginning, a beginning of the preparation for them to be the courier boys of redBus. Once the ticket was sold through the site, it had to reach the customer in time, and one cannot rely on traditional courier or postal service, especially when a company is in the start-up phase, where a positive experience with initial customers matter a lot.

redBus offered the service of delivering the tickets at home, at office, or wherever the customer wanted, in person. The engineers, who left their jobs and were still struggling with sales, could not afford a team of delivery boys. Hence, the trio decided to deliver the tickets on their own till the time they had achieved the critical mass required to hire delivery boys.

As they reached the Inner Ring Road, Sudhakar's eyes were set on a huge steel-grey and blue building from a long distance. A volcano of memories erupted in his mind. Two months ago, the giant IBM campus in Embassy Golf Links had been his workplace, but today, he was going there as a courier boy to deliver tickets to his clients. A sting of embarrassment stirred him. 'I am not going inside. I will wait for you here,' Sudhakar told Phani, with his eyes set on the watchman, who was looking at them suspiciously — the same watchman who used to salute him two months back.

'OK, don't worry. I will go in.' Phani gave a smirk and walked to the reception, only to be faced by a barrage of questions by the security guard and the receptionist. Once satisfied with the answers, the receptionist called the concerned person.

In the course of time, Phani was getting better at dealing with customers. 'Hello, ma'am, I am from redBus. Here is your ticket, ma'am,' he said. One couldn't sulk over it for too long; enjoying it was a better option.

He was humbled by the experience, and it left an indelible mark on him. He realized that every work, big or small, deserved respect because it has a contribution to make.

Jostled out of the trail of his thoughts, he saw a ten-rupee note being handed to him. It was his first tip as a courier boy. *'Kya din aa gaye hain.'* He smiled to himself.

~

All efforts bear fruit in time. Their hard work proved them right. Bus operators realized the efficacy of their plan and joined hands with them. Things started falling in place, but as every journey has potholes, team redBus also had to bear certain jolts. And Phani was quite efficient in finding the potholes before-hand to escape unscathed!

There were no credits, nor any exams, nor anyone keeping a tab of how much they scored, and yet Phani, Charan and Sudhakar were trying really hard to understand the workings of the bus industry to bring in a positive enforcement. For them, to say that the 'bus industry is unorganized' was simply an understatement. Day-to-day affairs largely ran on verbal communication and commitments. And since the days of *'pran jaaye par vachan na jaayen* (life can be sacrificed but not promises)' are long gone, it's hard to rely on them.

Moreover, this awesome mélange was served with a topping of illiteracy and lack of industry statistics. Considering this situation, Phani was worried because there was a limitation for a registered company — any payment above Rs. 20,000 had to be transacted only by a cheque, which translated into the bus operator paying tax on the amount received through redBus bookings. Since the bus industry was unorganized and most transactions were in cash, operators easily evaded taxes, which was customary.

'Will they agree for that?' Phani asked their mentor.

'Why not? You are helping them to increase their sales, and if they make more money, they will not mind paying a part of it as taxes. Even they want to sleep in peace without guilt, so don't worry.'

~

'Guys, guess what! My brother's friend Chatur knows the biggest bus operator in Hyderabad. He will introduce us to them; he was Chatur *bhaiya's* classmate. He can really give us a lot of information,' said Phani, proud of his resourcefulness. He continued, 'I think it is a golden chance, and we should not miss it. He might like our software and buy it. It can be a turning point for us. So, Charan and I are travelling to Hyderabad the day after.'

With 380 km already travelled and with four hours still remaining to reach their destination, embracing the potholes on the roadways, Phani and Charan were confident that they were finally on their route to strike gold.

'Are you sure this visit will be fruitful?' asked Charan.

'I know Chatur *bhaiya.* He is as sharp, true to his name, and has a strong connection with his transport units. He will not go back on his word,' Phani convinced Charan, confident of his brilliant plan.

As soon as they reached Hyderabad, Phani called Chatur. 'He has asked us to wait here in his office. He is busy in some meeting, and he will reach after an hour,' Phani informed Charan.

An hour turned into two, two to four and four to six. Chatur gave lame assurances: 'I am coming. You just wait', 'I have told my friend about you. Just wait for an hour', and the like.

They waited for Chatur the whole day, but at the end, realized that he was lying. Disappointed, they returned to Bangalore, having learnt a very valuable lesson — not everyone is genuinely helpful; many people like to weave stories without actually meaning to help.

While Charan wasn't really affected, Phani was genuinely disheartened. When Sudhakar opened the door, he couldn't help pitying Phani. Sudhakar empathized for some time, beyond which he could not control his laughter. Sudhakar couldn't help teasing Phani; with a serious face, he imitated Chatur, 'Don't worry, *bhai. Main hoon na.* I know everyone here.'

Sudhakar didn't stop there. Every evening, he would remind Phani of the incident. With a wink, he would say, 'So, Phani, any new golden chances you discovered?'

Phani had learnt his lesson — the hard way, of course!

~

At times, one tends to leave the most precious asset called the brain in the closet and lock it. Phani did the same when he thought he had discovered his second golden chance.

Two o'clock in the afternoon was rush hour at the Domlur bus stand. All the buses that stopped there always seemed to be overloaded with passengers. The shops and stalls were also bustling with South Indian breakfast enthusiasts. Phani was wondering whether he would be able to recognize Mahindra, his cousin's cousin and now their first employee, who was coming from his village. He vaguely remembered seeing Mahindra at some family functions. When the bus stopped and the passengers got down, Mahindra looked around and recognized Phani straightaway and shouted his name aloud as if he had met his long-lost brother.

Attired in loose pants, which seemed more like a legacy bestowed on him by his father, and a bright and fitted shirt, with his well-combed hair neatly rested on his head between layers of oil, he resembled Amol Palekar. With him, he carried a treasure — packed in an ancient steel box were bags of *daal* and *chawal.*

Mahindra was the first employee, the first milestone in the HR strategy of employing friend's friends or cousins.

redBus had reached a stage where they needed more hands to deal with the market. But they were engineers with almost no exposure to marketing or finance. To them, both marketing and sales were alike. The next problem redBus faced was how to recruit candidates for a particular position. Sudhakar, ever the intellectual, had a solution. He said, 'We should recruit people who gel with us culturally. What can be better than family and friends? Since we are in a learning phase, let us recruit people who will learn with us.'

Sudhakar's solution was accepted. They knew their mentors would not approve of the idea, but it seemed sensible and practical.

Their new home-cum-office was a three-bedroom apartment with two rooms and a living room dedicated to office work, and the other room was home for the three partners.

During office hours, due to their workload, none of them were able to go out and attend to the basic necessities like telephone and electricity. This burden was now thankfully off their shoulders as Mahindra took on the responsibility.

Mahindra arranged their place and took care of getting a telephone and electricity connection for their new workplace — redBus finally got its first dedicated phone line.

~

The phone rang... 'Hello, is it Mr. Phanindra Sama?' asked a mature voice.

'Yes, speaking. Who's this?' Phani replied.

'Hi, I am Sundar. I have been a part of the bus industry for the past 15 years. Like you, I am also looking for an opportunity to do something innovative and take this industry to another level. Maybe we can work out something with your technical skills and my exhaustive industry experience. Can we meet to discuss?'

It was decided that they would meet at Café Coffee Day at Forum Mall.

Phani was waiting for Sundar. When he saw a person in his mid-30s apparently searching for someone in the crowd, Phani waved his hand to draw attention.

'Hi, I am Sundar.'

'Hi, hope you are doing well. So what brought you here?'

'Well, I've been working in the bus industry for the past 15 years. I know it inside out. This is an unorganized sector. Every day, there is chaos. As there is no clear ticket allocation system, no one knows who would be having how many tickets. So when I heard that you are creating some software to address the issue, I was really glad. I can be a bridge between you and the bus operators. I know the industry and you know the technology, so we can think of doing something together.'

Phani was glad and thought that finally things were moving in the right direction. 'Since we are making a mark in the market, experienced people in the industry are now approaching us.'

Phani was now wandering in a dreamland...visualizing bus operators standing in line at redBus's office to buy the software, while operators on all phone lines of redBus attending sales enquiries. 'Wow, what if this brings such a turnaround!' thought Phani.

The meeting with Sundar lasted for seven hours. With the commitment that they would get in touch after 15 days, they parted ways. 'I am going to my hometown in Tamil Nadu. Please don't call me because I will not be able to pick calls on roaming. I will come back and call you after 15 days,' Sundar informed.

Phani returned home with a twinkle in his eyes, looking forward to meet Sundar after a fortnight. He told Charan and Sudhakar about his eventful day. Everyone was excited!

~

After many hectic days of struggling to sell tickets, approaching bus operators, facing rejections and getting accepted, they were all set for an eventful night out — it was for a meeting with SRS Bus Service, one of the biggest bus operators of Bangalore, who offered an entire gamut of bus and cab services to offices and call centers. The owner was available only after 1 AM, and the meeting was scheduled for 2 AM.

The alarm rang at around 1 AM, and soon they were up. After all, they didn't want to be late for the appointment.

They reached the SRS office at around 1.45 AM. There was a long queue of people waiting to meet the owner. After some time, he came out to stretch himself and casually asked Charan, 'Where are you from?'

'From redBus,' Charan replied.

'Oh, redBus, come...come.' The trio was happy to see that redBus was finally getting recognition.

As they stepped into his office, he offered them a chair and, pointing towards a person sitting on the other chair, said, 'Meet your competitor.'

Phani and Charan shared a nervous glance. Phani could not believe his eyes. Sundar, whom Phani had met at the coffee shop and divulged all the details of redBus, was sitting across the table!

Phani froze as he saw him. Sundar got up and left the room.

Phani was absolutely taken aback and was drowned in guilt over his over-enthusiasm to discuss the plans of redBus in such detail without the consent of its co-founders. Since redBus was a collective effort of all three of them, he didn't have any right to spoil things.

He wasn't able to concentrate on the discussion. Charan took over and discussed various aspects of inventory allocation. The meeting was successful. Charan was glad, but he kept on looking at Phani, who seemed perturbed. 'Why are you so lost? SRS has shown interest in allocating us inventory. We should be happy.'

'That guy whom SRS introduced us to was Sundar,' Phani said in a low voice.

Charan was shocked. 'What?'

As they returned home, Charan consoled Phani. They had learnt a valuable lesson — there were all kinds of people in the world, and at times, over-enthusiasm had to be curbed. This incident added the word *ati sundar* to their vocabulary as a reminder of Phani's mistake.

~

Phani was in *Dev D* mood: a room dimly lit by a ten-watt bulb, and a cerebral look on his face. It astonished Charan and Sudhakar.

'*Kya baat hai, break up ho gaya kya,* from yet-to-be-found girlfriend? (What happened? Did you break off with yet-to-be-found girlfriend?)' asked Sudhakar.

'Shut up, Su, my head is going to burst with the thought of getting broke. It's not working guys.' Charan and Su gave him a suspicious look.

'I am in no mood for jokes. A lot is going on in my mind. I am clueless about our future. In the last three months, our collective earning is paltry Rs. 7,500. We have not crossed Rs. 2,500 per month mark. If we continue at this rate, how many years will we take to recover our salaries? See, we need more and more people to buy tickets online. For that to happen, we need to create awareness. We have already exhausted our savings. From where will we get financial assistance? None of us have our jobs now. I know we have really worked hard on this. We have created the software too, but bus operators are not buying. There are not many people who are booking tickets through our website. Maybe we are fighting a lost battle. Maybe the Internet is still not as big or people are not comfortable buying bus tickets on the Net. We have given our best shot, but if it is not working, it is just not working.' Phani poured out his feelings in one go.

'But, Phani, our mentors are guiding us, and it has only been three months,' said Charan.

'Yeah, right, it's only a punch right now. Should we wait to get our bones broken and then go to hospital?' Phani retorted. 'Look, guys, I know it was my idea. I pulled you in it. I accept my mistake, but we can't get emotional about it and need to see the reality. Though we have started this journey with a lot of enthusiasm and hope, I fear we have boarded the wrong bus, and it is not taking us anywhere. I think we should get back to our jobs. We all know we were true and sincere with our efforts, but maybe we need to focus our efforts elsewhere.'

There was a deafening silence in the room. Charan and Sudhakar were in deep thought. Phani was restless. 'I think we should close redBus and get back to our jobs. We have tried enough, but it is not working out the way we thought, and there is nothing wrong in it. At least we gave it a shot. How long can we remain stuck like this?'

'It is only three months...' Sudhakar said, still looking down and thinking.

'Yes, but each of us were making Rs. 1 lac a month. Now we are barely making Rs. 2,500. Even if our business grows by ten times, it will still be Rs. 25,000,' said Phani, wondering at the futility of their efforts.

'Then why the hell did we leave our jobs in the first place if we are losing our confidence in just three months? We should not have committed ourselves for this cause. But once committed, we should not give it up midway. At least I will not give up; if you want, you are free to join me. Otherwise I will work on this alone.'

The overpowering aggression of Sudhakar killed the pessimism of Phani.

Content with the decision, Charan quietly smiled. He realized the importance of having a strong and determined cofounder who could pull one back from the downswing and get things back on track.

Charan encouraged Phani by saying, 'Relax, Phani. Don't get bogged down by initial hiccups and hitches. Our persistence will pay, so let us focus and work hard. Things will fall in place!'

Gradually, it did! redBus picked up pace!

~

It seemed that Mahindra, in some past life, had been associated with Saint-Gobain glasses, considering the way he cleaned the office, for one could even see their reflection on the floor. The intensity of his dedication had tripled since he came to know about the venture capitalist (VC) meeting at redBus office. All rooms other than those used as office premises in the flat were locked; waste items were put in the kitchen. Since there was no lock for the kitchen, the top priority in the wish list was to make the VCs glued to their seats and not allow them to enter the kitchen! That's what nervousness does to everyone.

redBus's mentors had arranged for VCs to raise funds for the start-up, and improving on the presentation became a major part of their daily chore. The mentors guided them on key points and did their best to sort out any issue they might face. Two crucial issues had to be decided before the VC meeting: the front face of the company (i.e. the CEO) and the profit-sharing ratio among the cofounders.

'There is one critical matter that you need to address,' said Anandram during the Monday morning meeting. All three cofounders gave each other inquisitive glances and waited for him to carry on.

Sanjay elaborated, 'Like a car, even in a company, only one person can be in the driver's seat. Your task ahead is to decide the person who will occupy the driving seat, that is the front face of your company.' After a pause, he popped the big question, 'Who will be the CEO of www. redbus.in?'

Sudhakar was relaxed, as this wasn't the problem he was anticipating! Charan said in a calm voice, 'I think it should be Phani. What do you say, Sudhakar?'

'Agreed,' said Sudhakar, wondering how Charan had managed to read his mind.

In this demonstrating of maturity and trust, they now grew from friends to business partners.

Phani, the CEO, was given the responsibility to document the ownership and profit-sharing among the founders before the VC meeting.

All three were anxious, and the anxiety was no less than proposing to a childhood girlfriend — after all, a lot was at stake: fear of losing one's friendship and hurting the other's sentiments were overpowering. They had shared room, food, money and so many memories, but the thought of sharing profits and signing a formal, written agreement made them uncomfortable. Though none of them wanted to hurt other's feelings, expectations could be very subjective and one could never anticipate the other's reaction.

To break the ice, they decided the time and venue for a formal meeting.

Phani worked on his opening lines that he had rehearsed before the meeting, but when they met, he forgot everything and said, 'Let's have it equal, one-third for all.' He had pondered over this matter for a week and was expecting a long discussion, meeting to run over hours, but listening to his suggestion, Sudhakar and Charan unanimously said OK and concluded the meeting.

'This conviction and reliance that we have in each other's decisions is our most precious asset,' Phani thought.

After addressing both the issues, they were ready to venture into the VC meeting. Niranjan, one of their friends who had done MBA, helped in preparing the presentation. They wanted to raise Rs. 30 lacs on an estimated turnover of Rs. 1 crore.

Bharati Jacob, the VC, came, and Mahindra's prayers were answered — she did not go to the kitchen! She saw the presentation. When she saw that the amount required was Rs. 30 lacs, she smiled.

Phani's mind started racing, and ifs and buts cropped up in his mind. 'Have we asked for too much? Do we really need so much money? What if she doesn't invest?' After going through the presentation, she said, 'One of my colleagues is visiting Bangalore next week. Meet him and he will take this discussion further.'

The next meeting was scheduled for the coming week. Though they kept wondering if Rs. 30 lacs were too much to ask for, they stuck to their presentation. The week passed with anxiety. The day had come to meet Pravin Gandhi, Bharati Jacob's colleague.

They showed him the same presentation, and it went very well. Pravin Gandhi asked a couple of random questions. They were confident that they would be able to raise the required amount, until Gandhi said, 'All this is OK, but can you make your presentation for Rs. 100 crores?'

For 100 crores! Did they hear it right? Is that what the VC had said? They went blank and looked at each other.

With a lot of difficulty, they had made the first draft of Rs. 30 lacs on a turnover valuation of a crore, but scaling it to Rs. 100 crores was simply beyond their imagination. It took them a few days to believe that they weren't dreaming.

Bharati worked with them and prepared seven versions of business plan. The seventh version said they would need Rs. 3 crores to fund the business for the first year of operation.

They got a cheque for Rs. 3 crores on a Rs. 10-crore valuation. It was a big day, and they were wondering where their lives were heading. Everything was happening so fast! Ten crores was too big an amount. They were overwhelmed.

However, after the initial reaction, a sense of responsibility gripped them. Somebody had put so much trust and money in their idea and ability that they must be focused and work hard to prove them right.

~

'With a cigarette in my hand, I feel like a man' was Sudhakar's favourite ad, which he tweaked to 'With the VC money in my bank, I feel like a superman!' All three of them used to chant it like a mantra until Phani visited Ramachandran, one of the biggest bus operators in the town.

'Rs. 400 for electricity bill! *Tum to mera diwala nikal doge* (you will make me bankrupt),' shouted Ramachandran at one of his employees. He was livid, as if the person had committed a Rs. 400-crore scam.

'What a weirdo, wasting his energy on such a trivial amount,' Phani thought, but soon he gave it a second thought and the importance of being thrifty dawned upon him.

He realized the value of saving each penny and curtailing wasteful expenditure as crucial to any business's success. If they had to ensure redBus's success, they must cut down on the extra costs, Phani realized.

That day, when he reached the office, he checked the electricity bill: it was a whopping Rs. 3,000. Then he glanced through the tea bill and his heart skipped a beat: it was Rs. 2,000. He decided that he would run his business with no frills, just like Ramachandran did, and cut down on unnecessary costs.

'Phani, I agree, but cutting down electricity and tea bills is just a tip of the iceberg. The real task we have is to get trained staff. Though we have enough money in the bank, we must save the money for our future expansion. We cannot afford to pay as per market standards.' Charan wondered how to solve this recruitment problem.

~

They decided to approach HR consultants. It turned out to be a worse experience than delivering bus tickets. At least there, they used to get tips in appreciation, but here, they became subjects of mockery.

'What! Do you know what you are talking about? We are doing business, not charity, and even a charitable organization cannot fulfill your demand. You want an English-speaking person who can operate computers at Rs. 2,500, and that too in Bangalore, where IT is booming. The average salary of such a person in market is Rs. 10,000. How can you even expect a person to consider your offer? Even a housemaid earns more than this?' exclaimed the HR consultant.

Though they increased the salary slab to Rs. 3,500, it was way below market standards, and hence the people they got were way below the average standards. Since they believed in the motto 'where there's a will, there's a way', they were able to find some alternative.

~

At one of their meetings, Sudhakar exclaimed, 'To get quality, either invest in money or invest in time!'

The redBus trio chose the latter option and thus started their training department. Since then, it has become a norm that the founders trained new employees for the relevant skill sets.

They made sure that they made best use of available resources and did not indulge in lavish spending.

With the amount of cash that they had raised from the VCs, the first thing they did was to come out of cycle of debt that they had taken from family and friends.

To kick-start the process of selling tickets through the Internet, they had to buy the bus tickets in cash. Since the selling of tickets through the Internet delayed the payment by 15 days, they were trapped in heavy debt cycle.

The VCs gave them the leverage to expand the team and open new offices in other geographical locations. Gradually, they expanded their wings from Bangalore to Hyderabad and then to Delhi.

By 2007, though redBus achieved a turnover of Rs. 20 crore, yet they were not profitable. Various unbudgeted costs surfaced out of nowhere. A new UPS for their Bangalore office costing Rs. 5 lacs was not estimated. Unexpected bills became a regular phenomenon.

'Why do we need so much money? This is a simple business. We don't need so much money to build it,' Phani remembered saying to his mentors when they made a presentation to raise Rs. 30 lacs, but now he knew the value of money better. The famous adage goes '*Jo dikhta hai who bikta hai* (what is seen sells)'. redBus's visibility improved with their marketing efforts. Media attention proved good for their business. With an increase in new clients, competition sprang up from unknown quarters. While some were regional players, others were existing travel portals earlier operating in air travel.

But one of them truly made Phani uneasy — one of the competitors had received a six-million-dollar funding. They started distributing computers to bus operators.

'What if these actions bring a shift in the long-gained loyalty of bus operators?' The same thought pervaded everyone's minds. They were brainstorming if a counterattack could be counterproductive. In two minds, they sought the refuge of their mentors.

'He will not value a free computer; he will value a paid customer. Keep solving customer problems,' Sanjay Anandram guided. He told them to focus on their core business: to build a popular consumer brand and drive sales for bus operators.

They followed their mentor's advice diligently and kept their focus on building alliances. By mid-2008, redBus was selling around 1,200 seats per day. They had tie-ups with around 400 bus operators across India.

Now running smoothly on their growth trajectory, the co-founders of redBus wanted to increase their product offerings.

They planned to launch BOSS (bus operators' software services), the first product that they had developed for bus operators. BOSS allowed bus operators to manage their inventory in real time. Multiple users could access and book tickets. Bus operators could sell tickets from their multiple offices across the city. They could also sell return tickets with the help of BOSS since they were in control of the entire inventory. But to launch BOSS, further funding was required, which, considering their growth and image in the market, they were confident of getting. VCs themselves had started approaching them for funding.

But it took a backseat when Anandram advised them to focus on redBus instead of BOSS.

But in business, the rule is always to expect the unexpected.

~

The Lehman Brothers collapsed. Stock markets crashed, panic engulfed the air like dark clouds, and it was the worst recession that had hit the world markets since 1929. It was a year of recession and job cuts. The trickle-down effect was extremely quick. Suddenly, the private equity space dried up, and it wasn't one of the best years to raise money. Consequently, nobody was ready to fund any start-ups.

Phani and team were not really worried. They needed money to scale up. They knew that no VC would give them a high valuation, resulting in a lower than actual valuation of their company. It was a difficult decision, but an important one nonetheless.

'Narayana Murthy and his family own only 5 percent shares of Infosys. What percent share one owns doesn't matter. You are here to solve a consumer problem. Just focus on that. A 5 percent more or less is not going to create much of a difference. You may hold 100 percent equity in a Rs. 10-crore company, but holding 10 percent equity in a Rs. 1,000-crore company is certainly more profitable,' Anandram emphasized.

Understanding this equation clarified what was at stake for them. They raised more money at just half of their actual valuation. While it was a strategically right decision, it drastically brought down the motivation of an otherwise charged up team. They suddenly realized that the valuation of their company was way lower in the eyes of their staff.

~

Phani was walking in the office preoccupied with something, and he didn't respond to Sudhakar's greeting.

Mystified, Sudhakar asked, 'What happened?'

'Rajesh resigned,' Phani conveyed in a sad tone. Rajesh, their business development manager, was one of the most important and committed member of the redBus team.

'Why?' Sudhakar asked.

'Well, he cited family issues as the reason, but I don't think it is the actual reason. I think our lower valuation has demotivated our team. I can sense that more number of people will leave.'

'That's a serious matter. I think we need to talk to them and clear their doubts,' Sudhakar advised.

Phani knew proper communication solved every problem, but never before had he seen it in action. At the end of the meeting with his team, he realized the importance of communicating the reasons behind crucial decisions that the top management takes to the employees in a clear and transparent manner to maintain trust among employees. Despite that, some important employees left the team, and this became one of the most humbling experiences.

The redBus team was young and didn't have much experience. Though a few employees' exits did shake the morale of the team, they learnt a lot. Even then, they had to interview people, train them and make sure that the team was motivated enough to drive growth. They understood that business is about managing and motivating people, and it took them around six months to get things back in shape.

~

Problems in business are like the rains in Mumbai — they can come anytime and turn everything upside down. First came the recession, followed by a lower valuation, resulting in a lower employee confidence and landing redBus in HR trouble. Also, they were faced with technological conundrum.

'It has taken two days to open the port on this server,' Charan complained.

'Even the last time, the memory size wasn't enough to service the workload, and the upgrade took more than a month, and our business took a hit. Moreover, procuring a new server or upgrading an existing server will take more than two weeks!'

'We should move to cloud computing,' Charan proposed.

With redBus's growth, the core team had expanded from three founders to eight members.

It was a small meeting room, and everyone was worried. Charan was standing near the screen across the table to discuss IT issues.

The pace of growth at redBus was just too much for the IT team to handle. They required a permanent solution to avoid firefighting every three months. Charan was concerned because most of his core team's time and energy went into circumventing scaling issues, such as procurement of new servers, upgrading existing servers and issues related to IT infrastructure, rather than in improving the system. Thus he suggested cloud computing as a permanent solution.

'What about the security of our data?' Phani raised one of the most important questions.

'What about the cost?' the finance manager asked.

'What about the capabilities? Has anybody in India tried this before?' Sudhakar enquired.

'No one ever tried selling bus tickets online as well before we did,' Charan said with a confident smile.

'We have to try this because maintaining the kind of data we have is becoming a problem. I suggest we make a gradual shift to cloud computing. It will give us the flexibility and scalability, both factors are very important for our business. Importantly, my team will focus on developing and enhancing the application that would improve our offerings to customers and not spend unproductive time on IT infrastructure. This, in turn, will bring more sales and profit,' said Charan confidently and winked at the finance head, who had no choice but to nod. Thus, redBus became the one of the first Indian company to move 100 percent of its operations to cloud computing.

Consequently, they won accolades from the chief technology officer of Amazon.com, who was very impressed with the architecture, the scalability and the robustness of the solution.

Mr. Phanindra Sama
Dear Mr. Sama,
You are cordially invited to be our guest of honor at the inauguration of the Kadamba bus transportation's first e-Kiosk.
Regards,
MD
Kadamba

Phani read the letter almost five times.

'Oh, cool. It isn't a love letter. It's just an invitation letter. After all, *ab to tum bade aadmi ban gaye ho!* (You have become a big man.) They don't know you yet; they should have written "guest of horror" instead of "guest of honour",' teased Sudhakar.

'I hope it isn't a prank. Someone inviting me to be the guest of honour, doesn't it sound funny?' Phani laughed. But soon he was off to Panaji(Goa) to inaugurate the first e-Kiosk operations by the Goa State Transport Corporation (Kadamba Transport Corporation). By the time he reached, the event had started. Making his way through the jam-packed crowd, he reached the front row.

'Now we invite Mr. Phanindra Sama, the CEO of redBus, to cut the ribbon and inaugurate the e-Kiosk,' the host announced.

Everyone's eyes were on the first row. People were guessing who among the oldies would be the CEO. In India, the word CEO is generally associated with a person in his early 50s with grey hair and bulging tummy. Phani just didn't match that image.

'I am going to change my designation after this event,' Phani thought. He sensed the amazement, or maybe disappointment, of the crowd when he cut the ribbon. How on earth could he be the CEO? What would he know about the bus industry? He is so young? Such questions would have been running through people's mind.

Phani had been invited by Kadamba for a reason.

A year ago, the Goa Road Transport Corporation had launched their luxury Volvo bus service between Goa and Mumbai. This route did not prove to be profitable due to their ticket distribution model. The bookings in Goa were taken care of by the local offices in Goa, but they did not have any booking offices in Mumbai, thus leading to heavy losses. Opening offices in Mumbai just for 40 seats didn't seem economically viable for the corporation. Thus, the officials at Kadamba were about to take a call to close the service when someone suggested that they use the service of redBus to sell their tickets. The proposal was accepted by the board for a trial period of six months.

Soon, the tickets started selling, and Kadamba's luxury bus started running fully. The initiative was applauded. The officials were convinced on using the online platform for all other interstate buses.

When the MD of Kadamba told him about the way redBus had benefitted them, Phani was overwhelmed as he realized that their efforts were contributing to a much larger ecosystem.

Their vision of making a difference in people's lives by making things convenient for them was coming true. redBus was aiding in increasing the profitability of another company. He vowed that he would work harder to increase the scope of their operations.

~

On returning from Goa, Phani was browsing through some mails when the business development head knocked.

'I was just looking at the monthly report. We are doing some real good numbers. Good show.' Phani appreciated the team's effort.

'Yes, and it will be better. Today I received a call from another state corporation. They want to tie up with us. This is the fourth state transport corporation that is contacting us. I think we need to put an extra effort and try to get them all on board.' The business development officer saw some promise in the future. He continued, 'We are trying, but technology integration from their side will take some time as most of the state transport corporations are not so advanced technologically to adopt our online platform. We are building on that. We hope that in another three to four months we will change the way people book tickets for government buses.'

~

'How dare you write on your site "Do not buy tickets from this operator"? I am giving you business and you are trying to put me out of business, eh? You don't know who I am. Who are you to rate me as not good,' said an enraged bus operator.

Neha, a newly employed front-office staff, politely requested the operator to calm down and said, 'Sorry for the inconvenience, sir, but the ratings are not by us; it is by customers who used your services last time. If you improve the quality of your services, we will change our ratings accordingly. We want to be honest to our customers, and your cooperation will improve things for all of us.'

Just two months into the system and Neha was well equipped to deal with the situation. Practice makes one perfect — this proverb rang true in her case. Every week, she dealt with two to three such horrid calls. But these experiences made her learn a valuable lesson.

'If you try to do good to one party, the other gets hurt, but if you are honest with them, they will stick with you,' and thus, despite the negative ratings, none of the bus operators left redBus because they were confident of the organization's transparency and honesty. They knew that redBus had not increased the 10 percent commission charged on every transaction. They had kept it fixed since the starting days. They could have easily demanded more due to increased volume and dependence of bus operators on them. But their decision to stick to 10 percent won the trust and confidence of the bus operators.

'The only thing of real importance that leaders do is to create and manage culture. If you do not manage culture, it manages you, and you may not even be aware of the extent to which this is happening.'

The mentors elucidated, 'For example, Wipro is a democratic organization. It promotes a culture of connecting and listening to its people. New ideas and innovations are appreciated and support is provided to transform it into action.' They then left it to the redBus team to decide the kind of culture and value system they would want to create. Inspired by the story, Phani, an admirer of Buddhist philosophy, opted for the middle way — neither an autocracy nor a democracy. They would thus build their organization's culture on quasi-democracy, with values like honesty, maturity and hard work.

~

It was Diwali, and Phani left for office early. The team had planned to decorate the office and ready it for Diwali *pooja* the next day. His office was just 20 minutes away, but today it took him 35 minutes to reach the office, courtesy the Diwali rush in the markets.

At office, he was the only one present, except for the security guard.

The office was clean, calm, bright, the color red made it vibrant, and the redBus employees breathed life into it. It was an official holiday; however, employees were invited for a little get-together and celebration. Everyone wanted to decorate the office and have *pooja,* as they did every year. Then Phani headed towards his cabin.

When he was through with his mails, he looked at his watch — the watch that his parents had gifted him on Diwali, the same Diwali when he couldn't get a ticket to go back to Hyderabad.

He stretched on his chair and slowly took a walk down the memory lane. There was still no sign of anyone; he has an hour to himself. He pulled his chair to the window; he had always enjoyed looking out, observing people, but today, he went back in time. It all seemed like a dream, and he wondered where he would be when he finally woke up ...in front of a PC at Texas Instruments? Five years back, he was there, desperate to finish off his work so he could take a bus and go off to Hyderabad to celebrate Diwali with his parents.

Today, it was the same occasion, and the same time of the year, but life had taken a 360-degree turn. In retrospect, the pace of change astonished him. From his dream of designing chips for Texas Instruments to running his own business — the last five years have been a roller-coaster ride for him. With friends, it wasn't that difficult.

Two years back, the entire spotlight had been on building the team. Last year, Charan was focusing only on technological innovations to support future growth. Yesterday, the core team was discussing plans to get into business with Bangladesh and Malaysia: geographical expansion was the first priority. Every year, business dynamics were changing, and the company was responding well to the change.

From a humble start to creating a Rs. 300-crore company, Phani wondered where the future would be. The morale and expectations of employees were at an all-time high.

Phani was shaken out of the reverie when the marketing manager greeted him. Phani smiled slowly.

'Sir, today's newspaper reports a travel portal coming out with an IPO. When do we plan to raise money from capital markets? Don't you think we should also get into airlines ticketing, where the margins are much higher. In any case, redBus is running smoothly, isn't it the right time to diversify?' asked the marketing manager.

'There is still a long way to go,' Phani said. 'You have a point, but I have a question. Do you think we have reached the stage of perfection — that is, 90-95 percent customer satisfaction? Or if a person calls, do we guarantee that his call and query is answered without fail? Is our site up and running every minute? Do you think that we have reached that level?'

'Hmm...Not yet,' the marketing manager mumbled.

'You know since childhood, I have had a very strong belief that instead of being average in all subjects and getting 80 percent, it's better to be master of one and get 90 percent in that one subject. Because to get 80 percent, you need to know the subject in and out, but to get that extra 10 percent, you have to put in three times more effort. It requires stamina, analytical skills, dedication and ability to sit up. It adds to so many other things that has nothing to do with subject. But that extra 10 percent gives you a competitive edge which is very difficult to replicate. According to me, at present, we are at 80 percent stage.' Phani paused, 'So what do you think should be the most important goal?'

'To work three times more and get to that extra 10 percent edge.' The marketing manager smiled.

After all, there were still many miles to be covered, many lands to be conquered and many horizons to be touched for team redBus.

REDBUS
KEY LESSONS
SANJAY ANANDRAM

Sanjay Anandaram has been one of the mentors to the entrepreneurs behind redBus. He brings 25 years experience as an entrepreneur, corporate executive, venture investor, faculty member, advisor and mentor. The views expressed here are his own. He can be reached at sanjayanandaram@gmail.com

The incredible story of redBus that created and then dominated a category within 6 years is inspirational. Having been closely associated with it almost from inception, here are, some associated lessons.

Be Obsessed about Customers, not Competitors
All too often entrepreneurs tend to have a knee jerk reaction to what competitors do and then bring all their energies to responding to competitors rather than on focusing on the reason for their existence, namely serving customer needs profitably.

It is important to keep an eye on competitors but more so to remain obsessed about your own customers! Customers come first!

Be Consistent
Once a policy is in place — treatment of vendors and partners — apply the policy consistently, uniformly and without fear or favour. redBus did not change its policy to accommodate the interests of partner; that would have been unfair to the large number of smaller partners.

Be Frugal

Inspite of having its entire VC funding in the bank, the fundamental character of frugality didn't change. Everything was negotiated and optimised. Better alternatives were sought. Lavishness and ostentation were discouraged.

Have Values

Inspite of many pressures, redBus didn't compromise on its core values of hard work, integrity and maturity. It preferred to challenge unfair and unethical practices — delaying and upsetting its operations many times — but in the process creating a value system that it is justifiably proud of.

Go and Learn

Seek advice and learn from others. Do not be inhibited. Seek out those who are more experienced and have more expertise. The important thing is to learn. Read as much as you can, ask questions and learn.

Be Humble

Humility allows for learning. Don't be hesitant to travel to meet partners and customers at short notice even if they are in at hard-to-reach places. Remember, they trusted you when you were young, inexperienced and learning. Don't be arrogant; it inhibits learning.

Learn to Let Go

There are moments when tough decisions must be taken. It is important to not to be emotional but to take decisions based on data and pragmatism, logic and reason. Having colleagues depart, voluntarily or involuntarily, is always an emotional issue but how one responds determines the winner.

Best Marketing

Marketing is what happens every day — when your customers speak well of you. redBus hardly spent any money on marketing for first several years of its existence.

Follow your Passion, Be your own Role Model

Don't be hesitant about rolling the dice if you have an insight. Don't be afraid of failure. Pursue your entrepreneurial dreams. The biggest risk is in not taking a risk.

the LOOT
Great Steals on Big Brands

Winner of Tata NEN hottest start-up of the year — 2009

In 2009 The Loot was recognized as the biggest thing to hit retail therapy in India and its founder Jay Gupta was invited by prestigious London School of Business to share his experiences of 'Great Steals on Big Brands'.

The Loot is a multi-brand discount store, offering customers a wide range of products in apparels, footwear and accessories with discounts ranging between 25%–60% — throughout the year.

During its peak The Loot had set up over 150 stores (approximately 3,00,000 sq. ft. retail carpet area) in 75 cities and 20 states throughout the country.

The Franchising World (2008) recognised The Loot as one of the top 50 business opportunities in India.

Founder Jay Gupta, was christened the 'Robinhood of Retail'.

5
THE LOOT

JAY GUPTA

Life is always tough, but one can make it easier by sharing one's dreams and creating co-dreamers to move up on the success path.

Jay Gupta

AFTER MAKING A FEW QUICK CALLS to his stores, Jay glanced at the daily sales report (DSR).

'In some stores, sales are up like-for-like, while in others, sales are down. Both scenarios are depressing,' Jay was talking to himself. 'On every sale, I am making a loss of approximately Rs 50. I am trapped in a vicious circle. How do I face this dilemma? Should I sell more or settle for less? If the sales increase, operational losses will increase; if the sales decrease, sooner or later I will be out of business. How do I save the business I have built from scratch? How do I save the jobs of my employees?' Jay was confused, frustrated and depressed. 'How do I get out of this mess?' he thought and picked up the newspaper.

The headline read *'Govt. Mulling Tweaking FDI Policy to Accommodate IKEA'*. Jay smiled.

'On the one hand, the government is easing norms for foreign retailers by relaxing the FDI policy, but on the other hand, there are no reforms to facilitate the domestic retail industry,' he remarked and read further. After a long time, the newspaper interested him.

The news about IKEA's ambitious plans for India with investment of Rs. 10,500 crore made multinationals bullish about the potential of retail in India. Jay, having experienced the bumpy ride of Indian retail for more than a decade, scorned at the ironic truth behind the announcements of investment, growth, hiring, revenues and the so-called national rollouts. It was all a façade.

'So, now one more international retailer wants to take his share of the Indian market, and why not?' Jay smirked. 'India is shining with its huge middle-class populace, increasing per capita income and consumption. After all, India is one of the fastest growing economies in the world. We all are in the middle of the consumption boom. It is a dream market for any retailer. Everybody falls into this trap.'

'I wonder why no one sees the other side of the coin. Retailers are having a tough time. Even retail chain giants like Subhiksha, Vishal Mega Mart, Koutons and Lilliput all are struggling, and some are even history. We are fighting every day to survive. It is blind euphoria, he reflected. There was no solace for Jay. He, like many others, had seen unprecedented highs and abysmal lows in the span of couple of years.

'Where did we go wrong? Was it poor policy by the government, bad planning or fate?' he questioned himself.

~

At 6 pm, the sun was about to set, and so were Jay's spirits. He ordered two cups of tea from the nearby tea stall. Restless, he scanned the room again. The stocks of western wear, sportswear, footwear, etc. were neatly stacked in the shelves and were categorized as per the sizes. The exhibition hall looked in perfect condition.

He turned towards Renu, wife of Ajay, his friend and partner in his first entrepreneurial venture of a garment exhibition. Renu had been observing Jay for quite some time; he was shuttling between the entrance of the exhibition hall and the corridor. She understood Jay's anxiety and said, 'Don't worry. Once people get to know about the exhibition, they will come,' she consoled Jay. 'You check with the newspaper vendor if he'd distributed the leaflets this morning.'

'I inquired about that in the morning. Even I went to check some areas. He has distributed the leaflets,' Jay replied.

'Maybe because this is the first day, and that too a working day, we have no footfalls. It could be that shoppers will come late in the evening and sales would pick up.' Renu maintained a confident smile.

'I hope so. Let me turn the volume up on the stereo. I hope the sound brings in some customers.'

Jay stared at the entrance of the exhibition hall they had rented. He saw a typical Navi Mumbai market; small shops and crowded streets. On one of the parking lots outside an apparel shop, he saw a Ford Ikon — the car he wanted to buy with the money he thought he would make from this exhibition, but he could see his dream shattering as they hadn't sold a single piece yet. 'I was a fool to be bullish about this exhibition. Forget the car, I might not recover what I have spent on petrol for my bike,' Jay thought.

'Sir, *chai,'* said a ten-year-old as he handed Jay a cup of tea.

'Give one cup of tea to madam sitting inside,' said Jay.

Sipping tea, Jay walked in. Renu was busy with the bill book.

'What are you doing? Counting chickens before they hatch? I hope our eggs hatch. We haven't sold anything to do any accounting.' Jay smiled at his business partner.

'Don't worry. What is the worst that can happen? Anyway, we stocks on consignment basis. We can return the unsolds.'

'We will have to give back everything, I presume,' said Jay, a little disappointed.

'Calm down. We won't make any losses. See, customers are entering the hall.' She braced herself for meeting the customers.

'Can you show me a pair of jeans?' asked an 18-year-old good-looking girl as she approached Jay.

'What size are you looking for?' he asked her politely. Jay, a college student in his early twenties, was overwhelmed by her good looks.

'I don't know. Can you measure my waist?' she said.

'Wow! I can officially measure her waist. Investing money here was definitely not a waste,' Jay thought. He looked at Renu, trying hard to hide his grin. Renu winked and smiled mischievously.

Finally, they sold stocks worth Rs 1,000 on day one. Though the sales disappointed Jay, the waist measuring experience was enough to keep his spirits high. He looked forward to the second day.

The next day was Sunday, and, to his surprise, they did business of around Rs 24,000.

'Renu, this is incredible! The game has changed within a day! I never thought that a weekend would make such a difference,' said Jay enthusiastically but Renu was exhausted after the day's work.

'Till today the only exciting thing about Sunday was Doordarshan's *Rangoli* and the evening movie. In our village, we used to finish our work and would sit in front of the television set ten minutes before the program started. Today I realize that Sunday in Mumbai is equal to *haat bazaar* we have in our town.'

'Haat bazaar?' Renu quizzed. It was a new word for her.

'Kaunse planet se aayi ho?' Jay was baffled, 'Miss America, *tumhe haat bazaar nahi maloom? Haat bazaar* is a weekly market that has stalls selling clothes, toys, eatables, etc. People from nearby villages and towns come to shop there. It's a high earning day, like our day today,' he explained.

'Do you have fitting rooms in *haat bazaars?'* Renu smirked.

'Well, we will pass a law that all *haat bazaars* have trial rooms as per Her Highness Renu's wish,' Jay retorted.

'For us, every customer is Her Highness, and we need to have quite a few fitting rooms. Our customers are educated, sophisticated and brand-conscious than your *gaon ki goris* (village girls). They want to try everything before buying,' Renu explained the logic.

'What is going on, Renu and Jay?' Ajay asked, entering the room and greeting them with a big smile.

'Well, your Bandit Queen — oops, I mean your Branded Queen is giving me lessons on retail,' said Jay with a naughty smile.

'She is qualified to do that. After all, she has credits to her name for participating in five exhibitions so far. By the way, she told me you had a good day today. Happy?' asked Ajay patting Jay.

'It was surely a good day, but I still cannot buy the car and she the jewelry, at least for now,' Jay told in a matter-of-fact manner.

'The good thing is that we have recovered our costs, and you can sleep in peace, Ajay. Jay, you don't complain. By now you know the waist size of half of Navi Mumbai girls,' Renu teased Jay, and he blushed.

'More importantly, it was a great experience. It never occurred to me that in apparel retail we need to focus on fast-moving sizes. There are few sizes that we couldn't sell a single piece of, and then there are few other sizes of which we don't have a single piece left,' said Jay.

'Actually, it was a win-win situation. We did not lose our money and learnt about the rules of the game. We will be better next time,' Renu concluded with a smile.

~

'What are you reading, Jay?' asked Devang, a close friend.

'The article in *Business Today* on the emerging sectors in India. It is very interesting. These sectors have done well in the growing economies of the world.'

'Which are the sectors?'

'Chain of value hotels, lifestyle retail stores, banks and allied businesses,' said Jay, musing over what would be a suitable business for him. 'I am thinking of getting into one of these businesses.'

'The projections made in the article are for a decade, not a year. Then why do you rush? First, complete your studies, take up a job, and gain some experience, then get into business,' Devang advised.

'College *karke kisne kuber ka khazana pa liya hai?* (There is no wealth to be got from attending college.) I will get my degree in tandem with my business. Warren Buffet said that one should start earning as early as possible, and I am already late. I should ask for a report from a consultant for starting a chain of affordable hotels,' said Jay, determined to make his mark on the world.

'But why business in the first place?' Devang wondered. He had seen most people taking up jobs rather than going headlong into business, and hence he could not understand Jay's urge to start something of his own.

'I belong to a business family. I have the *baniya* (traders') blood in my veins. I can't imagine myself taking instructions from someone else. Moreover, I have always dreamt of building a business on my own. *Yaar,* I have seen my father working day in and day out. Though he did well in his business and we had a comfortable life, I never saw him enjoying his life. He never had time for us or for himself.' Jay paused, cleared his throat and said, 'Some memories are too overpowering. I just lost track.' Jay had lost his father a year before he moved to Mumbai for his studies and memories made him nostalgic. 'So, what I am saying is that I want to build a business in the organized sector so that I achieve a work-life balance. I have already lost 20 years of my life, and I can't afford to lose more.' He smiled. Still in his second year of college, Jay started planning his way ahead.

'At least complete your graduation,' Devang advised him.

'*Yaar,* what's the purpose of graduation? It is just a degree, and I don't understand how and where we will apply what they are teaching us. I also don't know how it will help in case I want to take up a job,' argued Jay. Finally, Devang gave in to Jay's arguments.

Meanwhile, Jay hired a consultant for a feasibility study on chain of hotels. The report had cost him Rs 3,000. As per the report, the initial investment needed to start a chain of hotels was huge and was way beyond his financial capacity. Banking was beyond his understanding, thus leaving him with no other option but to choose retail.

~

A long train-journey from Raxaul to Mumbai forced Jay to relax. Raxaul, a town in Bihar, was his native place. After his father's death, the assets were divided among him and his brothers. Jay's share was Rs 5 lac. Jay announced to his family about his plans to get into the retail business, and his brothers encouraged him to pursue his plan.

With Rs 5 lac in his bag, which he was using for a pillow, he couldn't sleep a wink that night. Money was the key to his dreams.

Jay remained preoccupied during the train journey. He recalled his meeting with Kishore Biyani, MD of Pantaloon Retail. Jay, along with his friend Raja, had contemplated on opening a multi-brand apparel store. It was a new concept that was gaining prominence in Indian retail sector. Jay and Raja signed an agreement with Mr. Kishore Biyani to sell Pantaloons' merchandise from their retail outlet.

'Finally, I am all set to start my business. Once I deposit this money in the bank, I will call Mr. Biyani,' thought Jay as he looked at the bag that he was using as a pillow. 'I hope every brand is as accommodating as Pantaloons is.' He knew it was wishful thinking. Jay had initiated discussions to open franchisee outlets with Pepe, Lee Cooper, Spykar, etc., but they had strict guidelines, making it difficult for a newcomer to make a breakthrough. They required security deposits and a minimum sales guarantee, except for Lee Cooper and Pantaloons, which were extremely flexible. Hence, the first brand he signed was Pantaloons with Mr. Kishore Biyani.

Jay was excited about his first big breakthrough. He had started with his share of his father's assets, and had soon quit his studies, without completing graduation. His dreams kept him awake throughout the journey.

As Jay reached Mumbai, a shocking news was awaiting him in the form of a letter from the bank. The letter stated that the cheque that he had issued to Mr. Kishore Biyani for confirmation of the agreement had bounced due to lack of adequate funds. Jay had previously instructed Mr. Biyani not to deposit the cheque till he had said so, and Jay had rushed to his village only to make these arrangements.

Disturbed at the turn of events, Jay immediately called Mr. Biyani. 'Sir, I had asked you not to present the cheque till I said so,' said Jay.

'I am so sorry, Jay. It was just a mistake. I am so busy expanding business that it must have slipped my mind. We have just opened our first big store, and there are many things lined up. I am sorry,' Mr. Biyani said in a hurried voice and hung up.

'My first cheque bounced,' thought Jay. 'Pantaloons is sure to make headway in retail sector and so will I. After all, I am in the sunrise industry of India, with ambition and passion.'

~

'Hi, Devang, how are you?' Jay asked. Jay was in a jovial mood. Devang, the elder brother of Jigar, Jay's friend in college, had invested Rs 2 lac in Jay's first multi-brand store.

'Hi Jay, I am good. How is the business going?' Devang inquired about his new multi-brand store spread across 240 sq. ft. in Vashi.

'Our sales are on the rise,' Jay replied. 'Actually, I have come to pay off your loan. Thanks for your timely help.' Jay was able to pay back the loan in the first month itself.

'Great. I am happy to see that you are doing well. So what's next?'

'Brother, I'm sure of one thing: I will not stop with one store. I want to open more shops. Also, there is lot to learn.'

'You have just started. Don't worry. You will learn the tricks of the trade as you try newer things. How has it been till now? Are you facing any issues with brands?'

'No, not yet. The scenario till now has been encouraging. Brands like Lee Cooper have been very supportive. They have given me stocks on consignment basis. Basically, I pay only for what I sell,' said Jay. 'Big brands teach you a lot.'

'That's really good.' Devang was pleased to see Jay in high spirits.

'But not all brands are like Lee Cooper. Strong brands are very aggresive. They follow the "push strategy" and send stocks of their choice, not allowing us to choose what we want to stock. The problem with this approach is that I have to pay the brand for the stock they send, and if the product does not sell, I will land up having a large inventory and thus lowering my working capital. Also, if one brand pushes too much stocks, I wouldn't have enough money to buy stocks of other brands. This is not to say that I am capable or experienced in buying the right product. Sometimes, I am scared,' Jay shared his inhibitions.

'Well, I don't understand much about these issues, but I can tell you this. Last week, when I went to your store, I found a very limited collection in each brand.'

'Yes, that is another issue I am grappling with. It is a small store, and I cannot offer a wide spectrum of designs from any one brand. Customer thinks that if he wants to buy Pepe product, a Pepe store would be the best place. Maybe opening a single-brand store will help.'

~

Soon, Jay turned possibilities into reality by opening exclusive brand stores of ColorPlus and Weekender alongside his multi-brand store.

'Every day you learn something new.' Jay was sharing his experiences with the store manager of his ColorPlus store when a girl at the cash counter caught their attention.

'How much discount does the store offer on this T-shirt?' a girl in her early twenties asked.

'Sorry, ma'am, there is no discount right now,' Dimple, the manager, informed the customer politely.

'Oh,' she said, looked at the T-shirt again and walked out of the store without purchasing the T-shirt.

Soon, Jay realized that for most customers, a discount was more important than the purchase itself.

Jay thought that customers wanted a wider range of products with more varieties, so he opened exclusive brand outlets (EBOs), but the problem of selling persisted. Customers visited the store, spent hours trying outfits, and once they were satisfied with the fitting, they saw the price, and, in that eye-opening moment, realized that buying an expensive branded garment disturbed their monthly budget, abandoned the garment. Whether in multi-brand outlets (MBOs) or in EBOs, the conversion rate was very low. Only 10-12 percent of the customers who walked into the store bought the product.

'It's strange, but almost 70 percent of customers ask for discounts. They want a bargain,' the store supervisor told Jay in the meeting.

'About 70 percent of our people cannot be wrong. There is something that we are missing here. One thing is clear: people aspire for the brands but are not willing to pay the premium. They cannot afford to pay such a high price, so they ask for a discount, and that is the reason why the number of customers increases during the sale. The need gap is clear. We need to find a way to fulfill people's aspirations of owning the brand at a lower price,' said Jay.

'Sir, we could ask brands to give us their product at better rates so that we can offer discounts to the customers,' suggested the supervisor.

Jay smiled at him and said, 'We have to be their son-in-laws to be so lucky. Why would brands give a discount to us? What is so special about us? There are only two scenarios in which brands will give discounts. First, if they are not able to sell the merchandise themselves, and second, if they have large inventory and have surplus stocks.'

'Sir, we can buy their surplus stocks and open our own factory outlets. It could work,' said the supervisor. He was thinking of how the situation could be optimized.

'Bingo! That's exactly what we need to do. Our next store would be a factory outlet,' Jay concluded the meeting.

~

Jay was on a retail ride. From exhibitions to EBOs to MBOs to factory outlets, nothing seemed to satiate his thirst. He wanted to make branded clothing accessible to all. He thought that opening factory outlets would solve the problem, but was yet to understand the consumer psyche.

'Don't buy from these factory outlets. They sell defective pieces,' a pissed-off husband ranted his wife at the factory outlet of Adidas.

Manish, the store-in-charge, listened to the customer's ranting and tried to explain. 'No, sir, these are not defective pieces.'

'Then why are they so cheap?' the husband questioned Manish and looked at his wife assertively.

'Sir, this is surplus stock. When a brand is not able to sell merchandise for various reasons — like change of season, excess inventory or excess buying of a particular design — they give it to us for a lower price, and we pass it on to you,' Manish explained politely.

'So why can't they sell it from their stores?' He was consumed by the belief that these were defective products.

'Sir, for example, I have a blue trouser in different sizes, of which I have sold sizes 30, 32 and 34 but have not sold sizes 36, 38 and 40. What will I do?' Manish looked at the customer and smiled. 'I will remove those sizes that were not sold and bring another set of trouser which has all the sizes. Now does it mean that sizes 36, 38 and 40 were defective? No, they were as good as the other sizes which were sold. So you will find those leftover sizes in the factory outlets.'

'Then why don't you take returns and exchanges? You don't have trial rooms as well. If you sell original branded products, why don't you take returns?' The customer continued his debate while his wife was busy selecting merchandise.

'Sir, these are company policies,' Manish replied. He explained that if the brand offered all the facilities at a factory outlet, then no one would buy the product at full price. If a customer wants services, he should pay the full price.

While the husband was arguing with Manish, his wife picked up three Adidas T-shirts.

The husband paid the bill, and walking towards the exit, said, 'This green T-shirt is really nice. In such stores, you need to have an eye to pick the genuine brand.' Manish overheard and wondered that if the customers doubted the authenticity of a product, why did they buy from here?

'Customers think that either we sell rejected pieces or our products are fakes,' Manish narrated his experience with the last customer to Jay.

'Frankly, it isn't the best shopping experience for customers. They cannot try the garment. They cannot exchange the garments and there is no assurance of quality. Though customers buy from such outlets, there's always a doubt,' Jay concluded.

'That's true. Despite our conversion rate going up to 27 percent, customers are buying from factory outlets only because our products are affordable. In exclusive outlets, where we offer all the services, exchanges, returns, alterations, etc., our conversion rate is still 10 percent.' Manish had worked at the Weekender exclusive outlet before getting transferred to the factory outlet; he had been with Jay for the past four years.

'Maybe we need to change the current format on which we are working.' Jay, an astute observer and keen learner, was planning his next move.

'Sir, *aap kitni baar dukan badalenge?* (How many times will you change shops?)' Manish and Jay both laughed.

'Manish, I am not an astrologer. I cannot predict the market and forecast trends. The only way I learn is by getting into it, observing it and experiencing it,' said Jay. He paused for a moment and said, 'If customers want more brands, we open more MBOs. If customers want a wider range, we open EBOs. If they want discounts, we open factory outlets. If they demand better service along with discounts, we should improve and offer something better. Now we need to think what that "something" will be...' Jay was crystallizing his thoughts. His every move was driven by customers' expectations. He knew that he was reading the customer right, and to meet expectations he had to come up with something that no one had tried till now.

Manish nodded in agreement and said, 'Anyway, sir, some of the stock is damaged beyond repair.'

'Hmm. We can't do anything about it except book it as a loss.' Jay had experienced this before. Brands often played foul — they sent damaged stocks and blamed the franchisee. Franchisee outlets were dependent on brands for the stocks, and brands took advantage of this and dumped stocks on their franchisee factory outlets. The franchisee had only two options: clear those stocks or book losses.

~

'Arrey, sir, *loot mach gayi hai Loot mein.* Hundreds of people have queued up at the entrance of our store. It looks like our store will be looted today.' Vijay, the store supervisor, couldn't contain his excitement. It was becoming difficult to manage the crowd. 'Even

during the Diwali season, I have never seen such a rush. Sir, *itni bheed to langar mai bhi nahi hoti.* (We don't see such crowds even where free food is distributed.)' Vijay was thrilled.

Jay smiled and said, 'Finally, I've got it right. I've read the pulse of the people.' Over a period of time, Jay rebranded all the eight exclusive factory outlets as The Loot, for which he took a loan of Rs 5 crore. He was the first person to start a unique concept of a 'multi-brand discount chain'. These outlets offered 25-60 percent discounts throughout the year on branded apparel. It was the first weekend for The Loot, and the response was way beyond their expectations.

'That's why we have named it The Loot,' Jay replied. A few weeks back, he had read an article about a US store getting looted. As he read further, an image of crowd looting the store flashed in his mind. That image turned out to be a reality today.

'Sir, there is a long queue at the trial room. I think, when we are selling items at high discount, we should not keep the trial room open. Staff finds it very difficult to arrange the outfits from the trial room back into our regular stock. We are unable to attend to customers properly,' branch manager, Santosh, expressed his concern.

'Then how would we be different from other factory outlets, Santoshji? The innovative approach is not only to the change in the name but also to the entire business. *Chodo kal ki baate, kal ki baat purani, naye daur mein linkhenge, milkar nayi kahani.* (Leave the old school of thought, we need to change with the customer.) Even if the products are on discount, we need to offer all facilities like a trial room, exchanges, etc. We are no more a factory outlet of another brand. We are a brand of our own. We need to serve customers with all basic services that they expect. Even if they buy a Rs 100 product, we have to make them feel like a king.' The Loot was the brainchild borne of his learnings at single- and multi-brand stores.

During that time, the whole country was swept by the 'India Shining' wave, and retail was at an all-time high. Banks were funding retail businesses on a large scale. The first rebranded store came in Mumbai's upmarket college area, Marine Lines. Students of nearby colleges loved this novel retail concept of discounted branded goods.

'Sir, yesterday, we kept 100 pieces of Lee Cooper's white shirt priced at Rs 100 a piece on the table, and today the table is empty, all sold out. We are out of stock now. Shall we order for more stock?' the supervisor checked with Jay.

Jay and his team did not anticipate that it would sell so fast. 'Wow, now that's incredible! About 75 percent of our merchandise was of size 'small' and 'extra large'; these sizes generally don't sell too fast. If we can achieve selling these numbers in such quick time, then it's worth celebrating.' Jay was in a euphoric mood. 'Sir, we need to order more and stock up quickly,' the supervisor reiterated his demands.

'I will speak to the brand, but I don't think that they can replenish the stocks.' Jay knew his limitations. Since The Loot was selling the surplus stock, they did not have the liberty to choose from the fresh stock. They were completely at the mercy of brands for their inventory. 'Most brands don't know about their closing stocks, as they don't even have stock statements. So, how will they find the surplus stock of a white shirt?'

Jay was glad that the performance of all eight stores had improved drastically under the new, The Loot brand.

'Please make sure that we celebrate our achievement by cutting a cake after working hours. Everybody has worked hard to bring the changes in the stores. I will pass the message to all the stores.' Jay walked away brimming with hope and energy.

~

'How can a business operate at loss?' Jay was not able to comprehend the drastic change in his financials. 'Kanchan, give me the details of all the expense headers. Costs are sky-high. Where are we spending money?'

'Sir, all the overhead costs are up.' Kanchan gave the printout of the expense sheet.

'Where did we spend more?' Jay started looking at the sheet.

'The rentals are up as we have leased a warehouse. Earlier, we were only paying rent for stores. Also, our new billing system has a high cost attached to it,' continued Kanchan. As she spoke, Jay realized that his business was no more the same. The Loot had its own software (for billing) and a warehouse. Earlier, the marketing cost was borne by respective brands, but now they had to spend on marketing.

'I have been in the business for eight long years and I have seen it all: from MBOs to EBOs to factory outlets. How could I make such a mistake? Why did I not think of all these overheads before? I was so consumed by my idea that I overlooked the obvious,' Jay observed as he sunk in his chair. He was still pouring over the financial statements. 'I have seen so many companies with suicidal cash flows, and yet, here I am, despite managing my cash flows well, my profit-and-loss statement is at break point.' The factory outlets were profitable for Jay, but this new format raised his overhead costs exponentially. Even with higher sales, losses were incurring.

'Sir, can you please come to the storeroom?' the warehouse supervisor called Jay in haste.

'What happened? Why are you in panic?' Jay inquired while mourning over the profit-and-loss report, which showed depleting month-by-month profits. The 1,000 sq. ft. of warehouse suddenly looked like a white elephant, blocking his way ahead.

He walked towards the supervisor, who was staring at one of the open cartons. 'Sir, all these pieces have a brown mark on the right-hand sleeve. We cannot sell them as fresh stocks.'

'These brands! All they know is to push their damaged goods to us! We are the victims of typical Indian traits: advice and defective stock are distributed with absolute astuteness. The rules of the game have changed. Now it is no more a factory outlet. Our store does not keep defective stocks anymore. Brands will always push these kinds of stocks. What should we do now?' Jay started thinking about various options. Fundamentally, The Loot was supposed to offer better ambience, merchandise and services than the factory outlets, but Jay knew better. He knew that, sooner or later, a quality check had to be put in place, but setting up a quality check unit meant a further increase in operating costs.

'Please send them for dry-cleaning. Let's see if we can remove those stains and make the product salable,' Jay instructed the supervisor.

'Sir, getting so many pieces dry-cleaned would be so expensive. We can invest that money in setting up our own dry-cleaning facility,' the supervisor made a humorous remark without a second thought, but realized that Jay was lost in thought. He stopped suddenly.

'I think you are right; in fact, why set up only dry-clean? We need to probably set up entire unit for washing, stitching, dry-cleaning, etc.,' Jay replied enthusiastically, adding to the joke.

The supervisor wore a puzzled look; he did not expect his comment to be taken so seriously.

~

'Jay, what is keeping you so busy that you are unable to sign the offer letters. We need to close the hiring of the IIM graduates,' said Kanchan, the executive assistant to Jay, reminding Jay one more time about the new recruits.

'I remember. Please keep them on my table. I will sign them by the end of the day,' said Jay. He was extremely busy. For the past two years, he had taken a conscious decision to go slow and hence opened only three new stores, but now, confident of the road ahead, he wanted to speed up and expand his brand's wings. With the expansion came new challenges. He realized that for geographical expansion a supply chain management team, which would be very expensive, had to be put in place. Despite these challenges, growth was his only option as well as the motivating factor.

'With IIM graduates joining the team, we can set up efficient processes so that mistakes made in the past can be avoided,' Jay shared his thoughts with Kanchan, who was working with him for the past seven years. She was aware that the dynamics of this business were changing. The Loot's rapid expansion required employees who could scale up operations. He wanted people who had both the attitude and the aptitude to manage big businesses.

'I didn't go to any college or B-school, so I kept those funds aside so I could learn, and the only way I can learn is by making mistakes. That's the price I have paid for learning.'

'Learning by experience is a better option, so I suggest we hire some senior and experienced people as well. Anyway, we need to build the right team before we set out on our ambitious expansion plans,' said Kanchan. She could always be trusted for a level-headed opinion.

'I agree, Kanchan. No doubt about that. We need to hire a few senior managers from big companies like Adidas, Levi's, etc. I am sure you can work on that. Right now all my energy is consumed in arranging for funds and making presentations to raise them.'

'Jay, but your involvement is crucial in recruiting senior and middle-level employees.'

'I understand, but I am not a superman. My to-do list is never-ending. You know, all these talks about balancing work are a mirage. If I involve myself in everything, I won't be able to focus on anything. Now, arranging funds and recruiting employees are two equally demanding jobs, and for me, arranging funds is a priority. As far as recruitments are concerned, I trust you enough.'

Jay had been pitching to K.S.A. Raymond, a venture capitalist, for a first round of funding, and they showed interest in investing in The Loot. Like every other retailer, Jay needed funds to expand his business. Indian retail was booming, and all the major business houses of India — like Tatas, Reliance, RPG group — wanted to take their share of the pie.

'Jay, building a good team is as critical as raising funds. We can't take it lightly,' said Kanchan.

'I am not taking it lightly, Kanchan. I know it is crucial, but you need to understand that experienced people will come at a cost. How will we pay them? We need funds, don't we? About 40 percent of my time is spent in arranging funds, chasing the banks and investors and the remaining 60 percent spent in managing operations.'

'Yes, that's my point. How would you expand business if you don't have time and people?' Kanchan disagreed.

'That's why we are recruiting people from best of the B-schools and best of the companies. Once they come on board, I am hoping, a lot of things will be streamlined. The issues demanding my attention now will be addressed. It is just a matter of time, but raising funds doesn't leave me with much time. The market is huge, the opportunity is big, the growth potential is massive, but it needs to be grasped soon,' Jay said, knowing very well that opportunities won't last forever.

~

'Sir, I can't help it. The sale of platform tickets is closed,' the boy said to the ticket checker (TC) on New Delhi railway station.

'I know it is closed,' replied the (TC).

'*Arrey aapko pata hai?* (You know that?) How could I buy platform ticket? I came to drop my mother here. She has her ticket for the journey to Indore,' the boy tried to explain his situation.

'That is not my concern. I need a platform ticket or I will fine you,' the (TC) replied sternly.

'If they are not issuing tickets, how will I buy one?' the boy was confused. He was not a lawbreaker. Though he wanted to buy a platform ticket, he couldn't get one because authorities weren't selling tickets.

'If they are not selling tickets, it means that they don't want everyone to enter the railway platform. The platform is only for passengers. You should understand that,' the ticket checker said to the young boy.

'Sir, my mother cannot carry the luggage. I have to drop her.' With a helpless look on his face, the boy tried to explain his situation.

'What should I do? My job is not to create rules; my job is to follow rules. You can go and complain to the stationmaster. You can file a case against this kind of rule. I would also support that, but right now you need to pay a fine of Rs 500. Understand?'

'*Kuch kijeye,* sir, you also know it is not my mistake. I would have bought the ticket,' the boy requested.

'Stand aside and then we can discuss the matter.' The TC started walking.

The boy followed the TC behind a nearby tea stall. Standing near the tea stall, Jay listened to the entire conversation between the boy and the TC. He smiled at the irony. Sometimes rules were such that they conflicted with common sense.

'What is tougher in India — to know the law or to follow it?' he thought. Jay had received a few notices from government departments. A typical retail store requires more than 20 approvals or licenses from various government departments to have a legal operation in India. Thus, The Loot had no other option but to appoint lawyers to face the trials at various places.

'How do we avoid the legal notices?' Jay was searching for answer.

The boy came back to his mother and said, 'The fine is Rs. 50.' Jay couldn't help smiling.

~

'They don't have electricity in the town. They cannot provide air-conditioning to our customers,' Neeraj, the head of franchisee operations and a product of one of the best B-schools in the country, called up Jay in frustration. A large chunk of Jay's funds went as salary to these sophisticated gentry he recruited from IIMs and other top-league business schools.

'So?' Jay could not comprehend his concern.

'So, they want higher margins for generator and fuel,' said Neeraj.

'What an irony! These guys crack the toughest of exams in the country but can't crack a simple deal!' Jay thought. Jay knew that the client was taking him for a ride. MBAs like Neeraj were comfortable taking strategic decisions, and making expansion plans, but stumbled at the execution stage. The small-town franchisee owners were more street-smart than the likes of Neeraj.

'Neeraj, he is trying to squeeze us for better margins, nothing else,' Jay explained politely. In the last ten years, Jay had negotiated enough to know when to draw the line.

Jay knew that retail could not be won by mere PowerPoint presentations and boardroom meetings. One had to get one's hands dirty in these day-to-day operations. People like Neeraj, who came from top business schools, were too process-oriented. They were excellent drivers when the car and the road were in a good condition but lacked the art to drive a car on the bumpy Indian roads.

Jay was lost in his thoughts when Kanchan and Mr. Chabbra, the finance advisor, walked into his cabin with their laptops.

'Jay, please see the presentation, we have worked out some HR plans for the next three years.' Kanchan kept the laptop on Jay's table and opened the presentation.

'My dear Kanchan, as you know that from recent experience, my belief in presentations has been shattered. My humble request to you is recruit people from tier III cities; even if they are graduates. All I need is employees who can find the solutions and do not hesitate to do ground-level work. Our business requires more HMTs (Hindi-medium types) than IIM graduates. The Loot is an adventure, and we need people who can create things from scratch and get the job done,' Jay said sarcastically. He was not happy with high-profile IIM recruits and experienced hands who came from big companies.

'Yes, Jay, I do understand your plight, but you need to take a look at this presentation. As per your instructions, we have projected the increase in staffing, but that has a huge cost implication attached to it.' Kanchan looked at Mr. Chabbra for support.

'Jay, it will be expensive. We cannot afford to keep 15 percent extra employees,' Mr. Chabbra added his opinion.

'We don't have any option; our attrition rate is almost 50 percent — that means half of our employees quit within six months, and it isn't just us. The entire industry is struggling with the issue. On top of that, we can't even find skilled manpower. So it is better to hire and keep the extras,' Kanchan said.

'In any case, new recruits take three months to learn, another three months to master the skill, and only by ninth month they do show their full potential.' Jay paused, and with a frustrated voice, he continued, '... by the end of the year, he or she leaves the job.'

While The Loot was expanding, a lot of other national and international players were simultaneously flooding the Indian market with their brands, leading to a very high attrition rates.

'That's true, and I bet this attrition rate will increase further if you continue like this,' said Kanchan.

'What do you mean by "if you continue on like this"?' Jay was puzzled.

'Jay, you need to spend more time with the team. There has to be some sort of a connect, an emotional bonding with the company, and no one except you can build that.' Kanchan was concerned about the growing distance between employees and Jay. An invisible indifference was seeping into the company.

'But, Kanchan, I am always there for them for every task,' Jay defended himself.

'Yes, these days you are there for them but only for work. Earlier, you used to spend some time with them, and with such a high attrition rate, it has become all the more crucial. Paying them more isn't a solution, so we need to give them another reason to keep continuing with us, and that reason can only be loyalty, an emotional connection with the company,' explained Kanchan.

'I agree, but we are growing so fast. I am busy in opening stores. I myself want to bond with them, but I don't have enough time for everything,' said Jay. Jay, unlike his father, ventured into business so that he could find the time to enjoy his life, but his life was full of ironies: he was expanding so fast that his business consumed him. Leave alone time for his family, he didn't have time even for himself.

'Maybe, but I fear losing the foundation while we are busy building tall towers for our castle,' said Kanchan, forecasting the future. A critical exercise of team-building was overshadowed by the bright glare of aggressive expansion.

~

'I am glad to inform you that The Loot has opened its 50th store last week. We are...' the marketing head paused amid the applause.

For the past couple of months, the weekly meetings had become a significant and auspicious ritual. The stars were in their favour, and in every meeting, they had good news to share with their employees. The Loot was already an established player with its nationwide presence, but it was just a beginning. '...and we will be touching the 100 stores benchmark in the next two years.' The roar of clapping got louder. 'I am not finished yet. The most exciting news comes now.' He paused again and looked at everyone. Their eyes were popping out of curiosity. 'We have also decided to appoint a brand ambassador for our brand.'

'Who's that? Salman Khan?' the vice-president of sales and purchase asked with excitement.

'Hey, I wish it is John Abraham. He portrayed the role of a con in Dhoom. It will get with our name as well. What do you say?' another employee said with vigour. The room brightened with sparkling faces of everyone as they shared their ideas.

'Well, well, well, I know we have the brightest brains present in the room, but I think I will leave this for Jay to explain.' Head of marketing and Jay exchanged smiles.

'Thanks for your suggestions. I would like to take you through our thought process and share with you the direction in which we want to take our company. For The Loot, the brand ambassador should not be merely for a visibility campaign; the person should be a personification of our brand positioning, value system and brand appeal. To remind all of you, our brand does not stand for fashion and so we cannot choose a personality like Salman Khan.' Jay looked at VP (sales and purchase) and grinned. 'We want to create a concept similar to that of Café Coffee Day or My Dollar Store.'

'For any concept to register in the mind of the customer, it has to be more than just a discount store or a factory outlet,' added the head of marketing.

'Exactly, which means that we need to create the entire package, and our brand ambassador has to be part of this package. We need Robin Hood who loots the brands and gives it to customer at very low cost. A good man will not do that, and so we need a bad man. Do we have any guesses now?' Jay smiled and waited for the response.

'Don't tell me that you are signing Gulshan Grover as our brand ambassador!' said the head of operations in a sarcastic tone. Gulshan Grover is known as Bad Man of Hindi cinema; he had played many negative roles in Hindi movies.

'Why not? There won't be much difference in number of people who know Shahrukh Khan and those who know Gulshan Grover. The awareness level is the same, but the cost is not. While Shahrukh is extremely expensive, Grover is affordable,' the head of marketing.

'But we can't have a villain as our brand ambassador!'

'Sure we can, and in fact, we should,' Jay countered the suggestion. 'It is not only the most intelligent student of the class who gets attention but it is also the most notorious student. You know the backbenchers, right?'

'I always envied the backbenchers. The girls were always with them,' said the head of operations, regretting the fact that he was always studious and not a backbencher.

'I was a backbencher throughout. I gave my teachers a difficult time, and I am sure they still remember me.' Jay laughed. 'Coming to the point, we need a brand ambassador who can connect with at least three generations, and so, while thinking of the bad boys of Bollywood, we are left with three choices: Amrish Puri, Danny Denzongpa and Gulshan Grover.'

'Oh my God! I was guessing it right all along! It is Gulshan Grover,' the head of operations was amazed with how his guess was right.

'Yes. Unfortunately, Amrish Puri is no more. Danny is neither visible these days nor well-known in tier III and tier IV towns, and so we decided upon Gulshan Grover to be our brand ambassador,' the head of marketing explained the reason.

'...and so we will leverage the negative shades of Gulshan Grover to lure the consumers by influencing their desire for great steals on big brands,' concluded Jay. Soon, The Loot got a brand ambassador.

~

Dr. John, the professor, entered the class and greeted the participants. Around 100 entrepreneurs were participating in a one-week course run by London School of Business. The participants were from Young Professional Network (YPN). One could became a member of YPN only when they had their own business worth at least $20 million (Rs 100 crore).

'I welcome you to Day 3 of this course. It is my pleasure to be with all of you today,' Dr. John addressed everyone.

'Good morning,' the class replied.

'We have two more days to go for this week-long program. I hope your sessions were good till now.'

'We had some brilliant lectures,' said one of the participants, who was in his fifties.

'The upcoming sessions will be equally great, if not more,' Dr. John assured his class. 'As all of you know that the BRIC (Brazil, Russia, India and China) countries are the growth engines for global economy; remarkable business models are emerging from these countries. We will study one such case from India now.' Mr. John started his PowerPoint presentation. All eyes were on the screen.

'The Loot: The Loot is a multi-brand discount retail chain in India with 75 outlets and offers a mix of men, women and kids apparels ranging from formal, semi-formal, casuals and sports. It also offers a wide range of footwear, accessories and home linen. The Loot addressed the need of customers who aspired for branded goods but could not afford them...' He completed his 45-minute-long presentation. 'The house is now open for questions,' said Dr. John.

'How can it be profitable after selling stocks at such high discounts?' questioned one participant.

'How can a brand be created by keeping price as its only differentiator?' asked another participant.

'It is too dependent on dead inventory by brands,' said another.

'I can't clarify all your doubts. I do not work at The Loot,' smiled Dr. John, 'but I have someone in this room who can answer your questions.' Dr. John glanced at the last row and waved at Jay. The entire class turned to see him.

'Mr. Jay Gupta, the man who has created The Loot from scratch. He will himself answer all your doubts,' said Dr. John and introduced Jay to the class, who sat through the discussion.

He looked at the class: the participants were at least ten years older than him. 'They all are achievers, much more experienced than me and more successful than I am, and here I am, a college dropout, talking at one of the most prestigious business schools in the world to a class full of business leaders from across the globe. Life is amazing, everything is possible,' thought Jay.

'Good morning everyone. I thank Dr. John for giving me this opportunity to address achievers like you. It's a humbling experience,' Jay continued. 'I make money because somebody else made a mistake. Though it is true for all of us, it is rather obvious in my case.' Jay smiled and so did the entire class.

'When international brands have poor sales and excess stocks, we celebrate because we have better stocks to offer our customers.

'But after offering high discounts, how do you make money?

'The Loot's strength as a retail outlet lies in proper procurement and an excellent supply chain management. This helps in getting better pricing from the manufacturer and thereafter passing the benefit to the consumer. We are an opportunity bulk buyer, buying lacs of pieces of the same design at once. We buy stocks that have been produced in excess by brands, especially the designs in limited sizes, the large ones that didn't sell at higher prices in brand stores.

'We also make money due to the inefficiency of government departments, for example. At times, shipments from abroad get delayed due to customs clearance or other issues, and we pick up those stocks at throwaway prices.' Jay chuckled.

'What is the effect of recession on your business?' asked a participant.

'Well, I love the recession,' said Jay and looked at the participants. The entire class was taken aback by his statement. The United States was dealing with the subprime mortgage crisis and the whole world was heading towards one of the worst possible recessions. All of them just had one question: How could recession be good for anyone?

'When people have money, they buy branded clothes, but during a crunch, their brand aspiration is still there. They spend cautiously and start shopping smartly. The average discount offered by us is higher than what is offered during the sales season, and so a discount retail chain like ours does even better business,' explained Jay. 'Retail has five major costs: manpower, real estate, taxation, electricity and advertising. When the markets are down, we get good talent for less than what we would have to pay otherwise. Real estate prices and rents have dropped, too. Thus, recession is good. At least for us,' said Jay and smiled at the class.

'What if brands don't have excess or surplus stocks?'

'I agree with you. No brand can guarantee us continuous supply throughout the year, and so we introduced private labels to fill in the gaps,' said Jay, explaining the rationale for introducing private labels, which contribute over 25 percent to the company's revenues.

'Did you face problems when you started scaling up your business?'

'You can safely say that our path was laden with obstacles. We could not have grown like the "multinationals" did, by laying out a huge infrastructure at the very start and expecting profits after four or five years. We were trying out a new concept, and growing at the gradual pace was our best bet. On our way, we got mired by questions such as "should we build a team first and increase our costs, or expand and develop revenue streams. It was a chicken-and-egg dilemma". Often, we had no choice. We dealt with circumstances as they came our way. There were times we did not have funds to invest in planning and so we went firefighting.'

As soon as the session got over, all the participants gathered around Jay to talk. He was overwhelmed. Jay, a college dropout by choice, was thrilled that his business was being appreciated by some of the finest brains of the business world. After the session, when everyone had left, he sat on one of the classroom chairs and smiled. 'Life is amazing,' he thought. Never in his dreams did he imagine that he would achieve such an honour. The hard work, the sleepless nights and the anxious days seemed to be worth his effort. He called his wife and family in India. Even though ISD prices were sky-high, he couldn't contain his excitement: he had to share his joy with his close ones.

~

An evening of glitz and glamour: it was the party for the Tata NEN Hottest Start-ups, one of the biggest competition for Indian start-up companies. The room was full of India's Next Gen entrepreneurs. They all showed a lot of promise; while some would sustain the stormy seas and rewrite the rules of the game, others would succumb to the high tide of the sea and be lost. No one knew the future, but as of now, Jay was one among the many new age entrepreneurs participating in the contest. Though Jay had already won four different awards at the beginning of 2009, he was still very nervous. 'If I win this competition, it will reaffirm the belief in The Loot's business model. This may open new avenues to explore funds for further expansion of the brand.'

'We are one of the top five finalists.' Jay's face was glowing when he informed the good news to his CFO. Getting nominated to the final five was itself a great achievement for Jay (The Loot team). The Loot was selected from among hundreds of Indian start-ups. 'We have come so far, so we can't lose this one,' said Jay to the CFO and kept his fingers crossed.

Everyone set their eyes on the jury who was about to announce the name of the winner. 'It must have been a difficult choice. There is no dearth of talent in India. Each business idea deserves recognition. What a tough battle! We have to make it,' Jay thought. As the jury opened the envelope, Jay gripped his chair in nervousness and looked at the other four finalists. 'Please let us know, fast,' thought Jay. Every minute was a wait of a lifetime.

'The winner is a true-blue entrepreneur. When it was started, the company received neither any financial support from any investor nor any supply chain support from the brands it sold. It didn't have any industry recognition as well,' the announcer was in no mood to kill the suspense. 'After four years of surviving the highs and the lows of the sector, it has created a benchmark for itself. Ladies and gentlemen, the winner is...' he paused, which seemed to be a very long pause to Jay, '... the winner is The Loot.'

Jay jumped off his feet. His prayers had been answered. Silently, he thanked God. As he moved towards the podium, he heard the thundering applause in the background. Though he was conferred as a winner at 'CNBC Young Turks Awards', won the 'Most Promising Entrepreneur Award' by Asia Pacific Entrepreneurship Awards, 'Young Achiever Award' at Global Awards for Brand Excellence and plethora of other accolades, winning the TATA NEN Hottest Start-ups Award was the most prestigious feather in his cap.

His company was recognized as best among the emerging start-ups, and as he walked to the stage to accept his prize, he looked at the audience — it was overwhelming. As he accepted the 'trophy', and the audience stopped clapping, everything came to standstill. Jay wished for a time machine so that he could press the 'pause' button to experience the glory for a few more minutes. Though he was bubbling with excitement, he controlled his emotions, and, with a calm but firm voice, thanked the jury, sponsors and event organizers.

'It feels great to know that there are people in the industry who recognize perseverance and sincerity. The awards not only motivate us to work harder, but also let us know that we are on the right path. I thank TATA NEN for creating such a platform for start-ups. These platforms will encourage entrepreneurship and motivate people to propel new initiatives in India. I thank everyone who voted for us. I thank all our vendors, partners and all those people who believed in us, and, most importantly, I thank every employee of The Loot without whom this journey would have been impossible. It is our victory today. We promise that we will work harder to offer our customers high quality for a low price. Thank you all for the award.'

~

'Why is the signboard not lit?' asked Jay to the salesgirl at the counter on one of his unannounced visit to one of his stores in Nasik. The Loot was on a rapid expansion mode, and Jay was so busy opening new stores that visiting old ones had become a rare occasion: he visited this store after many months. After covering the metros, The Loot made its entry into tier II and tier III cities. Between 2007 and 2009, 100 new stores of The Loot were opened across the length and breadth of the country.

'Sir, the switch is not working,' she replied.

'Since when?' asked Jay in a stern voice.

'For about 15 days,' she stammered nervously.

'What, 10–15 days! Why?' he couldn't control his anger.

'I don't know, sir. I had informed the store manager,' she justified herself.

'Call the store manager,' Jay yelled.

The store manager came running.

'Good evening, sir,' the manager greeted him with a big smile.

'Why is the signboard not working?' Jay demanded an answer. Though he was angry, he kept his voice low because he did not want to shout in front of the customers.

'I have informed the electrician, sir. He will come in a day,' the manager replied casually.

'OK, let's go to the back office and talk.' Jay lost his temper at the manager's callousness, but remained calm.

'I want to see the financial reports. I will audit everything in your store right now,' Jay said, controlling his anger.

'You took a fan on rent and paid Rs. 8,000 for it? What is this?' Jay was stunned on seeing bills of this kind.

'Sir, the AC was not working, so we rented the fan,' explained the manager.

'What? Have you lost your brain? You paid Rs 8,000 for a fan on rent? You could have bought a new fan for just Rs 2,000. What kind of stupidity is this?' Jay was disturbed with lack of ownership among his employees.

'Will you wait for ten days to change a bulb in your house? Then why can't you do it here? Is it not your store? This is ridiculous!'

While everybody — from top management to the sales staffs — were working very hard for the company's growth, the middle management was lackadaisical and not aligned with the organization's goal. Jay wanted to break the barrier, but didn't know how to go about it. Soon, Jay realized that his hunger for expansion had come at the cost of a fatigued organization with disoriented and disconnected employees.

'Damn, how much can one person do? Build a business or build teams first? Ideally, both should happen simultaneously, but do I have the strength to do everything single-handedly? It all boils down to balancing, but the mere thought is so unbalancing.' Jay was caught in a trade-off once again.

~

'Like football, life is a game of inches. The margin for error is very small. One half-step too late or too early and you don't make it. One half-second too slow or too fast, and you don't quite catch it. The inches we need are everywhere around us,' quoted R. P. Chabbra, the CEO of The Loot, while addressing the employees in the annual meet to discuss the future course of action. The Loot had opened its 150th store the previous week. The management was aiming at another 100 stores in a year's time.

'We are playing our most important innings now. With expansion as our target, we have to be more aggressive in our approach. Since our inception, we have 150 stores pan-India. In the last year alone, we've added 75 stores. While a lot of companies have shut shop, we have moved forward at an express speed,' said Chabbra, referring to Subhiksha and Vishal Mega Mart, which had closed down. 'What is interesting is that in a recession-afflicted economy, we have grown because we responded to the need of the consumer to get greater value for money. With "Highest Quality at the Lowest Price" as our fundamental proposition, we are one of the very few businesses that are not just recession-proof but actually recession-friendly!' Chabbra quipped, and everybody in the room smiled.

'Looking ahead, the next two years are very crucial for us. We aim to add another 100 stores and, to manage the expansion, have invested in IT infrastructure. We have tied up with TCS (Tata Consultancy Services) to develop the back end to implement our own SME-ERP (small medium enterprise-enterprise resource planning) solution in order to make systems more efficient. A fully equipped and technologically upgraded warehouse has been set up at Bhiwandi to help us meet the challenges of expansion,' Chabbra continued. He looked at Jay for affirmation, and Jay nodded. The room was charged up, and the entire team was excited with anticipation of the future.

Jay stood up from his seat and looked around. 'Six years back, all I had was a small franchisee, and today we have crossed the 150-store mark. The unparalleled growth could not have been possible without all of you. Each one deserves a pat on the back. We have done an excellent job till now, but as they say, the bottleneck of the bottle is at its top. As we grow, it will become increasingly tough to improve our performance. The only way to achieve our goal is to invest in our people, and with this goal in mind, we have tied up with S. P. Jain Institute of Management and Research to train our team. This will give an opportunity to our 900 hardworking employees to better themselves,' said Jay, a firm believer in improving oneself continuously.

'As far as funds are concerned, we will take a call once the sensex settles down at 18,000 points,' said Jay, referring to the Rs. 100-crore initial public offering (IPO) that was postponed last year because of the economic depression. Instead they funded their expansion plans through bank loans.

~

'Sir, the journalist has come for the interview,' called the marketing executive.

'We have had our share of publicity, I don't want anymore. Inform the journalist that I am busy shifting the office right now. Our focus now has to be only on business. Our sustainability is in question. I don't have time for anyone except business,' said Jay. In just one year, the game had changed. The Loot was under tremendous financial pressure. The markets were depressing, and an IPO to raise funds was out of the question. The cost of interest took its toll on The Loot. To add to their woes, as Subhiksha, Vishal and other retail chains had closed down the banks had withdrawn funds from the retail industry.

Jay and his team had to cut the company's expenses. He was moving from his spacious 5,000 sq. ft. office to a smaller 1,000 sq. ft office. Jay had shifted his office for the fourth time since 2004. The Loot was a homegrown retailer. When funding and the market was good, they had bigger office spaces, but when times are bad economically and financially, they made their adjustment with smaller office spaces.

'Jay, I have analyzed store performances. We should close three more outlets in Gujarat. That will reduce our operational costs,' said Sunil Rathi, VP (finance).

'We have already closed so many stores. Now the strength of our employees have dwindled to a mere 200. Even then we are not able to pay them their salaries on time,' said Jay. Jay had ventured into retail business with the hope of an easy and happy life, but he was sinking in the quicksand of deeper financial troubles with every passing day.

'Yes, but these stores are cannibalizing our other profit-making stores. We have opened two stores extremely close to each other,' explained Sunil.

'Did you speak to the banks? Did anyone agree to give us a loan?' Jay knew that it wasn't just cannibalizing; the lack of working capital was another major reason why stores had to be shut down. Financial assistance from the banks would give them liquidity to battle the business slowdown. Also, with time, stores would become profitable and a lot of jobs could be saved.

'No, I don't think we will get any funds from banks because they are not funding the real estate and retail sector anymore. None of the Indian retailers are making money. Why will anybody, leave alone banks, fund this sector?'

'How everything changes so rapidly! Till last year, retailers like Vishal raised money through IPO and were oversubscribed, and now, we are not even getting loans,' said Jay dejectedly. He was desperate to make it work.

'Yes, inspite of an IPO, Vishal has gone for a complete lockout. Banks have even more reason to worry.'

'But the change is too drastic. I mean, all of a sudden, the entire sector looks depressing. There is so much pessimism around. Till last year, retail was booming and we were winning awards,' reflected Jay.

As George Orwell once said 'whoever is winning at the moment will always seem to be invincible'. Nobody predicted the rapid downfall of these retailers. The Loot and other retailers had seemed invincible.

~

Jay was standing in front of one of the closed store of The Loot. With tears in his eyes, he was shutting down one more unprofitable store. His survival looked bleak. The bait of easy life in business proved to be a mirage. In the last seven years, he has touched unprecedented heights, won multiple business awards and was hailed by media all across, but the easy life eluded him now. There was a time when he felt like a criminal even if he took two days off from the business.

The speed with which his stores were closing down was much faster than speed with which he opened them. Devastated, he drove to Marine Drive. It was around 1 am when he reached there. The darkness made him wonder if the night was darker or his future. Battling his emotional turmoil, he found solace in the silence of the sea. He kept gazing at the waves. It was a high tide. He felt a splash of water on his face. He kept looking at the tides. A few years back, he and many others were swept away by the high tide of retail, but just as the tide subsides and leaves the debris behind, Jay's world was torn apart. All he did these days was closing stores and attending court cases.

'Where did I go wrong? How would I have predicted retrospective tax on rent, introduction of excise duty and ever-changing compliances?

It was a sunrise industry that saw many illustrious entrants start with a lot of enthusiasm. Organized retail is increasing the tax net for government, generating employment opportunities and offering better products to the end customer. Instead of getting encouragement and incentives, the industry suffered due to poor policies.'

Every budget during the last three years clean bowled the retailers. Everybody involved in organized retail thought that, over time, the central and state governments would see the importance and merits of promoting a more efficient, modern retail distribution system and work towards simplifying, updating or eliminating archaic policies and systems such as the APMC and the MRP regime that forced retailers to sell goods at the same price at the ultra-high cost places like Colaba (Mumbai) or South Extension (Delhi) as in a tier IV town of Madhya Pradesh or Odisha. Around 20 different approvals or licenses from different government departments to open a store did not help the matter for anyone.

On top of it, the companies dealing in discounted readymade garments were subjected to dual taxation — they had to pay an excise duty on MRP for the production of garments and a service tax on 70 percent of expenses.

The additional cost of service tax on labour and retrospective service tax on rent made life miserable for retailers. The ever-growing fuel prices swelled the cost of running business and put pressure on profitability. The lesser growth in revenue, coupled with high taxes and interest cost and reduced operating margins, resulted in a distress situation for many companies. To make matters worse, the introduction of excise duty amplified the negative effect on already subduing purchasing power.

'Whatever could have gone wrong has gone wrong with retail. Was it completely about compliances and policies? Or was it about cutthroat competition in the industry? Maybe we could have planned better? Maybe we should not have scaled before ensuring sustainability. Perhaps dreaming too big and too fast was sin.' Jay knew that he was not alone. All major leading icons of modern retail were shutting down their stores. Only a few giant groups who had the capability of sustaining the onslaught of dual tax and other policies were able to survive, but many companies and groups were virtually wiped out.

Jay believed that he could have outperformed others if he had the required funds, the banks did not give further loans, and the interests were too high. Post recession, an IPO was also out of question. With enough funds for future, the The Loot's story would have been a different one.

'We are going through a rough time. We have never faced before what we are facing today. This experience is a good learning process but I don't want to go through this process ever. I have not bargained for all this trouble.' For Jay, it was not only a battle to salt away the business but also to fight a lot of legal issues. Vendors, brands, and banks had sent their notices on the issue of nonpayment.

'What will I do if there is no The Loot?' Detachment from the brand proved to be very difficult. As an entrepreneur, Jay has not lost hope yet. But he was no more the fearless Jay from Raxaul. Jay Gupta, the MD of The Loot, was apprehensive of his future.

The Loot was fast approaching complete lockout, and Jay and his team were trying very hard to revive the company. Losing patience was not an option for them as the entire process was time-consuming, and there was no magic by which the company that has suffered such serious setbacks could revive overnight. The only goal for Jay was to get The Loot out of this crisis and keep the brand alive.

~

'Damn, where did I go wrong? Should I blame the government's unfriendly policies or my own over-ambition?' Jay said aloud; there was no one to hear his plight. Retrospection and introspection were his only allies.

'How could have I fought the 12 percent labour tax, which raised labour cost? To add to it, the government added VAT (value-added tax) with the false hope that CST (central sales tax) would be withdrawn. I should not curse the government, but greed is not a virtue to appreciate,' he thought. 'These taxes could not satiate the government, so they introduced 12 percent service tax on rental property and that too retrospective for three years. To add to the misery, petrol prices went skyrocketing, messing up the entire distribution and supply chain. The great Indian laws!' He threw a large stone in the water, venting out his frustration.

'But I can't blame the government alone. Maybe I could have planned better. Maybe I ran too fast. I could have reduced my pace of growth. Maybe I overestimated the feasibility of my stores. The more stores I opened, the more sales got divided. The proportionate increase in cost was higher than the increase in revenue. I wish I had enough funds for the future.

'What an irony! I wanted an easy life which gave me a lot of time for myself and my family but the easy life eluded me.' He laughed at himself. 'In the past six years, I had everything but time. In good times, I was busy opening stores; in bad times, I am busy closing stores,' murmured Jay to himself. He remembered the time when he won almost every award held for entrepreneurs and retail innovation and how proud he felt when The Loot was ranked ninth in 'India's Fast Growth 25' survey conducted by AllWorld Network and Professor Michael Porter of Harvard Business School. All the fame and glory had now come to an end.

His eyes were dry now. He purged himself of his emotional heaviness. Slowly, the silence seeped in and he felt a sense of tranquility. He lay down on the sand and looked at the sky; its vastness was cooling.

As the dawn approached, he looked at his watch. It was 6 am, and he realized he had been sitting on the beach for hours. He stood up to take a walk. 'I am a businessman. I am bound to face business crisis. Right now I am going through a phase of depression, but I will soon recover and rise up again. I know I will,' he said to the sun and smiled.

'The reign of The Loot may have come to an end, but not mine. I am just 39 years old. I can start all over again.' He stood calmly and watched the sunrise.

THE LOOT

KEY LESSONS

KISHORE AHER

Kishore Aher is Founder of www.mygreatstay.com and www.primeservicedepartments.in. My Great Stay is pioneering the concept of home stays in India. He was head Buying and Merchandising department for Globus. He has seen Indian retail from close quarters and has always been a keen observer. He is an electrical engineer and did his MBA from IIM Ahmedabad.

~

This fascinating story of 'The Loot' is like an action packed movie. It's a tribute to indomitable spirit of Indian retailers who keep struggling hard to maintain cash flows and profitability.

Get Going

You live only once, so if you have an idea and the passion for that idea, then just get going. This is not only true about business but also about other aspects of life like writing a book, singing, climbing mountains, dancing or even proposing to your beloved.

Many of us have better financial and academic background than Jay, but we never start. He did.

Plan well in Advance

When you start, make a basic plan with some broad rules, and provide for possible scenarios. Be flexible to change the plan, as it will never be perfect at the first go.

Identify Problem Areas

Whether you hit success or failure, there are problems associated with both outcomes. Try to identify them in advance, so you are not surprised later. When in thick of action, there is no time to plan and reactions maybe hasty, which is not the best way to progress.

Operate at Brass Tacks

Hands on approach gives maximum knowledge. Till such time as company feedback systems become stable and efficient to output actionable data and information, it's better to be hands on. Be patient. It is easy to hire talented people, but for them to learn essence of the business will take time.

Don't Get carried Away

Whether times are good or bad, don't let any situation dominate you.

Maintain Reserved Capacity

This is true not only about capital but also about people i.e. keep a team ready, who can tackle difficult situations and are your most trusted resources.

Spirit of Enterprise Matters

Success and failure are part of the game. No one can predict market situations, government policies, rules and regulations and competition. Retrospective tax is the worst thing.

Keep the Spirit alive. Failure happens

As a nation we do not promote enterprise, so we think failures are a stigma and our financial institutions, government policies are not supportive to accommodate failures. It is very difficult to close a limited company in India.

If USA creates most innovative companies, who in turn create massive wealth for that nation, then it also has most number of bankruptcies declared. At the end, what matters most for all of us to succeed as a society; is to keep spirit of enterprise alive.

It was 'The Loot' as a venture which may have failed but not Jay. I am sure he would be back with a bang and I will wait for the day!!.

Brand is more than a brand name.

Yo!China is India's largest chain of Chinese restaurants with 60 points of presence in trendy locations across 22 cities.

Moods Hospitality Pvt. Ltd., the parent company has expanded through Yo!China Cafe, the large format cafes and Dimsum Bros, the premium fine dining restaurants.

To capture the market further, the founder Ashish has also launched an e-commerce venture called dreamcanteen, to deliver gourmet food and ingredients in Delhi-NCR.

The brand has big plans to launch 140 outlets in 50 cities in the near future.

6

YO! CHINA

ASHISH DEV KAPUR

When you want something, the entire universe conspires in helping you to achieve it.

Paul Coelho, *The Alchemist*

ASHISH CLOSED THE BOOK and got up from his bed. With blankets wrapped around himself, he looked out of the window. Outside, gods were pouring their wrath on earth. A steady stream of rainwater was hitting the window panes and smoothly flowing down. The road was empty, and the sound of raindrops falling on the road was deafening. He opened the window and put his hand out; the freshness of the freezing rain filled his entire being, and his mind contemplated on a fresh start. He closed the window and turned towards the study table to keep *The Alchemist* that he'd just finished reading.

The Alchemist is a book about a shepherd crossing a desert in search of a treasure and having strange experiences, only to realize that the real treasure was in his backyard, a realization that leaves an indelible impact on him. The treasure was finding one's destiny.

'What is my destiny?' Ashish thought. The question kept him awake through the thunder-filled night, thinking about the options he could explore. Ashish, at the age of 22, was contemplating his way ahead, or probably, his way back. A bright student throughout his academic life, he completed his engineering from McGill University, Canada, and had been working with General Electric (GE) North America for the past three years. At GE, he got a chance to work with various departments in different parts of the world and had bright chances of climbing the ladder quickly.

However, deep down inside something was missing. Coming from a family which had served India — many of his relatives having been posted at various government departments and civil services, he had an inherent pride for his country. He always wanted to come back to India and start his own business that would make his country proud.

He stared at the book. It was his moment of truth; it defined the journey that he had to take in pursuit of his destiny.

Everything looked possible. He picked up the phone and dialed Meghana's number.

'Meghana, I want to tell you something. I have decided to move back to India,' he said with excitement.

'Are you going by the next flight?' she asked in her sleepy voice.

'No, but why?'

'Then you can wait till morning. Bye, Ashish.'

'It's already 3 AM. See, I can't wait. It's crucial for our life. I need to discuss it right now,' he said with urgency.

'See if it's crucial, don't you think we should discuss it with fresh mind. A lack of sleep makes brain cells work slowly. We can't take this chance. What do you say?'

'We have to take this chance. You get up now and keep the coffee ready. I am coming in ten minutes,' he said and hung up. Ashish picked up his jacket and stepped out of the house. As he moved to the road, he realized that the rain had stopped. He took a deep breath, smiled and thought, 'The world is already reaching out to help me.'

~

While walking, it occured to Ashish that everything auspicious in his life had connection with a storm. When he met Meghana for the first time, Montreal was hit by a winter storm and there was a power failure due to the heavy snowfall. The local government had requested people to stay with friends or community as a group in one house to conserve electricity.

Ashish's roommate took him to his friend's place. His friend, the only Delhite in a group of Mumbaikars, was a victim of constant bantering, and so he took Ashish, an ace debater, to settle the scores. But even before he could lay open his cards, Meghana, a Mumbaikar, offered him a sandwich, and with one bite, he laid out his heart and thus started the classic tale of love at first sandwich.

~

He was totally engrossed in his thoughts when he reached Meghana's doorstep. It was chilly. 'No wonder she didn't want to wake up,' he thought and rang the bell.

'Good morning,' he greeted her with a beaming smile.

'Well, I am not sure about good, but it is definitely a very early morning,' she said bringing two cups of coffee and handing one to Ashish. 'OK, shoot,' she said with a straight face. In the freezing winter, if getting up at 4 AM was torturous, then pushing someone to make coffee was suicidal, so Ashish preferred to focus on the agenda.

'Well, as you know that shifting to India was always on the cards, but I wasn't able to muster the courage to take this decision.' He paused to see if Meghana was listening or nodding sleepily. Seeing her attentive, he continued, 'After reading *The Alchemist* I have made a conscious decision that it is the right time to pursue my dream.'

'Finally, you have decided to take the Bollywood route,' she sighed.

'No, I have dropped the plans as of now,' he said and looked at Meghana, who seemed more interested in the conversation now with a wide smile and sparkling eyes. 'I am pondering over three business ideas, out of which we need to choose one. The main reason I came here is to discuss which one is the most appropriate.'

She straightened her back and tied her hair and geared herself for an intelligent discussion.

'I see a huge scope in budget airlines like Southwest Airlines. India doesn't have any. In fact, I studied about the low-cost airlines model while working in GE. In India, the success rate of such a model would be very high. I wonder why no one has started a budget airline. What do you say?'

'What a phenomenal idea!' Meghana said. 'I am sure the Indian government would be indebted to you for this, and Tatas and Birlas would come at your doorstep to invest in you. A 22-year-old engineer with no experience in aviation wants to start a low-cost airline business in Indian market with zero financial backing!' Meghana teased.

'Don't be sarcastic. Everything is possible as long as one believes in it,' he defended.

'Move on to the second idea,' she cut him short.

'Other option is an IKEA kind of do-it-yourself (DIY) furniture store. There is a clear gap in need for such store in India.'

'DIY stores! That's a refreshing idea from a lazy Punjabi guy who can't even keep a glass of water in place,' she quipped.

'Stop bantering! This is a serious discussion,' said Ashish.

'OK, OK. On a serious note, Ashish, this idea again calls for a huge capital investment, and considering your credentials and age, I don't think we would get investors. It sounds too ambitious. We may revisit the idea a few years later. What's the third option?'

'Unexpectedly, it's an intellectual response,' he teased. 'Well, the third idea is a chain of restaurants. I have not zeroed in on the cuisine; it may be either north Indian, or south Indian, or Chinese.'

'Yes. This sounds perfect. You won't even need much of capital to start with.'

'But, Meghana, are you fine with my leaving everything and going back to India? I would be unemployed and would have hit rock bottom,' he asked, as they were thinking of getting married.

'Hey, it's not you, it's we who are going to India, and reaching rock bottom. Besides, opening a company is still better than reaching rock bottom and struggling to be an actor.' She smiled, and he was relieved.

~

'Mom...Dad...' shouted Ashish as he banged the door and entered. His parents ran towards him and saw his swollen leg, bruised face and torn school shirt.

'What happened?' his mother exclaimed.

'Don't ask what happened, ask why it happened,' Ashish was livid.

'First of all you sit. Let me get the first aid box and then you can tell me how it happened,' said his mother.

'It all happened because of you. Why do you have to take so many transfers in your job? I was all set in India, in a good convent school. I was well recognized, I used to win every debate competition, but you took me to Iran and made me study in a gurdwara-run school. It was more like a Punjab *ka pind* (a village of Punjab), where even a word of English hurt Punjabi pride.' He moaned.

'But, my dear son, you were the main lead in almost every play and you made so many good friends. Why do you have to cry about it now?'

'That's OK, but then you brought me to Italy. I jumped from Class VII to Class XI. Every time I enter the class, I feel out of place. On the playground, I feel like a dwarf playing with body builders,' he said getting up from sofa and standing in front of his parents. 'See what those hulks did? You won't be able to count the wounds. My back is aching, ouch!' he cried and collapsed into the sofa.

'Stop crying like a baby and don't blame us. Did we not give you the option of staying in India and completing your studies? You could have resumed from Class VIII. You were well aware of the education system here. It was your choice. So why are you complaining now?' said his father in a strict voice.

'Now that is unfair! You took me to Iran without giving me an option, and when it came to a country like Italy, you gave me a choice. Why would I give up Italy and live in India alone?'

'Then face it. Even if it is not your choice, you need to learn to face the situation, fight it out and win. My son, heroes don't cry and complain. They invest time in thinking how to make things better,' his father consoled him and stroked him on his shoulder.

'Ouch!' he cried in pain. 'When I am in pain, you want me to be a hero. Otherwise, you are always against it,' he defended himself.

His father laughed and said, 'It isn't about physical pain, son. It is about the fighting spirit of a hero. Even if you are hurt physically, never let your spirits get hurt, no matter what.'

Though he mellowed down at the mention of being a hero, his heart wanted to rant a bit more 'But, Dad...'

'No ifs and buts. Don't make a mountain out of a molehill. You will face tougher situations in life and you have to succeed.'

~

Ashish and Meghana boarded the flight for South Africa. It was a long flight, and a lot of thoughts raced through Ashish's mind. It was a difficult decision; he had tried to approach various investors but had no luck. He could not convince them to invest in his idea, but after each meeting, his conviction increased. All investors raised questions he had not thought about, and each time, he pushed himself to evaluate the business proposal in a new light.

'Ashish and Meghana, what a pleasant surprise! We are so glad to see you,' his mother said with excitement.

After they had settled in, his father asked, 'I feel you have come here for a specific reason. This is not just a surprise visit. There is something on your mind.'

'Yes, Dad, I have been thinking about something for a long time.'

'You rest now. We will discuss it over dinner,' said his father.

Meghana and Ashish's mom sat for a chat while Ashish crashed in bed, but he could not sleep. He was speculating on his parents' reaction. His parents had already tagged him as eccentric. His passion to be an actor was beyond their comprehension.

He fondly remembered the incident when his parents were so worried that they took him to an astrologer, 'Please do something so that he gives up his craze for acting.' Coincidently, that astrologer happened to be a distant relative of Karan Johar, the movie director.

He started praising Bollywood and showed them the letter of appreciation by Karan Johar, who had also sought his advice. The look on his parents' face flashed before his eyes, and he laughed.

At dinner, his father asked, 'Tell me, what's going on in your mind?'

'I have decided to go back to India,' he said, paused and looked at his parents. Their calm turned into an expression of horror. 'I want to open a chain of restaurants there.'

'Now, what is this new idiocy? First, you wanted to become an actor, and now you wish to become a waiter. Moreover, do you want to leave a prestigious company like GE in America and want to go to India and open a roadside restaurant? Can't you think straight?'

'Dad, first, it is not a roadside restaurant, I want to open a chain of restaurants, and second, I have already left GE,' he broke the most difficult piece of news. His mother looked at him with disbelief.

'Are you mad? You are about to get married. What will you say to Meghana's father? And, Meghana, do you want to marry an unemployed man with the crazy dream of opening restaurants? Ashish, do you even remember when you last visited India? Do you have any idea how difficult it is to start a business in India?' She was shocked with this news.

'Yes, she has a point. Why can't you start your chain of restaurants in America? You could have done that while you were still in job, and once things have settled down, you could have left your job. Why did you have to leave your job before everything was in place? Can't you act with maturity?' Ashish's father wanted to know.

'Dad, I want to serve India the way you have done, the way everyone in our family has done. It is not just about profit. I want to do my business for both pride and profit. An American food chain opens in India and India goes mad on it. I want to take an Indian food chain to America. Maybe, one day, I will open my restaurant in Times Square. You will see that,' he panted as he finished. His mother offered him a glass of water.

'Well, since you have already decided, it's fine. I am happy that you gave up the idea of becoming an actor and thought of a start-up,' his father was relieved.

'You don't know Bollywood will be missing a superstar. I am being generous to the business community,' Ashish said.

Ashish's parents knew that now there was no stopping for their son. Once he decided something, he wouldn't waver from it, and so they focused on the practical questions.

'How much would be the initial investment?' his father enquired.

'It would be around Rs. 70 lacs.'

'That is a huge sum. Your father is in service. How will you manage the funds?' his mother enquired.

'We need to search for an investor.'

'OK, did you try to find an investor in America?' his mother asked.

'Yes, I met one, but he was more interested in hooking up his daughter with me... Meghana would have killed me.'

'Hmmm...' his father took a deep breath. 'I have a person in mind. I suggest you meet him. His name is Arun Chadha, and I am sure he will help you,' his father said searching for Mr. Chadha's number in his mobile.

Ashish's face brightened. 'The great Indian parents!' he thought. 'Once you decide to work on something, even if it's against their wishes, they will always support their child.'

'You have a meeting with Arun tomorrow at 8 PM. Join him for dinner. Give your best shot. We are always there with you.' His father hugged him.

~

The next evening came too soon. Ashish was nervous, but confident.

'Sir, I want to build Moods Hospitality, a company which would own a chain of restaurants. The unique feature of these restaurants would be their ambience, and the menu will change as per the mood...' he continued to explain his concept for the next half an hour.

'Agreed, but you are an engineer. What value can you add in the food business?' said Mr. Chadha.

'Sir, the very fact that I have identified this opportunity is a value addition. No one else thought of it. As far as rules of the game are concerned, they can be learned, that's not rocket science. You don't need to be a pilot to start an airlines business. The greatest value addition, I think, is the vision itself.'

'Have you done any research on this?' he asked.

'Yes, I have evaluated and compared the offerings and price points of at least 50 restaurants in the category.' He remembered how Meghana and he went to restaurants to steal the menu. In every restaurant they ordered French fries, as it was the cheapest item on the menu. After three days, he vowed that he will not eat any more French fries for next three years.

'Hmmm...Well, to be quite honest, I don't understand this restaurant business much, but I see the passion and sincerity in you, so I will invest in you. Whatever support you require from my side, ask for it and I will provide that,' said Mr. Chadha.

'Thank you so much, sir.' Ashish was overwhelmed.

'In fact, I suggest you meet Mr. Joydeep Singh when you go to India. I am sure he will help you out. I will give you his number and will tell him about your proposal.'

The auspicious meeting concluded. Ashish was glad that he chose to fly down to South Africa to meet his parents. It was a blessing in disguise that he found his first investor in South Africa.

~

'Hey, Meghana, what do you think? Will he like our concept? I think he will appreciate out-of-the-box thinking,' said Ashish, excited about his meeting with Sanjeev Kapoor, one of the most renowned chefs in the industry, anchor of a cookery show *Khana Khazana*. Meghana knew Sanjeev Kapoor and his wife, and she had fixed his meeting with Ashish so that he could get an expert's view.

It was Ashish's most awaited dinner: he was waiting eagerly to have Sanjeev Kapoor's feedback.

They reached the restaurant 15 minutes early. Ashish browsed the menu and quietly kept it in his bag. Meghana gave him a stern look, but she was aware of his habit of collecting and preserving the menu cards of all the restaurants he went to.

'I am confident that with the speed with which you collect menu cards, you will soon have your name in the *Guinness Book of World Records* for the largest collection of menu cards from all over the world,' Meghana teased him.

Soon, Sanjeev came with his wife. After exchanging pleasantries, Sanjeev asked him about his plan. For half an hour, Ashish vividly explained his concept of a restaurant wherein ambience and menu will change daily as per the mood of a customer. When he finished, Sanjeev smiled at him.

'It is definitely an interesting idea, but to evaluate whether or not it will be financially viable or not, you have to answer a few questions. Let us start with understanding the psychology of a person who wants to eat out. Primarily, a typical Indian goes to a restaurant to enjoy food, and so the first thing is to decide the cuisine he wants to eat. If the menu and ambience are changing, how would a person decide? Initially, out of curiosity, one may want to visit and revisit, but for how long? Curiosity is not a strong emotion to base your business model on. The biggest flaw of your model is unpredictability. A majority of people don't like guessing, especially when it comes to eating out. Even if we discount this factor, tell me what your brand would stand for? What would you specialize in? You won't be able to give an answer because the experience that you offer to the consumer is inconsistent. People need to know what you are about, so keeping the focus becomes very important.' He paused and waited for a response from Ashish, who looked a bit fazed by his comments.

'I don't mean to discourage you. It is just that I want to give you a different perspective. There may be some points that you haven't thought through, and I am just shedding light on those. Talking about logistics, if your offerings change every day, how will you manage so many menus? The more the number of menus, the more will be the inventory required. Every item on your shelf represents a possibility for loss. It can be stolen, mishandled or stored incorrectly and thus spoiled. The less the inventory items, the less will be the waste,' finished Sanjeev. By this time, Ashish was choked up. 'Perhaps, I was so obsessed with my idea that I overlooked the obvious,' he thought.

'Ashish, the restaurant business is very complex, and your model is adding to the woes. It looks impossible to me. This industry is very tough, and succeeding here is even tougher.'

Finally, he ended his questions and analysis. More than food for the stomach, he had food for thought.

'Your questions are very valid, sir. I will rework on my initial thoughts and see how I can make it work in this industry. Maybe I need to unlearn and look at my model with a fresh perspective, but I'm grateful to you for the clarity you have given me. It will help me to improvise on my idea,' Ashish said with determination.

'I just want to tell you again that it isn't as easy as it looks. It is very complex, and what you want to do is even more complicated.'

'I understand, but everything is complex initially in any business. Complexity is not a good enough reason to give up on any idea.'

Sanjeev paused and then smiled. 'You know, Ashish, I am glad that your belief in yourself is much stronger than the negativity around. I wanted to test that, and that is why I was so negative. If you can survive the pessimism around, you will succeed. If you gave up your idea just because I told you, the idea wasn't worth it. When you start a business, you are bound to face a lot of difficulties.'

For Ashish, this meeting served as a reality check. Earlier, he felt proud of the uniqueness of his concept. After this meeting, he thought that if no one had thought of it even in countries that were much more advanced in retail, there must be something wrong in the idea.

The perspective that Sanjeev offered pushed him to re-evaluate the idea and unlearn what he had learnt till now.

After the meeting with Sanjeev Kapoor, Ashish reworked on his presentation and geared himself up to meet the investor Mr. Chadha from South Africa has referred. Joydeep Singh, living in Delhi, was Mr. Chadha's brother-in-law.

'Sir, I am Ashish. Mr. Chadha must have told you that I would call.'

'Oh yes, he told me about you. How are you doing, Ashish? Indeed, I was waiting for your call,' he replied.

'Sir, when is a convenient time to meet you?'

'We can meet right away. I am at the golf club right now. We can meet outside Saket Golf Club. How much time will you take to reach there?'

'About half an hour.'

'Done, see you in 30 minutes or so.'

Unlike any other meeting with an investor, their first meeting happened under the pole light near the golf club. It was a casual conversation, and Ashish explained about his plans.

'I am working on building an indigenous chain of Chinese restaurants where we will be serving authentic Chinese cuisine. Right now there are a lot of restaurants serving Chinese cuisine, but they are largely owned and operated by a single person, and thus their authenticity is in question. My focus is to establish Yo!China as a quick service restaurant serving authentic Chinese food at an affordable price. It will be a brand for the youth with the target group mainly comprising the student community, young working professionals and families. My aim is to have a national presence in the next five years.'

'Why did you zero in on Chinese cuisine?' Joydeep Singh enquired.

'I did extensive research, and as per the results, Chinese emerged as the most preferred choice of cuisine among youngsters. In fact, it is the second-most ordered food in India. There is a lot of scope for innovation. For example, American chopsuey is available neither in America nor in China but sells a lot here in India. Moreover, I want to offer food that people generally don't cook at home. So taking all these factors into consideration, Chinese was the best choice.'

Mr. Joydeep thought for a moment and asked, '...and why did you choose the name Yo!China?'

'Yo!China sounds youthful and trendy and spells out energy. It's also simple and direct in meaning.'

'Apart from engineering and entrepreneurship, you also have a creative instinct — Yo!China... interesting,' Joydeep remarked.

'No, no, it isn't my idea. We had taken the help of two advertising professionals, Fredy and Navid, who suggested this name. They are working on other communication elements and will help us with their insights on how to build the brand,' Ashish informed.

'Actually, investment isn't a problem. I will invest, but I think I can also add value. Would you mind if I come in as a marketing consultant? I have more than a decade of experience in marketing. I see a lot of scope in this idea.'

'Oh sure. In fact, I am looking for people who can share their passion. You are more than welcome.'

Without any presentation or formal pitching, Ashish got his second investor and a team member.

~

'Meghana, life is actually the way Paulo Coelho had described. When you really want to do something, the whole universe opens up. Not only did I get investors, but also my first co-founder. Remember, I told you about Mr. Joydeep Singh. Apart from investing, he wants to work with us. He believes that Yo!China is a great idea.' Ashish was exhilarated.

'That is great news!'

'There is more! God has been really kind, and everything is falling in place. I was in discussions with Sampat Talwar and Mandhir Soni, and fortunately, they are also joining us as co-founders. Not only this, remember, I told you that I needed a person from food industry. One of my friends introduced me to Ajay, the owner of Turquoise Cottage. I met him today, and guess what! He agreed to join us. So now we are a team of six.' Ashish was excited.

'Wow, that's wonderful news! Ajay is running such successful restaurants. I wonder why did he agree to join you? You have not even opened a restaurant yet and still he agreed. What magic did you do?' Meghana was surprised.

'That's my style, you see. What if I am not a reel-life hero, I am a real-life hero.' He winked.

'Now can we cut the crap...' she snubbed him.

'In fact, I made it clear that it will be a private limited company and all of us would be co-founders not partners. Though they are 10-15 years elder, I would be the managing director and all reporting and procedures would be as per the organization structure.'

'OK, that is good,' she remarked.

'It seems like we are on our journey from good to great.'

'Are you talking about our marriage or Yo!China ?'

'Both,' said Ashish and smiled.

Ashish and Meghana got married two months before the first Yo!China outlet was opened, but the long-awaited event in their life was the opening of their first restaurant.

~

'Joy, it's really nice of you to invite Kapil Dev for our launch.' Ashish was excited when Joydeep informed him about Kapil Dev's confirmation on attending Yo!China's launch.

'He could not have refused. I told him Yo!China was one of its kind. It is a restaurant that matches international standards where you would find display kitchens. Besides Kapil Dev, I have invited a 100 more guests,' said Joydeep.

'In total, we have invited almost 350-400 guests. I wonder how many will turn up. Ajay, do you have any idea?' Ashish enquired.

'I don't think the number will exceed 70,' his words were taken as final as he was the veteran in the industry.

Suddenly Shalini, who looked after business development, came running. 'Ashish, we are in trouble. I just received a call from our furniture vendor, and he won't be able to deliver the furniture today.'

'What do you mean "he won't be able to deliver today"? We have our launch tomorrow. What will we do without furniture? Where will people sit? And how could he back out at the last moment. He had given the confirmation,' remarked Ashish. Faced with an unexpected situation, even before he learnt restaurant management, he had got himself into disaster management. The excitement of launch turned into terror. Ashish called up the furniture vendor and scolded him. Ajay and Mandhir called up other vendors to arrange the furniture for rent.

Ashish wondered even having done everything as per *Vaastu Shastra,* chosen Wednesday — an auspicious day for launch, he still found himself in the middle of mayhem.

'Ashish, fortunately, a vendor has agreed to supply us furniture immediately, but he has office chairs only,' Ajay informed after contacting almost 20 suppliers.

'What the hell? We will start our first restaurant with office chairs. That means a complete screw up of ambience.'

An emergency was declared. Everyone cross-checked everything and followed up with the furniture vendor every hour.

Finally, by the end of the day, the restaurant was set with office chairs.

'It's a pain to see our dream coming true with a compromise,' Ashish said to his wife, Meghana, who was assisting him in setting up the restaurant. After marriage, Ashish and Meghana had not taken a break but immersed themselves in setting up Yo!China.

'Sometimes things don't go as planned. Relax. Just make sure that you compensate it through excellent food so that people forget about ambience,' she consoled him.

'I really hope we get good reviews.'

~

On May 7, 2003, at MGF Mall, Gurgaon, Yo!China was launched. The co-founders, Meghana and the staff were busy arranging things for the big day.

Suddenly, Ashish felt drops of sweat on his forehead. 'How come I am so nervous today?' he thought and then realized that the air conditioner wasn't working.

‘Hari, switch on the AC. It’s so hot,’ he said.

‘Sir, neither the ACs nor the exhaust is working,’ Hari said in a shaky voice.

Everyone turned towards Hari. No one said a word. Ashish looked at his companions in disbelief. ‘First, it was the furniture and now the AC, bad omens,’ he thought, remembering *The Alchemist*.

‘Sir, last night, I checked all the ACs and exhausts. They were in perfect working condition, but today, when I switched the AC on there is a water leakage and some other technical problem. Though I can fix this problem but it will be time-consuming, and we are short on time. I am sorry, but we can’t do anything about it now,’ said Hari, the in-house electrician, confirming everyone’s fears.

‘When something has to go wrong, it will go wrong. I am not saying so, Murphy said so. It is Murphy’s law,’ said Ashish, looking at Ajay, who gave him a blank look. ‘Ajay, I am really worried about our invitations. We have invited around 400 guests. What if even half of them turn up? How will we manage that kind of crowd? We estimated a turnout of 70 guests. On top of it, the air conditioners and exhausts are not working. It is scorching hot outside. We have a display kitchen. What will we do with the billowing of smoke?’

‘We can only pray that my estimates go wrong,’ said Ajay, half-concerned and half-baffled at the turn of events.

At around 7.30 PM, people started coming in, and soon, there was no stopping them. Till 9 PM, they greeted the guests. Soon, the situation went beyond their control.

‘Ashish, more than relishing this food, people would be cursing us for this torture. What do we do about the smell and smoke? Our exhausts are not working. Everyone’s eyes are smarting from the smoke. Look at Kapil Dev. His eyes are red. He is eating with spoon in one hand and a tissue in another to clean his eyes,’ said Joy. The excitement turned into visible disappointment.

It was utter chaos; no one knew how to handle the situation. Everybody’s eyes were red and pricking. The smoke, due to tangy Chinese ingredients like vinegar, soya and chili sauce, increased the irritation.

Finally, the longest four hours of their life ended and they returned home disappointed. It was a disaster of a kind he had never imagined in wildest dreams.

'Meghana, today was honour killing in its literal sense. We messed up terribly. People must be laughing at us.'

'It is just a matter of time. This isn't such a big issue. People have a short-term memory. They have even forgetten bigger scams. Next time, give them a good ambience and great food and they would eventually forget what happened yesterday,' she reassured him.

'I just hope so.'

~

At 11.30 PM, after bidding goodbye to last customers for the day, the chairs were pulled aside and the restaurant's lights were changed to disco lights. Though staff parties at Yo!China was a common occurence, this one had a special purpose.

When all the staff settled in, Ashish addressed everyone.

'Guys, I know that at this late hour you are in no mood to listen to any kind of speech; you must be craving for food and dance.

'I will come to the point. Despite a horrifying start, we have recovered our capital within seven months, which is both great and unexpected. We had a humble beginning: I used to take orders, Meghana took charge of reception, Ajay took over the kitchen, Joy handled the cash, Sampat and Mandhir looked after other operations and financials. Now all of you have replaced us and have done an extremely good job. There have been Sundays when we had to close down during lunch because we run short of supplies. It's great to know that we are able to pull in that kind of a crowd, and it's also worth appreciating that now we have geared up ourselves to face a much larger clientele.

'Even the media has started acknowledging our efforts. Recently, the editor of *HT City* came to Yo!China, and they will be publishing our review on Sunday. They liked it so much that they had sent their special photographer to take pictures. I request all of you to read this Sunday's *HT City* issue and ask all your friends and relatives to read it. That will be a proud moment for us. Now let's party to celebrate our success and efforts in advance.'

The party went well into the wee hours. Ashish made sure that his employees had a great time. He always gave priority to employees' bonding. Whether it was an employee's birthday, or any festival, their team was always together.

~

It was a Sunday morning and Ashish woke up earlier than usual. The previous night, he had a dream: big front-page article flashing accolades about Yo! China. 'People say morning dreams come true,' he thought, and with a smile on his face asked Meghana to get the newspaper. 'Meghana, give me the paper,' he demanded.

'Just leave it,' she said hesitantly, holding onto the newspaper rather tightly. She was pale.

'What do you mean? We have our review on the front page.' He was puzzled by her reaction.

'Actually, it's not best of the reviews,' she said while handing him the newspaper. Ashish read the article and was horrified.

'It's not the best! It is the worst review I have ever read. It's restaurant's first review and he has screwed me up on everything — ambience, food, service! How can everything go so wrong?' He had been shocked to see the headline 'Yo No No.' He read it again in disbelief.

Meghana waited for him to speak. Finally, after about an hour's silence he spoke. 'You know it feels as if someone has slapped me hard. It was not the same with GE. I mean, I would not have taken it personally if someone would have abused GE. Maybe when a person becomes an entrepreneur, he becomes inseparable from his business. It's like when a movie is a hit, all the credit goes to the actor, but when it flops, it is the actor who is blamed.' He paused and continued, 'You know, I requested almost everyone I knew, to read the newspaper today.'

'Ignore it now. We can't do much about it.'

'We can,' he said as he got up to dress. Meghana was surprised.

'Where are you going?' she asked.

'I am going to meet the person who wrote this article. I will ask him to walk me through each and every point. For me, he is a disappointed customer, and I need to know the reasons for his disappointment so that I can work on them. I am sure I will win him back,' he said and left.

~

'What is happening? It's our first day in home delivery division and already this phone refuses to stop ringing,' said the receptionist, Karan to Ashish in frustration. 'It's just 2 PM and I have already received almost 40 orders. By the time I note down an order, the phone rings again. It is maddening. How do I keep track of all these orders?'

'This is beyond our imagination. We have received orders worth Rs.15,000 within two hours. We are still receiving orders. Ajay, how do we handle such a huge number of deliveries? We are just not prepared to cater to so many people. How did you handle the rush at Turquoise Cottage?' asked Ashish.

'We did not have home delivery facility there,' he answered.

'Then why did you suggest it here?'

'Ashish, now don't get angry. We always wanted to cross the barrier of physical space and reach out to more number of people. Home delivery was always the right strategy for expansion, helping us increase our market share. The actual problem is that we are not equipped to handle such huge number of orders,' Ajay said objectively.

'Sir, we have 60 orders so far, and customers have already started complaining that they haven't received their orders yet. Some of them are livid. They are shouting at us,' the manager said in haste. Even the staff could not match the pace of the orders they received.

'What do we do now? There is no way that we can fulfill these orders as per the customer's preference,' said the chef.

'This will be a major blow for Yo!China. How do we save our image?' Ajay asked, trying to think of the repercussions it could have.

'We need to think of a solution fast,' said Ashish.

'I think we should make two types of parcels: vegetarian and nonvegetarian. We will go to each house, apologize for the delay and deliver the parcel as per their preference for free,' Joydeep came up with a solution.

'Joy, are you OK? You are asking us to deliver orders worth more than Rs. 20,000 for free!' Ajay was stumped.

'Ajay, actually, it is a great suggestion. It will serve two purposes. It will not only conceal our mistake, but also delight the customer. Look at it as a marketing activity. As entrepreneurs, we need to have the thick skin of a rhino and the heart of a lion,' Ashish finished.

'Yes, you are right. Let's arrange the parcels in my car. Gosh, among this chaos, how will we serve the guests today?' Ajay wondered.

At 11 PM, after delivering the last order Ashish took a sigh of relief. Instead of being angry, people were amused that meals were delivered by the restaurant owners and that too free of cost.

'This was the second most chaotic day of my life, the first day of home delivery service. The calls were far more than expected, around 100 callers ordered food, and we served them all... This country offers such an infinite scope. You never know it unless you do it. I am glad that I did it,' Ashish said to Meghana while driving back home.

Soon, restaurant and home delivery operations were streamlined. Staffing and recruitment issues were also sorted out. The time was ripe to take the next step.

~

'Ashish, Ajay, Sampat and Mandhir, the agenda to call this meeting is that we should now focus on expansion. We have tested the waters, and I think now is the time to swim. What do you say?' said Joy.

'Yes, Joy, you are absolutely right. It's the time for opening our next outlet. I think we should refer to our initial plan. We had identified the areas where we would open our restaurants. But we need venture capitalists (VCs) to invest in our next outlet. We don't have enough internal accruals, and only if we get backing from VCs, we can scale up faster. What do you think?' Mandhir suggested.

'Precisely, we were always clear that we need to make Yo!China a chain of restaurants, and approaching VCs was inevitable for us,' Joydeep reaffirmed.

'Then our first step is to start working on presentations right away,' Ashish said and smiled at Joy, who gave an annoyed look.

'Why can't these VCs understand a business proposition without a presentation? Is it rocket science? I wonder how the entrepreneurs who don't know computers woo the VCs,' said Joydeep. He was inept at computers. Ashish taught him how to open a mail account but Joydeep had a tough time learning the basics of computer.

'Don't worry. You have a GE guy with you, who also happens to be a master in MS Office.' Ashish smiled.

'Coming to the point,' Ajay interrupted, 'we need to be equipped to answer the questions that the VCs will ask. They can ask us anything, ranging from "what Yo!China stands for" to "who are we targeting" to "what our USP is". So let's pen them down.'

'Let us focus on what Yo!China stands for. Well, Yo!China is a young brand that offers a variety of authentic Chinese food, and not Indian Chinese, at an affordable price,' Sampat said and checked with all of them, if it sounded fine. '...along with international ambience and great service standards,' he further added.

'Actually, they are the four pillars of Yo!China. First, is "quality" — we serve authentic Chinese cuisine. Second, "affordability" — the whole experience is more value for less. Third, "superfast" — like our growth, our service is also superfast. Fourth, its "international ambience and standards",' said Ashish noting every point.

'What will be our differentiator?' Joy asked.

'Our four pillars will lead to our differentiation. Our ambience will not have those Chinese dragons which we find in every other Chinese restaurant. Like our first restaurant, we will offer sophisticated and bright ambience, and we will make our service unique. Right now in India, Chinese food is served in bowls. We will serve food more gracefully and properly in plates, and in our menu, we will focus on combo meals,' Ashish replied.

The whole month was spent on polishing the presentation. Even before they could approach the VCs, the VCs approached them, and soon, they got their first round of funding. With funding came the stake, expertise and guidance of the VC in the company.

~

'The profitability of one restaurant is fine, but the profitability of chain of restaurants is a different ball game altogether. I want to know your approach towards expansion,' asked one of the VCs.

'We plan to set up a base kitchen,' Ajay explained, 'so that every product is standardized across geographic boundaries. From our food colour to taste to aroma, everything remains the same.'

'Well, once you fix the taste and set the processes, you need to get your hands on to supply chain and inventory management. But these are operational issues. What will be your approach towards branding? What would you want people to perceive Yo!China as?'

Ashish took the charge to answer the question. He passionately explained the four pillars. 'We want to create an aspirational brand for the youth of this country. We want Yo!China to be synonymous with a cool and trendy hangout.'

'But why do you think that youth of this country will spend on an aspirational brand?'

'Sir, the disposable income of the middle class is increasing, and around 45–50 percent of our country comprises of youth. With the call centers and BPO culture, youngsters are spending like never before,' Ashish explained.

'Yes, the great Indian middle class! What do you think the brands like Big Bazaar, McDonald's, Koutons, Vishal Mega Mart, etc., are doing? Are they selling for aspiration or need? See, I am trying to drive the point home that aspiration product is a value game, while a need fulfilling product is a volume game. Imagine in a country like India, where volumes are huge, what scale can a business achieve? So I would just like to advise you to rethink. Do you want to go for an aspirational product or a value proposition?'

'How can he ask me to redefine the basis of Yo!China?' Ashish was lost in his thoughts. 'Our concept is right, our performance testifies it, but he is an experienced person. If he is putting across a point, there must be some logic. I should not be biased. He knows the market better than me. He has been funding companies and mentoring entrepreneurs. I should probably go the way he suggests.'

'Ashish, are you there? Are you listening?' the VC asked, seeing that Ashish was lost in thought. 'Oh yes, very much. I guess you are right,' Ashish said, looking at Joydeep, who didn't seem to be impressed.

'There is one more concern. When you expand geographically, the rules of the game change. If you are not prepared, please don't take the step. The set of stakes are higher than what you have been exposed to so far. There is a difference in creating a company and expanding it. At every class in school, the level of difficulty increases and the student needs a competent teacher to guide him through the examinations. Similarly, when business expands, one needs experienced people to take them through that phase. To hone your skills and understand the business dynamics better, you and your co-founders might need to work under somebody. I hope you would not mind it because that is in the interest of your business.'

Ashish looked at Ajay and Mandhir, who were totally baffled with the VC's suggestions.

'They did not buy the theory of bringing bosses above us, but isn't the business above all of us?' Ashish thought.

~

Ashish was at his first outlet at MGF Mall, Gurgaon. It was lunchtime and the seats were empty. It was Yo!China's star outlet, where during peak hours, there would be long queues outside. Suddenly Ashish remembered the day the restaurant was reviewed badly in *HT City*. He was absolutely disappointed, and yet when he came to the restaurant, there were queues outside. Today, he waited for around 40 minutes and not a single person entered the restaurant.

Most of the profitable outlets were going down the drain, and they were slowly heading towards bankruptcy. The feedback, which used to be outstanding once, had turned negative. 'Horrible at Yo!China', 'Deteriorating service' and 'Yo, No and never' were a few feedback mails they had received on the website. The customer feedback in the restaurant register was another sad story.

'Success is like sand. No matter how much one tries to hold it, it slips through our fingers,' he thought and looked at his hands. He realized that he was holding an envelope. He opened the envelope, read and re-read it. It was the resignation letter of the head of operations. He had recruited four people and each of them quit their jobs.

Though Ajay and Joy were not in favour of his decision, Ashish persisted. Ashish wanted the business to grow. He was sure that differences in opinion will never lead to differences among them.

'Ashish, the VCs have a lot of experience, and it is important to learn from them. At the end, it is our call whether or not to follow them. There is difference between their perspective and ours. There is nothing wrong with that, but what is wrong is that you doubt yourself and us. I don't understand why you are hell bent on changing our brand positioning. It's our idea. We have made it work, and we are capable of taking it further,' Ajay argued.

'At times we underestimate our own capability and those around us,' he thought, looking at the poster which read 'Chinese Food at Chinese Price'.

Often accidents happen when one goes at high speed and the probability of going wrong increases. The same happened with Yo!China's reputation. In seeking a mirage of expansion, Ashish failed to understand the difference between being aspirational and being cheap. Also the positioning of 'Chinese Food at Chinese Price' diluted

Yo!China's brand image. Ashish called Ajay and told him about the resignation of the operations head and confessed to his mistakes.

~

'Ashish, let us meet post lunch. It's high time we take drastic measures to improve the situation. We are on the verge of bankruptcy. I have a few things in mind that we need to discuss. Inform Joy, and I will also ask others to join in. See you after lunch.'

When Ashish disconnected the phone, he had a smile of satisfaction on his face. 'We have gone wrong, have argued and have disagreed, but each co-founder has been with me and has shared the passion. That's the greatest asset any entrepreneur can have.'

Everyone gathered in the conference room during the post-lunch session. Ajay announced the agenda of the meeting.

'As all of you would know, our company is going through a tough time. On our growth path, we took some wrong turns and lost track in the middle. This meeting is to assess where we went wrong and take the decisions to undo what has already been done. Ashish will now take us through the mistakes that we have made in the past, and together we will brainstorm on the corrective measures.'

Ashish wrote the word positioning on the white board.

'Our first mistake was that we deviated from our initial plan and positioned ourselves as a "cheap" restaurant. The Indian customers are value conscious, but we misinterpreted it. Value is not only about price but also about package of food quality, freshness, ambience, and experience. Not only did we lose customers but we also lost the charm of selling Chinese cuisine with an aspiration value.

'We also made a few operational mistakes. We served eight dimsums in our high-selling category of dimsum baskets instead of five while reducing the size of the dimsums. We thought the customer would be happy to see an increase in quantity, but it backfired. People started complaining that we were using cheap tactics to lure them. Hence, we were further tagged as being cheap.'

'The first task for us is to do an image makeover. Let's brainstorm over how it can be achieved.'

'On the positioning front, we need to go back to our original thoughts and position ourselves as selling Chinese cuisine with an aspiration value attached to it,' said Sandeep, the operations head.

'Exactly! It's high time we cremated our tagline "Chinese Food at Chinese Price",' Joy added.

'What if we bring changes to our menu? Maybe we can add few new dishes to the menu so that our customers have something new,' Sampat suggested.

'Absolutely! We should bring changes not only to the menu but also in the ambience. When customers enter, they should feel the change,' added Joy.

'Yes, that is workable. Any more suggestions?' Ashish asked and waited for the reply. 'OK then, the next issue that we made a mistake of investing heavily in pursuit of aggressive growth. In the past few years, real estate has developed across categories — in malls, airports and metro stations. Every destination looked lucrative for business and so we invested and spread ourselves too thin.'

'While some of the malls did not open, some did not get the promised footfall. Our strategy of expanding fast backfired. We thought that malls will always be the right location but that was a mistake. Ideally, the location should be based on where our target group stays, and that place can just be a street. We have learnt the lesson: growth is not measured by the number of outlets, but by the number of meals we serve in the outlets, and at the right location,' said Ashish.

'To be true, in our drive to open more number of outlets, the existing restaurants suffered,' Mandhir added.

'As a corrective measure, we need to take a tough call on closing down the loss-making outlets. It is something that we have built with so much passion and effort, and yet we have to shut them. Closing down, parting with the employees, is a situation that no entrepreneur should go through. It's terrible to even think that the employees whom we have wooed for six months have to leave.' Ajay got emotional and lost track. 'Most time, people believe holding on and hanging in are signs of strength. However, there are times when it takes much more strength to know when to let go and then do it.'

'We need to cut down the number of restaurants and rather consolidate on the cities,' Ashish took over.

'Why do we have to close our restaurants? Can't we make the loss-making ones profitable? We need to think of ways to retain our employees. Why can't we raise money through VCs and channelize our operations?' asked Sampat. The pain was visible in his eyes.

'What you are saying isn't improbable, but we need to understand that raising money should be a need and not an event. Just because we can get funds doesn't mean we raise it. We cannot build the business by simply throwing away the money. Right now, we need to get our funds right, and our fundamentals are all about restaurant operations,' Ashish clarified.

'The focus should be on fixing the per unit economics, making each restaurant profitable, and for that, we need to cut the corporate cost. The first step should be to shift to a smaller, no-frills office. Our business is about the front-end. Ideally, everyone should spend more time in restaurant so we don't need a swanky office,' Joy suggested.

'We need to stop growth in order to stop losing money,' Ashish added. 'We have made terrible mistakes, but as we all agreed initially, we will not make the same mistakes again, but we might make new ones on our way,' Ajay joked.

'We have no room for new ones as of now. The burden of past mistakes is already too heavy. It sounds crazy now when we think of it, but we became standardization freaks. We were obsessed by the fact that even a size of chicken in our soup should be same across restaurants, and, to ensure that, we carted the raw materials from our base kitchen to the other locations. We were so fanatic that to ensure that the taste of ice cream remains consistent, we shipped Mother Dairy ice cream all across. Even Mother Dairy doesn't do it, but we did and it increased costs beyond our imagination,' Ashish finished and Joy took over.

'We should focus on localized supply chains. No more shipping. Let's be content with slight variations in taste, as long as we can monitor guest experience, ensure satisfaction and get good reviews.'

'Lastly, I think the most important thing is to believe in ourselves and our concept,' Ajay said and smiled at Ashish.

'Absolutely! Since we have discussed the reasons the corrective measures that we need to take to bounce back, our only agenda now should be its execution.'

'Execution, execution and ruthless execution, even if it means sleepless nights. We have no option but to bounce back,' Ashish insisted.

~

Ashish and Meghana went for a drive. A long drive was a stress buster for him. On the way, they stopped at Sai Baba Temple at Chhatarpur. This temple had a special significance in his life. After worshipping, they both sat on the temple stairs.

'Are you expecting a *laddoo* today as well?' Meghana asked, looking at Ashish mischievously. He smiled at the recollection of the incident when his mother took him to a Sai Baba *Satsang* in South Africa. He was reluctant to go, but his mother did not relent. Finally, he surrendered and went with her. For the first time in his life, he experienced a paranormal moment when the guruji read his mind. When he came back to Delhi, he visited the Chhatarpur temple one day, and mystically, a lady came and handed him the *laddoo,* telling that guruji had sent it for him and he may open his restaurant now.

'Ashish, come back to reality,' Meghana knew him well.

'Sometimes such mystical events happen in life. Probably it's true that sometimes, the whole universe conspires to help you.'

'True, but before that you need to help yourself,' said Meghana.

'Yes, that is exactly what we are doing. Things are looking better for Yo!China. We are implementing the changes, and within next four to five months, I am sure the situation will turn around. Though closing restaurants is painful, it is helping us to focus. Earlier, if we had to think of putting up a hoarding, it was ten hoardings for ten cities and so we were never able to do it. Now, putting up one serves the purpose because our focus is more on number of restaurants per city and therefore managing is easy.'

'Thankfully, the frequency of your travel has also reduced,' Meghana breathed a sigh of relief.

'At least I am able to visit my old outlets! It was maddening the way I was travelling to different cities to open the new restaurants. Who knew cutting ribbons would lead to cutting profits! Fortunately, things are looking positive. Our first outlet, at the MGF Mall, has come back on track. It's bliss to see your old customers coming back. Well, we are doing our best and leaving the rest to the *universe,'* Ashish concluded with a hopeful smile.

'What if guruji is not there? I am giving you the "good luck" *laddoo,* with my blessings that you will soon bring back the profit and the pride.' She had a bright smile on her face as she handed him the *prasad.*

~

'We are on the 60th, 61st, 62nd and, wow, 63rd floor! Finally, we have reached the world's largest open-air restaurant. Yo!' Sandeep couldn't contain his excitement. Every team member was animated about the team's outing. It was the much awaited dinner. After a year of struggle, Yo!China was back to its original glory and pride.

To celebrate it, Ashish took the whole team to Bangkok and arranged for dinner at Sirocco, the world's largest open-air restaurant in Thailand's second tallest building.

On entering the restaurant, they were mesmerized by the breathtaking view of Bangkok and the Chao Phraya River in the backdrop.

'Ashish, this is heaven! I have never experienced such breeze beneath the starry skies. The sky is so close!' Ajay said.

Slowly, dusk approached. The evening lights heightened the lovely orange-red shades of sky and the live jazz added life to the night. Every team member was vivacious and full of energy.

As everyone explored the restaurant, Ashish went to a secluded corner to capture the aerial view. What he saw was a treat for his eyes. When he looked down from the 63rd floor, everything looked miniature sized. That was the phase he had been through for a year. He remembered how he fought his way through bankruptcy. The whole team put their heart and soul to revive the brand. Closing down outlets, firing employees, hiring young blood directly from college: each experience made them stronger and brought them closer to establishing their brand. Each outlet was micro-managed to ensure that food and services offered were above the set standards. A positive feedback from customers had become a treasured incentive.

Suddenly, a loud applause brought him back from his thoughts. He turned and saw his team opening a bottle of champagne. He realized that they had been calling him while he was lost in his thoughts. He was glad to see his team laughing, joking and having fun. He smiled and murmured to himself, 'That's all Yo!China is about, having fun and enjoyment.'

'I have never tasted food that is better than this, of course, barring food at Yo!China,' said Sandeep, lost in the blissful experience.

'Sandeep, how many pegs down are you?' Ashish asked. 'You are eating Mediterranean cuisine. Don't compare it with Chinese.'

'Is it so? Then my next order is Chinese! I love Chinese and I am on a high,' said Sandeep while taking tequila shot.

'We are all on a high because Yo!China is on a high,' said Ashish with a content smile.

After a few hours of drinks and food, they called the chef.

'Sir, we are bowled over by your delicacies. We have never tasted better food than this. Everything, the choices in the menu, the preparation and the presentation, is just outstanding,' said Ajay.

The next few hours were spent chit-chatting with the chef. During the conversation, Ashish told him about Yo!China and his next dream of getting into fine-dine restaurants. The discussion proved to be very insightful. The chef talked about the nuances, challenges and complexities of getting into the fine-dine segment. The chat was so engrossing that they didn't realize that the dawn was approaching and the restaurant was about to close.

The trip to Bangkok proved to be not only a great unwinding experience but also a strategically crucial one.

~

Ashish wanted to expand vertically by starting a chain of fine-dine Chinese restaurants, but he was unsure of the way ahead. An evening in Sirocco gave him a clear picture on the approach that he needed to take. Fortunately, he and his team were able to strike a great rapport with the chef, who, a few months later, flew down from Bangkok to assist in setting up Dimsum Bros, a chain of fine-dine Chinese restaurants.

Ashish was reading the newspaper attentively. After all, it carried a brilliant review that said 'New face of Yo!China with Yo!China Café'.

'Yo!China has come up with a casual dining restaurant Yo!China Café with its tagline "Chilled Out Chinese", which is completely a fresh concept and is targeted at young generation. Yo!China Café is indeed a fun and chill out place to be with close pals and relish Chinese food,' the review said.

He read and re-read it and recalled his first review 'Yo! No No'. It was the worst review that any restaurant could ever have.

One shouldn't fear criticism. Instead, they should fear silence. Criticism is healthy. It gets people thinking about one's work. Even better, it gets them talking and arguing. But as for silence — it is the greatest killer of brands. Criticism can bring back the focus on improvement.

The highly critical review made Ashish more agile and focused. He took it as a challenge to win his customers back. He worked on every weakness that the editor at *The Hindustan Times* pointed out and moved from strength to strength. A year later, the same editor bestowed Yo!China with the Best Fast-Food Chain Award conducted by *HT City Guide*.

Ashish glanced at the shelf where all the awards were kept. All awards stood as recognition of their hard work and efforts, but the award given by *HT* was the one he cherished the most.

This award was his real test. It was testimony to the fact that he won his dissatisfied customers back and that too in style. Ashish was a strong believer that the growth of a company was directly proportional to the number of satisfied customers.

~

Ashish looked at the watch. It was 2 PM. Post lunch he had a training session for new employees. Though Yo!China had expanded across 14 cities with 51 restaurants, Ashish had made sure that during the induction program, he addressed the new employees himself.

After the introduction with employees and briefing them about the company, he said, 'One thing that you guys should feel from your heart and also reflect from your every action is the focus on customer's delight. We strongly believe that dining is not merely about eating. It is an experience. We not only make cuisines from across China and other Oriental cultures and offer delight in tastes and aromas, but also create delight in services. Though our ambience is cool, we have to win our customers through our warmth. Keeping the customer's delight as our goal, we should pledge to make our every customer happy. We will serve 100 percent authentic Chinese, and ensure that our customer is 100 percent satisfied 100 percent of the time! Always remember our growth is not driven outlet by outlet. It is driven meal by meal,' said Ashish and concluded his talk.

YO!CHINA
KEY LESSONS
PANKAJ ACHARYA

Pankaj Acharya is Founder and Managing Director of Purple Focus Group, an Advertising and Marketing Communications company. He is a serial entrepreneur and has also co-founded two more successful businesses like Saints and Warriors Communications Pvt Ltd and Fusion Events Pvt Ltd. He has also been conferred upon 'Most Promising Entrepreneur Award' at prestigious 'Asia Pacific Entrepreneurship Awards'.

~

The Yo!China story presents some very important lessons in branding. The mistakes they committed on positioning, repositioning and business decisions are worth learning from.

Brand is Business

Brand and people are always in dialogue, both overtly as well as covertly. It is important that a brand's conduct be uniform, focused and strategically planned to eventually occupy the desired mind-space and heart-space of the consumer.

Consistency is the Key

If the genesis of Yo! China brand was based on the pillar of cool, authentic Chinese experience, it would have been better not to veer away from it, but to build on it. That would have been the right thing.

Understanding the Aspiration

'Even a hungry beggar will dream of sweetmeat and not basic bread.' This phrase pretty much sums up the human psyche and hence any business's approach towards brand positioning. All our transactions are governed by two primary motivation triggers — greed and fear. Aspiration is a fragment of greed. As human beings we are conditioned to be progressive and hence aspire. Aspiration has become a latent human need. No brand can avoid the aspiration pillar in its positioning, even if it is a mass appeal brand.

It's About Value, Not Price

People confuse aspiration with premium. Aspiration is an emotion and can be an integral part of value positioning. It is how a brand conducts itself. How it is perceived to fulfill a deep-rooted emotional need. Even value positioning is about experience and not low pricing. People are value conscious and not price conscious. 'People always buy the best they can afford.'

Value = return on investment. It can be decoded as 'experience I will derive at the cost I will accrue on it'.

'Chinese Food at Chinese Prices' as a brand tells a customer that it is cheap. It doesn't say its great value. Even when Ashish and team wanted to peg the brand around low pricing for reasons of increasing the perceptual reach, they should have been very careful on the brand promise which is more centric to great experience at lower prices rather than be so in-your-face.

Brand is More than Brand Name

The brand positioning decides business positioning and has a long-term impact on the business. Much larger than anyone expects. So it is imperative to be very, very cautious while choosing the positioning. It is not merely a statement sitting under the brand, but the philosophy and conduct of the brand.

Yo!China story leaves us with important lessons on branding. It also demonstrates that it is possible to rebuild and realign the brand with customer aspiration and expectation, as Ashish did.

❐